MW00527821

Parliamentary
America

Parliamentary America

**THE LEAST RADICAL MEANS OF RADICALLY
REPAIRING OUR BROKEN DEMOCRACY**

Maxwell L. Stearns

JOHNS HOPKINS UNIVERSITY PRESS BALTIMORE

© 2024 Maxwell L. Stearns
All rights reserved. Published 2024
Printed in the United States of America on acid-free paper
2 4 6 8 9 5 7 3 1

Johns Hopkins University Press
2715 North Charles Street
Baltimore, Maryland 21218
www.press.jhu.edu

Library of Congress Cataloging-in-Publication Data is available.

A catalog record for this book is available from the British Library.

ISBN 978-1-4214-4833-6 (hardcover)
ISBN 978-1-4214-4834-3 (ebook)

Song lyrics from "Brave" appear in an epigraph to the conclusion.
Words and Music by Sara Bareilles and Jack Antonoff. Copyright ©
2013 Sony Music Publishing (US) LLC, Tiny Bear Music and Ducky
Donath Music. All Rights Administered by Sony Music Publishing
(US) LLC, 424 Church Street, Suite 1200, Nashville, TN 37219. In-
ternational Copyright Secured. All Rights Reserved. *Reprinted by
Permission of Hal Leonard LLC*

*Special discounts are available for bulk purchases of this book.
For more information,
please contact Special Sales at specialsales@jh.edu.*

To my children
And yours

CONTENTS

Parliamentary
America

Happier Birthdays, Better Parties

Imagine you're a parent to a young daughter who, thankfully, along with her friends, regards your home a happy destination. Among your family traditions is hosting a New Year's Eve sleepover, which happens to be one month before your daughter's birthday. This year, she'll turn seven. You use the New Year's celebration as an opportunity to improve her upcoming party.

You ask the eleven friends and your daughter, a total of twelve children, to help choose the flavor of the birthday cake, one you might make or buy. No judgment here. And you offer four choices: chocolate, vanilla, red velvet, or carrot. Five girls vote chocolate, four vanilla, two red velvet, and one carrot, leaving eleven girls wondering why their friend, or you as a parent, would seriously consider serving a vegetable as a birthday cake.

The little girls feel strongly about all of this, and so those preferring chocolate or vanilla begin pressuring those who chose red velvet and carrot to tip the balance in their favor. You might think you'd have been better off limiting the choices to two. And it's not too late. You could still accomplish that by having the girls list their preferences over the four types of cake in order. Then you could drop the flavors that get the least support one by one. First drop carrot, then red velvet, and then tally the rankings of the two flavors that remain: chocolate and vanilla.

An increasingly popular proposal for election reform is ranked-choice voting, the system just proposed, but few parents use it when planning their children's birthday parties.

Now, picture this instead. The girl who chose carrot says, "I have an idea. How about cupcakes with different flavors?" And you respond, "Why didn't I think of that?" It turns out there's a way to make all the girls happier.

Let's return to elections. With respect to our nation's highest office, the presidency, the Framers of the Constitution devised a majoritarian voting system: the candidate who received the majority of votes in the Electoral College would win. It was all or nothing. They did so because majoritarian voting was both familiar and intuitive.

In middle school, and maybe high school, you might have been told that a remarkable group of men met in Philadelphia to fix the Articles of Confederation, but instead they ditched it and wrote the Constitution. The Framers believed the governmental system they constructed, based on separation of powers and federalism, would avoid factions, which we can think of as precursors to political parties. You might also have been told that the Constitution's brilliance is marked by its having long outlasted other constitutions throughout the world. That account is grounded in a larger narrative involving American exceptionalism. In that account, our unique history and our special institutions immunize us from so many challenges that other democracies have faced. There's only one problem: it's not true.

In a classic scene from the 1989 hit movie *A Few Good Men*, Lt. Daniel Kaffee (played by Tom Cruise) cross-examines Col. Nathan R. Jessup (played by Jack Nicholson) in a murder trial. In a heated exchange, Kaffee demands a candid answer, to which Jessup responds, "You can't handle the truth!"[1]

American citizens are looking straight ahead at a constitutional crisis. And countering the flawed American exceptionalism narrative is critical if we're to come out of it and emerge a thriving constitutional democracy. Citizens are desperately seeking genuine solutions. And yes, we can handle the truth.

True, our constitutional system has endured longer than others throughout the world. For several reasons, our nation has thrived despite our Constitution's flaws: geographic isolation, a steady and constant influx of immigrants, westward expansion (with tremendous pain imposed upon displaced Native Americans), and the profoundly tragic forced labor of enslaved persons brought and maintained here in truly unimaginable conditions. It's past time to recognize that to the extent the story of our nation is exceptional, it's in spite of, not because of, our constitutional design. This is especially so for our electoral system and system of executive accountability.

You might think of this counternarrative as a hypothesis. There's a way to test it. Ask yourself which electoral systems have been widely replicated across the globe. The answer is clear: not ours.

We've been very powerful in exporting democracy, just not our form of democracy. By contrast, other systems, those characterized by proportional representation and parliamentary selection, have been widely embraced throughout the world. There's an important reason why. Those systems, like the girl who chose carrot, recognize there's no need for all the children to enjoy, or suffer, a single-flavor cake, or even a choice of two flavors. The majoritarian winner doesn't always have to get everything. Parents can throw better birthday parties, making the children happier. And we can produce a stronger and more responsive democracy, with more and better political parties for ourselves and future generations.

American democracy is in crisis. We are wracked with growing polarization, a lack of confidence in our most basic institutions, and a gnawing sense that the true justifications for political and legal decisions are routinely masked beyond recognition. Political leaders decry the legitimacy of the very institutions through which they gained power. At the same time, growing numbers of people who regard our democracy as under threat are also convinced it's so damaged that it can't possibly be repaired.

Many serious ideas for constitutional reform are being proposed. Among the most popular proposals are ranked-choice voting (like sequentially eliminating birthday cake options and allocating preferences over the remaining choices); eliminating the Electoral College in favor of the national popular vote; enlarging the House of Representatives; at-large voting in multimember congressional districts; eliminating or bypassing the Senate; imposing term limits on members of Congress; and imposing term limits on US Supreme Court justices. Determining which proposals might resolve the crisis we face is a serious challenge.

I've been teaching constitutional law for over thirty years. I promise to be honest with you. I can't predict when we might hit the inflection point that will require making ultimate choices over the menu of proposals. It might happen soon, in a few years, or perhaps after you and I are no longer living. There's no way to know. Constitutional crises don't happen in a moment, and they aren't necessarily resolved in dramatic fashion. They can fester for years, even decades.

Here's what I can tell you: most high-profile proposals, including those I've mentioned, won't end our constitutional crisis. Yes, proportional representation is an important part of the solution, but it's not the entire solution. And the most popular proposals for infusing proportional representation are unlikely to succeed.

I agree that our democracy is in crisis. I wrote this book for those who remain hopeful, as I am, that it's not too late to fix things. In the pages that follow, I provide a comprehensive analysis of the failings of our democracy rooted in our history, constitutional structure, and the special challenges posed by the information age. After providing you with a tool kit letting you better understand how competing democratic systems function, we'll travel the world. The heart of this book is a tour of several present and former democracies. We'll candidly assess the strengths and weaknesses of competing systems and learn how to adapt the best features as our own. And I'll explain how and why this can be done.

For now, let's go back to New Year's Eve. This time imagine those little girls divided over different flavors of birthday cake as political parties. Our goal is to figure out how best to harness their energies to improve other decisions they might make, not about a birthday celebration, but about governance. The choice between chocolate or vanilla, like Republican or Democrat, provides too few options. We'll also see that democratic systems can fail by offering too many options. As with "Goldilocks and the Three Bears," a central question for democratic reform is how to get things just right.

We must first get past the idea of American exceptionalism. We must open our eyes to a simple fact: there are important aspects of democracy that other nations do far better. We must be open to reframing what the Framers framed wrong.

Some say every journey begins with a first step. Writing this book was a long journey. It required this author, a professor who has spent a career teaching Constitutional Law and Law and Economics, to explain in a clear and accessible manner the causes of our democratic crisis and the strengths and weaknesses of alternative electoral systems and systems of executive accountability. Because you're reading this, you're concerned about our democracy and finding a path forward. I've written this book for you.

I'll be taking you on a world tour. As the book goes to press, political events are rapidly evolving in virtually every nation we'll visit—England, France, Germany, Israel, Taiwan, Brazil, Venezuela, and here at home—among others discussed along the way. Even so, the insights I convey in the chapters that follow, helping to explain competing political systems and how we can adapt their best features as our own, will remain decades from now. The framings I offer in this book will outlive current political events.

To save our democracy, we need an educated citizenry capable of seeing, with clear eyes, the serious challenges we face. Voters must understand that when people use terms like *democracy, parliamentary government*, and *presidentialism*, they're speaking in broad generalities that inevitably overreach. It's essential to grasp differences across actual systems and to appreciate how and why competing democratic institutions work as they do.

There isn't only one system of democracy, parliamentary democracy, and even multiparty democracy. There are several competing systems of democratic government. And every single one of them is flawed, even antidemocratic, in some important way. This too is something our educated electorate must come to understand.

This book will help you appreciate the distinguishing characteristics of these systems—their differing strengths and their inevitable imperfections. You will not only learn how and why alternative democratic institutions work as they do; you will gain invaluable insights into what has worked and what has failed in the United States throughout our long history. But more than anything, you will come away uplifted, knowing what we can do, and must do, to make our system work better. We can produce a thriving Parliamentary America.

To do so, we must embrace reforms along two axes: how we elect members to the House of Representatives and how we structure presidential accountability. I'll demonstrate that reform along either axis alone cannot extricate us from the crisis we face and why reforms focused only on voting protocols aren't worth the candles.

Even before the first step, the most important journeys begin with a leap of faith. That includes turning the page. My ask isn't small, but it's essential. I want you to join the ranks of thoughtful citizens not merely frustrated with the challenges our nation faces, but also armed with an understanding of why and what to do.

Unless we take radical steps to transform our democracy, our children and grandchildren might not continue living in the United States as we have long known it and as we aspire for it to become. Together we can fix this.

To begin, we must be willing to learn from the experiences of others. And sometimes, we have to listen to quieter, more thoughtful, voices. Like that little girl.

PART I

How We Got Here

CHAPTER 1

The Third
Constitutional
Crisis

We are a nation in crisis. Our constitutional system is broken. Without radical reform, the United States risks the fate of so many other democracies throughout history: collapse or dictatorship. The threat is genuine and existential. Many see the crisis.[1] Few know how to fix it. I propose three specific reforms—each corresponding to a constitutional amendment—that together can save our constitutional democracy.

My proposal is radical, introducing change along two axes: first, the system for electing the House of Representatives, our lower of two legislative chambers; and second, the system of executive accountability, meaning how the president and vice president are chosen and how the president may be removed. These amendments double the size of the House of Representatives, with half continuing to be elected by district, a new cohort elected by party, and the entire chamber based on proportional representation. The amendments transform the processes by which we choose the president and vice president, incorporating features of parliamentary democracy. And finally, the amendments provide a new mechanism for presidential removal based on maladministration. Reform along both axes—electoral rules and executive accountability—is essential. There are several additional important details, and I will explain them.

Some critics will claim that this proposal is too radical; others will claim that it's not radical enough. I hope to convince you that what I'm proposing—Parliamentary America—is the least radical means of radically repairing our broken democracy. I also hope to persuade you that the unique features of my proposal make it more politically viable than most proposals that have gained considerable attention yet cannot accomplish their goals. Beyond all that, I hope to enlist you in persuading others to rethink constitutional reform so that our children and grandchildren may live their lives in a thriving constitutional democracy.

Rock, Paper, Scissors, and the Unicycle Constitution

In classrooms across America, children learn that the Framers of the Constitution constructed a system we call separation of powers. A central tenet is checks and balances. This means that each of the three branches—the legislature, or Congress; the executive, or the president; and the judiciary, and most notably the Supreme Court—jealously safeguards its prerogatives against encroachments by the other branches.

Consider the childhood game of Rock, Paper, Scissors. Paper covers rock; rock smashes scissors; scissors cut paper. What makes the game work is that no option invariably wins or loses. For whichever option a child selects—separating the middle and forefinger for scissors, a flattened hand for paper, or a fist for rock—each player has a fifty-fifty chance of winning. It's a game of pure chance. The Framers envisioned a Rock, Paper, Scissors Constitution, with some added tweaks. Teachers convey this when they describe a government comprising three coequal branches.

As in the childhood game, a coequal branch can't always win or always lose.

Schoolchildren also learn that our system rests on federalism. Each of the fifty states jealously safeguards against encroachments by the federal government, and the federal government likewise resists encroachments on the powers it claims. In this happy story, the Framers constructed a complex system resting on two forms of never-ending rivalries. Institutional rivalry pits the branches of government against each other, and geographic rivalry does the same for competing state or regional interests, and between states on one side and the federal government on the other.

The childhood game creates a peculiar dynamic. Scissors defeat paper (cutting it) and paper defeats rock (covering it), implying that scissors should also defeat rock. When children move from middle school civics to math, they learn that this is called transitivity. Ten is greater than five; five is greater than two; and yes, ten is greater than two. But not all relationships are transitive. Some relationships instead produce a cycle, including this childhood game.[2] Scissors defeat paper (by cutting), paper defeats rock (by covering), and yet, rock defeats scissors (by smashing).

The Framers' game is even more confounding. Imagine the children layering on another set of rules: *sometimes* paper covers scissors; rock punctures paper; and scissors sit on a rock. This too thwarts transitivity, producing a cycle, just in the other direction: scissors defeat rock (by sitting), rock defeats paper (by puncturing), but rather than scissors defeating paper (by cutting), this time paper defeats scissors (by covering). By combining both sets of rules, each option can now defeat or be defeated by any other.

In this cycling game, it's more helpful to envision a unicycle than a bicycle. When riding a bicycle and pedaling backward, you still move forward. In this game, though, as on a unicycle, when you pedal forward, you cycle forward, and when you pedal backward, you cycle backward. A better characterization than a Rock, Paper, Scissors Constitution may be a Unicycle Constitution.

Here's how it works: The president can veto bills; Congress can override a veto. The Supreme Court can strike down a federal statute as unconstitutional or construe it narrowly; Congress can start the constitutional amending process to restore the statute or amend the statute to broaden its reach. The Supreme Court can strike down the president's favored legislation or executive orders as unconstitutional; the president can appoint Supreme Court justices, hoping for better luck the next time around.

And so the Unicycle Constitution works like this: Congress defeats the president (by overriding), the president defeats the Supreme Court (by appointing), and the Supreme Court defeats Congress (by striking), producing a forward cycle. And yet, Congress defeats the Supreme Court (by amending), the Supreme Court defeats the president (by striking), and the president defeats Congress (by vetoing), producing a backward cycle. Each branch can defeat or be defeated by any other branch.

Oh, and one more thing: the Supreme Court decides whether the states or the federal government have exceeded their powers, starting the unicycle game—backward or forward—all over again.

The Framers extolled the virtues of endless unresolved tensions. They believed that these complexities—no one always winning or losing—would promote compromise and avoid entrenchment. If a group, or what they called a faction, loses today, that's okay; there's always tomorrow. And since the institutional actors will play again and again, those who are high-minded, looking to benefit society rather than narrow interests, will far more likely succeed.

Rather than promoting fixed rivalries among what they called factions or what we call parties, the Framers imagined that the system they created would be fluid. Shifting alliances with endless unresolved tensions would encourage accommodations or play in the joints. And—this is key—the game doesn't only benefit the players. Instead, it helps all of us.

The Supreme Court has reinforced these lessons. Relying on the Federalist Papers, a series of essays written to get the Constitution ratified, Justices Anthony Kennedy and Sandra Day O'Connor emphasized that separation of powers and federalism aren't designed to protect the branches of government or the states. Instead, these features—the Unicycle Constitution—are designed to protect us all.[3]

An Uncomfortable Truth

As a professor of constitutional law for over three decades, I've taught thousands of students from across the United States and around the globe. Over the past several years, I've found myself compelled to acknowledge an uncomfortable truth. As familiar, and perhaps appealing, as the preceding account of how our constitutional democracy operates might be, it's simply false. Separation of powers and federalism do not describe how our government functions. This has become especially true in the information age, a period that began in the early 1990s.

Checks and balances and separation of powers have yielded to fierce partisan loyalties among Republicans and often intense fragmentation and infighting among Democrats. Neither party can effectively govern. Few, if any, politicians are committed to separation of powers or federalism as a consistent matter of principle, although politicians claim to be when it suits them. Instead, they are committed, in varying degrees, to one of two dominant parties—the Democrats and the Republicans. The divisions separating the parties have grown so sharp, and our politics so closely divided, that Congress has become dysfunctional. Along the way, the Supreme Court, an institution designed not to be political, has become our nation's most coveted political football.

Rather than compromises arising from shifting coalitions affected by checks and balances and federalism, we experience ever-widening policy swings based on which party takes control of the White House in increasingly combative elections. Executive orders, often met with judicial challenges, have replaced legislative compromise, even on the most pressing of matters—immigration, the border, the budget, climate change, infrastructure, the COVID pandemic, interstate travel for reproductive rights, and the list goes on.[4] State political leaders, no less than members of Congress, pay homage to or vehemently oppose the president. The president is not merely the leader of the free world; he (thus far always he) is the leader of one of two parties upon which all political fortunes rest. Our rivalries are increasingly tribal, pitting two opposing camps in virtually endless warfare, with vanishingly few limits on the rules of battle.

The Framers didn't intend a two-party system. They didn't intend parties, or factions, at all. And yet the constitutional structures they put in place paved the way for our entrenched two-party system. We managed to accommodate this system for more than two centuries, but today it has failed. It is undermining our constitutional democracy and ripping apart the fabric of our society. Many media commentators and academics recognize the crisis.[5] Virtually none have properly diagnosed the ultimate cause or prescribed the necessary cure.

The Way Out

In this book, I'm advancing a singular claim: to survive as a democracy, we must change our electoral system and system of executive accountability. We must infuse features of parliamentary selection in choosing the president and vice president, and we must blend districted and proportional representation in electing members of the House of Representatives, the body that should be given that task. Only this will end the two-party system and let meaningful third parties emerge, adapt, and thrive. For third parties to be meaningful, they must play an essential role in forming the government.

The changes I'm advocating are essential to ending the partisan entrenchment destroying our democracy and convulsing our society. I've written this book to explain why these changes are vital to our nation's continuing as a democracy and how we can bring about these needed reforms.

The fundamental difference between presidential and parliamentary democracy involves the timing of coalition formation. In the United States, we have two election cycles. In the primary/ caucus cycle, the parties select their candidates for president. The winners each choose their running mates. In the general election, these candidates face off, competing for a majority of votes, but not among the electorate. Instead, they compete for a majority in the unusual institution called the Electoral College. (More on that later.)

In our system, the coalitions that become governing parties form in the primary/caucus stage, and thus before the general election. In the first round, candidates generally earn their party's nomination through a system of plurality voting, meaning the candidate who gets the most votes wins, even if not a majority. In the second round, the candidate who earns majority support wins. In House elections, we count ballots cast by voters. For the presidency, we count the votes of electors in the Electoral College. Our electoral system encourages two parties to unite behind a single candidate. Although the Electoral College creates other problems, replacing it with a national popular vote won't end the two-party system.

Voters preferring third parties face what I call the third-party dilemma, namely, supporting a spoiler or a randomizer (see chapter 2). A spoiler risks throwing the election to the disfavored major party candidate. Ralph Nader was a spoiler for Al Gore in the 2000 election. A randomizer risks rendering the choice between the two major party candidates a roll of the dice. John Anderson threatened to be a randomizer in the 1980 presidential election between Ronald Reagan and Jimmy Carter, as did Ross Perot in the 1992 election between Bill Clinton and George H. W. Bush.[6]

By contrast, parliamentary systems choose the head of government indirectly. Voters in those systems often cast ballots based on party, generally expecting no single party to capture a majority of legislative seats. A majority coalition chooses the head of government, typically called a prime minister, who develops and executes policy. Sometimes the head of government is also head of state, representing the nation on the world stage. More typically, these positions are separate, with a ceremonial head of state performing honorary functions. In England, the ceremonial head of state is embodied in the monarch.

In a parliamentary system, the dominant party is generally invited to negotiate a governing coalition after the general election. To win a majority, that party routinely brings third (or fourth, or fifth) parties into the coalition. Because smaller parties play a vital role in forming the government, voters supporting those parties benefit from doing so. In parliamentary systems, unlike our own, third-party candidates aren't spoilers or randomizers. In exchange for joining a governing coalition, smaller parties help their constituents, for example, by negotiating favorable policies or securing favored ministerial appointments (see chapters 5 and 6).

Three Amendments

I am proposing three Constitutional Amendments, which I call the Electoral Reform Amendments. Together these amendments will infuse parliamentary selection and coalition building into our system while retaining and preserving our most essential institutional structures. What I propose is radical, but *least* radical. The accommodations to several existing structures and power arrangements are critical to enacting these vital reforms.

The First Electoral Reform Amendment doubles the size of the House of Representatives, with each voter casting two ballots. The first ballot is for candidates in geographic districts, and the second is by party. The amendment provides for adjustments to ensure that proportional representation (the second ballot results) controls the entire House chamber to the extent feasible while seating all districted (first ballot) winners (see chapter 7). The amendment embeds a mechanism designed to counteract a scourge of democracy—hyper-partisan gerrymandering. Sitting members of the House and Senate remain incumbents after the amendment takes effect.

The Second Electoral Reform Amendment empowers the House to select the president and vice president from party slates by inviting up to five party leaders, in descending order of representation, to negotiate a majority coalition. Whereas the First Electoral Reform Amendment doubles the size of the House, this amendment and the third greatly enhance that body's institutional powers (see chapters 8 and 9).

The Third Electoral Reform Amendment empowers the House to remove the president with a 60 percent no confidence vote. The amendment promotes regime stability through existing succession rules, which determine who replaces a president failing to complete a term (see chapter 9).

The combined scheme breaks the two-party deadlock, avoids partisan gerrymandering, creates space for genuine third parties to emerge and thrive, and avoids the risk of regime instability. In parts III and IV, I explain each amendment in detail along with the politics of getting them passed. The appendix provides drafts of each amendment.

Why Our Eighteenth-Century Electoral System Fails in the Twenty-First-Century World

Today's partisan divisions are as constant and familiar as our never-ending news cycle. It's easy to imagine that things were always this way. But they weren't. In the mid-twentieth century, the American Political Science Association published a famous study, and its major criticism of our politics was nearly opposite.[7] The study declared the central challenge of our politics was a lack of distinction between the parties. In 1952, both major parties even courted the same candidate, Dwight D. Eisenhower, as their presidential nominee.

To understand how these party dynamics changed, we must explore their root causes. Without a proper diagnosis, we can't prescribe the right cure. So how did a system that we managed reasonably well for nearly two hundred years suddenly go off the rails?

Our late-eighteenth-century Constitution collided with twenty-first-century technology. The information age has eviscerated our electoral system in two distinct, yet interlocking, ways: hyper-partisan gerrymandering and algorithmic social media newsfeeds.

First, partisan gerrymandering is the process of drawing district lines to enhance the representational strength of the party in power (see chapter 3). Most commonly, state general assemblies are responsible for approving districting maps both for their own elections and for electing state delegations to the House of Representatives. Drawing lines that benefit the controlling party is hardly new; indeed, it's older than the United States. But more advanced technologies developed in the past few decades accomplish the task with stunning scientific accuracy.

David Daley, of FairVote and former *Salon* editor-in-chief, described the extraordinary hyper-partisan Republican gerrymandering plan that immediately followed Barack Obama's 2008 presidential election. Daley recounted the remarkable political distortions produced by what's now known as REDMAP. He captured the unprecedented extent to which the scheme violated all prior accommodations in an unbridled quest for partisan gain with his unceremonious book title: *Ratf**ked: Why Your Vote Doesn't Count*.[8] Through hyper-partisan gerrymandering, elected officials choose their constituents, not the other way around.

Second, social media platforms, especially Facebook (now called Meta) and Twitter (now X, and well before the Elon Musk takeover) fundamentally transformed the business model for news and news-like information (see chapter 4).[9] These news media conduits, meaning platforms that convey content created by others, operate on a fundamentally different business model than traditional print media.[10] These platforms thrive, deriving maximal advertising revenues, by ensuring that subscribers remain glued to the screen. News media conduits accomplish this with content that motivates active user engagement in the form of clicks, likes (or other reactions), and shares.

To succeed, these platforms have developed customizing algorithms based on past subscriber behavior to produce individualized newsfeeds that attract and engage readers for as long as possible. This includes content that excites readers either positively or negatively. An effective strategy involves conveying over and over that the subscriber is part of a team, or tribe, embracing a worldview and enthusiastically, and self-righteously, vilifying those who reject it.

Such content correlates to hyper-partisanship and a corresponding lack of reliability for accuracy. Investigative reports have demonstrated that the creators understand what motivates subscribers to remain actively engaged.[11] As with partisan gerrymandering, these platforms rely on increasingly sophisticated technology to generate what the program identifies as content likely to maintain such ongoing subscriber activity.

Media sources—very often exclusively online publications with streamlined staffs—know that playing to one or the other side's political base is more likely to trigger the algorithm, drawing in readership and advertising dollars. Just as partisan gerrymandering lets legislators select their constituents, not the other way around, these platforms let news media choose their readerships, not the other way around.

The information age has inverted the dynamics of political engagement, creating a crisis in our constitutional democracy. These combined dynamics—partisan gerrymandering and algorithmic social media newsfeeds—have divided our electorate and threatened our society, producing an ever-growing wedge between two increasingly distant and hostile camps. The divides have grown so intense that each side routinely accuses the other of having illicit motives and lacking basic intelligence.

The Framers' Deck of Cards

Imagine an evenly split deck of shuffled cards. Partisan gerrymandering and social media newsfeeds push the two half decks further and further apart. Solving the constitutional crisis demands reshuffling, but not just once. A reshuffle leading to a second permanent split does no good. We need more meaningful reform, ensuring that each time such a split recurs with the half decks separating, the deck can be reshuffled.

Although the Framers failed to fashion such a system, they shared this concern. They weren't so naïve as to imagine that different groups, or factions, would never form.[12] Rather, the Framers envisioned a system without permanent factions. More than factions or parties, they feared entrenchment. And although they unwittingly structured a system inviting a split deck increasingly entrenched over time, we can fix this.

Revising our electoral system to let multiple parties negotiate in selecting the president won't make everybody happy. But it will create better institutions that truly serve us all. Within the Democratic party, Alexandria Ocasio-Cortez and the Squad for the progressive wing; Joe Manchin, perhaps joined by former Democrat turned Independent Kyrsten Sinema, for the few conservatives; and Joe Biden, Kamala Harris, Hakeem Jeffries, and Chuck Schumer for the centrist leadership, will fragment into separate parties. So will Republicans. Social conservatives, fiscal conservatives, and Libertarians will no longer be bound together or with Donald Trump's Make America Great Again ("MAGA") base, which has gripped the GOP.

With multiple parties required to negotiate in forming the government, leaders may also discretely align on specific issues. Coalitions will form, but this process will allow greater fluidity, with coalitions developing and evolving over time rather than per-manent, and ever-widening entrenchment.

The First Two Constitutional Crises

This is not the first time our nation has faced a constitutional cri-sis. On two prior occasions, the Framing period and the Civil War and Reconstruction, we faced division or collapse. To avoid those outcomes, political leaders seized the moment, turning cri-sis into opportunity. This required a citizenry sufficiently well-informed to allow transformative change. Although written in late-eighteenth-century prose, the Constitution was intended as The People's document, even as the people were then narrowly confined to white men. To pull out of the crisis we face today, the Constitution must regain that status with a broader, more legiti-mate, citizenry. An educated citizenry must understand the Con-stitution's failings and what's required to fix it.

The nation's first constitutional crisis followed the American Revolution, after which the thirteen original states formed the Ar-ticles of Confederation. The Articles, which governed from 1781 to 1789, recognized states as the ultimate sovereigns, making Congress—the sole branch—entirely dependent on state legisla-tures to raise taxes or regulate commerce.[13] States erected trade barriers that protected local industry. Trade wars gutted the econ-omy. Congress lacked the power to demand requisitions. Absent revenues and a head of state, the US risked failing to negotiate or honor its debts.

The Philadelphia Convention, assembled in 1787, was never intended to write a constitution. It was instructed to propose amendments. But the Framers ditched the Articles altogether, including its amending process. The convention sent its newly minted constitution for ratification by popular conventions the fol-lowing year. The Framers declared "We the People" a higher sovereign than states. Rejecting the premise that states were the ultimate sovereigns, the Framers cut state legislatures from the ratification process. And they succeeded. Forming a meaningful union took several more decades, first adding a Bill of Rights and then a series of landmark Supreme Court rulings giving effect to separation of powers. Ultimately, strong leadership and an educated citizenry extricated us from this early crisis.

The second constitutional crisis encompassed the Civil War, 1861–65, and the fraught period of Reconstruction, 1865–76.[14] Intense disputes regarding slavery, our nation's original sin, and state versus federal powers persisted throughout the antebellum period. Following Southern secession and the shot at Fort Sumter, over six hundred thousand men died before General Robert E. Lee's unconditional surrender at Appomattox. Southern states were eventually compelled to accept three constitutional amendments ratified from 1865 to 1870—ending slavery, vastly expanding federal powers, and formally (although not actually) affording African American men voting rights. Historical events such as Lincoln's assassination, a Southern sympathizing successor, limiting judicial constructions, and a premature Northern troop withdrawal obstructed the Reconstruction Amendments. Giving the amendments meaning took decades, with unpredictable outcomes that ultimately transformed nearly every aspect of our constitutional system.

Notwithstanding the brutality of slavery prior to the Civil War, states were considered the guardians of individual rights and liberties, at least for citizens. After Reconstruction, a new set of constitutional Framers rejected that premise even as it took a full century to begin realizing their vision. The federal government, variously aided or thwarted by the Supreme Court, was called upon again and again to protect our most vulnerable populations from deprivations at the hands of states.[15] Once more, strong political leadership and a well-informed citizenry proved central to this ongoing process (see chapter 3).

Each constitutional crisis is unique. And yet, all three—including ours—share a disjuncture between a central premise of

THE THIRD CONSTITUTIONAL CRISIS　**25**

the existing constitutional system and the nation's exigent needs, threatening our ability to endure as a thriving democracy. Periods of productivity can arise amid constitutional crises. When they do, as with a bandage masking an infected wound, such periods risk accompanying and dangerous complacency.

In the first two crises, political leaders overcame complacency and seized the moment, transforming essential aspects of constitutional design. The opportunity for such change is exceedingly rare, last occurring a century and a half ago. At best we will have one opportunity to get this right. Tinkering at the edges of our constitutional system will not do.

Imagine the run-up to a presidential election in 2024 or 2028, with key states Texas, Arizona, and Florida adopting laws banning nonmilitary mail-in ballots, demanding mailing addresses lacking in Native American communities, insisting on government-issued IDs absent documented voter fraud, limiting drop-off ballots to inaccessible locations, and banning third-party ballot collectors. In 2020, Republican states tried all of these tactics, even prohibiting giving water to voters waiting in long lines in the heat.[16] Imagine another pandemic, once more making in-person voting a matter of life or death. And imagine that without these restrictions—all targeting Democratic base voters—these states would throw the election Democratic, but that with these restrictions in place, the Republicans seize the White House, expand control of the House, and take over the Senate. Now, Democratic activists storm the Capitol. This time, the most committed supporters of the Republican nominee, whether Trump or a successor chosen to capture the MAGA base, gather to stop the Democrats in their tracks. Following the attempted US Capitol insurrection on January 6, 2021, we can spin out even more dramatic scenarios that risk feuds on social media turning into actual political violence.

Today's crisis arises from unique historical circumstances. Our antiquated approaches to voting and executive accountability, which we managed to accommodate for nearly a quarter millennium, can no longer be managed. They must be changed. The information age has transformed the two-party system into something sinister. It hasn't merely undermined our basic constitutional structures, superseding separation of powers and checks and balances with hyper-partisan loyalties; it has also ripped apart the fabric of society to the point of splitting families and communities, and ending decades-long friendships.

Other Reform Proposals Will Not Work

For the first time since Reconstruction, serious conversations are underway about foundational constitutional reform.[17] For example, four major constitution projects and several independent works propose broad reform to the Constitution and to the institutions it established. Prominent proposals include replacing the Electoral College with the national popular vote, deploying ranked-choice voting, reapportioning the Senate, holding multimember district House of Representatives elections, tweaking congressional terms, abandoning primaries, expanding the Supreme Court, and limiting and rotating Supreme Court terms, among others. Some of these are good ideas; none will solve our constitutional crisis.

The goal of reform is not to throw out so many ideas that everyone is happy. Instead, it is to take on the singular problem from which all others derive. The latter approach is bolder, addressing what really matters, and less speculative, not imagining that after reform, the problems we experience or anticipate today will necessarily persist or that others we can't foresee will fail to arise.

Over the course of my teaching career, if I have learned one overriding lesson, it is this: although we can identify problems and modify institutions to address them, we're far worse at predicting future problems apt to arise as a result of the change. This is a fundamental lesson of the first two constitutional crises. In each instance, those supporting constitutional reform to resolve or head off a crisis failed to anticipate other problems that soon followed.

Identifying the root cause of failure in any complex system is a challenge. We consult physicians and other health care professionals for our bodies and minds, electricians and plumbers for our homes, and mechanics for our cars. There are no doctors or engineers of democracy. It's hubristic to imagine that a group of constitutional law professors, especially sorted ideologically as various constitutional reform projects have done, hold the key. The project of democratic governance is not about getting like-minded academics to agree. It is about creating institutions that motivate non-like-minded people—people often at each other's throats—to govern. Together.

Voters singularly committed to the environment, racial justice, women's reproductive rights, socialism, religious liberties, libertarianism, gun regulation, or whatever else moves them, will no longer be admonished not to waste their votes on a third party. Constituents will not be locked in, paying homage to a party ill-suited to their needs. Genuine competition will provide more opportunities. And yes, the system will require ongoing adjustments, only some of which we might anticipate.

Constitutional reform demands careful attention to how groups make decisions and how actors respond to incentives. Two subfields of political science and economics—social choice and game theory—address these very questions.[18] I have dedicated my career to integrating learning across these disciplines. One needn't enroll in law school or graduate studies in political science or economics to gain the essential insights needed to reform our failing Constitution. I promise to explain all of this clearly. I ask for only one thing—an open mind.

The Endurance Myth

Part of the folk wisdom surrounding the Constitution is that longevity corresponds to unerring insight by the Framers, whose document endured so much longer than others around the world. Thomas Jefferson's admonition that each generation should draft its own constitution so as not to foist a father's suit upon his son is ridiculed as folly.[19] But that's unfair. The average lifespan of constitutions across the globe is about seventeen years, almost precisely as Jefferson claimed.[20]

The true test of institutional success is not endurance, especially isolated endurance. Instead, it's replication. Replication implies a universal quality that lets others benefit through adaptation. The most successful technologies and businesses are routinely mimicked and sometimes copied outright. But our Constitution, especially its combined methods of elections and executive accountability, has remained a recluse on the world stage (see chapters 5 and 6). This raises the prospect, indeed the likelihood, that the United States thrived for other reasons—its unique geography, the brutality of prolonged slave labor, its relative isolation from notable military threats, its western expansion, its periodic influx of immigrants, its robust access to expanding domestic and international markets—and thus in spite of, not because of, its rare constitutional design.

Customized social media news algorithms and scientific partisan gerrymandering have, once more, made the premises of our eighteenth-century Constitution ill-suited to the twenty-first-century world. Data from the Pew Research Center demonstrate that beginning in the 1990s, the centers, or modes, for the Democratic and Republican parties have grown further and further apart.[21] Along with others, *New York Times* reporter Ezra Klein has documented parallel cultural divides on nearly every salient issue: COVID-19 vaccines, masks, and social distancing; the 2020 election; the January 6, 2021, Capitol building attack; voter fraud; immigration; Critical Race Theory; climate change; the Iran Nuclear Deal; the Afghanistan troop withdrawal; abortion rights; and more. The simultaneous developments of algorithmic social media newsfeeds and hyper-partisan gerrymandering, both products of the information age, have upended conventional understandings, wreaking havoc with our constitutional scheme.

To many commentators, and undoubtedly to many readers, the resulting divides appear insurmountable. Our institutions provide today's Republican Party disproportionate power compared with demographics. Senate apportionment provides two senators per state regardless of population. Each state's Electoral College vote equals the sum of its House and Senate delegations. Rural midwestern and southern states, the Republican base, have outsized power in nearly every institutional setting. California, with nearly 40 million people, has the same number of senators—two— as Wyoming, with a population under 600,000, an astonishing ratio of sixty-seven voters to one. As Joe Biden's 2020 victory demonstrates, the Republican Party is threatened by its shrinking base, even with these structures in place. The 2020 election reveals that in addition to egregiously manipulating district lines, Ratf**king turnout has become a favorite Republican strategy.[22]

Unlike Vizzini in *The Princess Bride*, skeptics claiming constitutional reform is inconceivable know what that word means.[23] People rarely relinquish money or power on their own. The way to make reform conceivable is to devise an alternative that radically alters the stakes by changing the rules of the game. This entails ending the power dynamics that, as with colliding trains, ensure tragic consequences, minus the certainty of knowing precisely when the crash will occur.

The path we're on is unsustainable. In the *New York Times* bestseller *How Democracies Die*, political scientists Steven Levitsky and Daniel Ziblatt make one lesson astoundingly clear. The worst thing we can do is wait until it's too late to figure our way out.[24] No one can predict the precise moment at which vital choices must be made—this year, 2028, or beyond. To survive as a democracy, We the People must understand what has caused our democratic system to fail and how to fix it.

No democratic system is perfect. All three major systems— presidential, hybrid (including semi-presidential and semi- parliamentary), and parliamentary—are flawed. Each embeds features one might credibly describe as antidemocratic. Foisting a choice of two problematic candidates upon voters is not more or less democratic than having voters select parties more closely aligned with their worldviews and letting legislative negotiations produce the winner. These systems are differently democratic, each with its own strengths and flaws. But parliamentary democracies, unlike ours, ensure an opportunity for shuffling and reshuffling the cards rather than guaranteeing an ever-widening split deck.

The Road Ahead

In considering alternatives, it's mistaken to compare the flaws of one system to the strengths of another. We must instead assess the strengths and flaws of each system and then compare.[25] When buying a home or shopping for a car, we make visits or take test drives. Online reviews help, but they can't really let us know how a house feels or a car performs. Changing democratic systems is costly. We can't test run competing systems here at home. We must instead take a second-best approach.

After explaining how we came upon our present constitutional crisis in part I, I conduct a virtual world tour, taking you to England, France, Germany, Israel, Taiwan, Brazil, and Venezuela, discussing other nations along the way, in part II. In so doing, this book will explore specific features of electoral and executive design that affect the number and nature of political parties. I will demonstrate why parliamentary list voting allows third parties to emerge, adapt, and thrive; why presidential systems render third parties spoilers or randomizers; and why hybrids such as semi-presidentialism, blending features of presidentialism and parliamentarianism, along with multiparty presidentialism, are prone to problematic results. And I'll demonstrate how to avoid having those problems arise here.

This book will explain why parliamentary selection generally improves voter satisfaction, with voters expressing sincere political preferences rather than being forced to choose within a simplified, hyper-partisan binary.[26] Parliamentary systems expand the scope, or dimensionality, of politics, letting voters express preferences on policy or economics along one dimension and culture or identity along another.[27] This avoids the dire consequence US voters face of having their electoral choices forced onto a simplistic right-left divide. Splitting these dimensions improves voter happiness, political signaling, and governmental responsiveness.

Certainly, parliamentary systems can and do face crises. A difficulty confronting some parliamentary regimes is too many parties, which can be as problematic as too few. In our world tour, we'll see how to achieve a helpful balance.

I'll also introduce a concept called valence, which plays a transformative role across political landscapes. Originating in chemistry, valence is the force combining atoms into molecules. In politics, the concept conveys the magnetic quality of particular candidates positively, pulling voters in, or negatively, repelling voters.

Valence works differently across electoral systems.[28] Because of the differing institutional barriers to threatening populist impulses, valence generally plays a more benign role within parliamentary systems than it does in presidential systems. In the information age, our two-party system is especially vulnerable to the threat that a high valence candidate, such as Donald Trump, poses. Trump managed to confound voter choices by stressing identity politics and by forcing the economics and policy dimension to yield. Along the way, he left those repulsed by populism yet distrusting of Democratic policies politically homeless. Although certainly not immune to populist impulses, parliamentary systems ameliorate these risks by expanding the dimensions of political choice, by inviting richer options in more competitive political markets, and by providing a filter between voters' registered preferences and the ultimate electoral choice.

Each democratic system has its own rules. As in any high stakes game, those playing it develop sophisticated playbooks.

Some playbooks rest on norms designed to promote fair play. But when conditions change, norms erode. Admonishing fair play cannot succeed. What's needed is a change in the rules. And changing the rules changes the game. Parliamentary America is a better game, for us and future generations.

When serious choices must be made—and they will—our electorate must know the stakes. Careful preparation is essential. There's no time to waste. Tweaking at the edges of a deeply problematic system won't do. We need transformative change for our democracy to thrive and for our society to mend. The project is urgent. Let's begin.

CHAPTER 2

The Third-Party Dilemma

The breakdown of our constitutional democracy is connected in intricate ways with how we select the president. Our voting process rewards strategy over sincerity, and it increasingly plays to the base of each party rather than the center of our politics. For a long time, most voters reconciled the tension, knowing that voting for the major party candidate who represents their second choice over a more appealing third-party candidate who is a spoiler or randomizer promotes a better outcome. But especially in recent decades, more voters have found this to be an ongoing struggle. Even those accustomed to choosing between the two major party candidates are routinely unhappy with the choices they face. The third-party dilemma arises from the tension between a voter's desire to hold fast to her or his sincere political values at the ballot box versus playing by the rules of a game that rewards unity and punishes division.

In the United States, we select the president in a two-stage electoral contest. After the major parties elect their candidates in the primary-caucus cycle, the candidate who receives a majority of votes in the Electoral College wins. When casting our ballots, we aren't actually voting for the candidates whose names we check. We are voting for people whose names we'll never know, specifically electors who, if our candidate wins, will cast their ballots in the Electoral College on our chosen candidate's behalf.[1] Despite its quirks, the Electoral College doesn't change one of the most significant implications of our majoritarian voting system. We still end up with two major parties.

In the Electoral College, each state is allotted a number of votes equal to its congressional delegation—two for the Senate plus the number corresponding to its membership in the House of Representatives. In all but Nebraska and Maine, which apply a proportionality rule, the state delegate results are winner-take-all.[2] Whichever candidate gets the majority of popular votes receives all the state's Electoral College votes. This peculiar method of counting votes distorts outcomes as compared with the national popular vote. Low-population states have disproportionate voting power. Sometimes, as in the 2000 and 2016 elections, the distortion is sufficient to elect a president who lost the popular vote.[3]

American voters learn early on that the ultimate electoral choice comes down to either of the two major party candidates, as only they have a realistic possibility of winning in the Electoral College. In each presidential election cycle, voters are reminded that supporting any other candidate is wasteful. In our system, it is wise to divide the opposing side, never one's own. This feature of our electoral system—the third-party dilemma—relates to an insight called Duverger's Law.

In a series of papers published in the 1950s and 1960s, Maurice Duverger, a French national who was a jurist, sociologist, and political scientist explained that first-past-the-post systems tend to produce two controlling parties.[4] Although commentators sometimes use Duverger's Law to describe our system, Duverger envisioned a different voting method. First-past-the-post voting implies a single-round contest in which the candidate who captures the most votes wins. In a multicandidate race, this is often a plurality, not a majority. The post metaphor is from horseracing:

the first horse to cross the finish line, or post, wins. Despite the name, Duverger's insight is more a tendency than a law. Plurality voting schemes sometimes produce more than two parties.[5]

US elections take place in two stages, with the first round governed by a series of plurality contests and the second by majority rule. The combination of single-member congressional districts and a president elected by voters (even as processed through the Electoral College) rather than a legislative body, entrenches a two-party system. Once more, voters realize that it's generally beneficial to stand united behind one candidate and to fragment the opposition with the goal of capturing a majority in the general election. Because both sides face these incentives, two parties emerge as dominant. This explains why presidential systems, where voters rather than legislators choose the head of government, are called majoritarian.

Majoritarianism doesn't mean an absence of third parties. Rather, it conveys that third parties play a confounding role, with effects that are difficult, even impossible, to predict. Quite often, those supporting third parties risk undermining their sincere ideological commitments and policy preferences. In our majoritarian system, voters are admonished again and again to vote strategically.

To illustrate the third-party dilemma, let's take a look back. We will begin with a famous 2018 congressional race and then consider three presidential elections: 2000, 1992, and 1980. These elections reveal the confounding nature of our electoral system.

AOC and the Squad

In a stunning 2018 New York Democratic congressional primary, Alexandria Ocasio-Cortez, a 2016 Bernie Sanders staffer who had never before run for elected office, defeated ten-term congressman and chair of the Democratic Caucus, Joe Crowley. A self-identified Democratic Socialist, AOC, as she became known, handily won the general election. She joined with Representatives Ilhan Omar of Minnesota, Rashida Tlaib of Michigan, and Ayanna Pressley of Massachusetts to form a group of newly elected progressive congresswomen known as "the Squad."

With Ocasio-Cortez as its most prominent voice, the Squad took on the Democratic establishment. Its members attempted unsuccessfully to unseat Congresswoman Nancy Pelosi as Speaker of the House; threatened primary contests against moderate Democratic members of Congress; and pushed several progressive policies such as The Green New Deal, a fifteen-dollar national minimum wage, and public college funding. In the 2020 presidential primary, AOC again supported Bernie Sanders until it was clear that Joe Biden would secure the nomination. Ocasio-Cortez ultimately, if grudgingly, endorsed the future president. She also declared that in other countries, she and Biden wouldn't be in the same party.[6]

The 2000, 1992, and 1980 Presidential Elections

In the 2000 presidential election, consumer activist Ralph Nader ran a third-party campaign. Nader described the choice between the major party nominees, Republican George W. Bush and Democratic Vice President Al Gore, as Tweedledee or Tweedledum.[7] Gore's campaign, like Nader's, focused heavily on market reforms and climate change. Seven years later, Gore's commitment to the environment earned him the Nobel Peace Prize. Even so, Nader took enough votes from Gore in key states that the outcome of the presidential election turned on Florida. Whichever candidate received Florida's twenty-five Electoral College votes would meet the critical threshold—270 out of 538—required to win. With the help of a divided Supreme Court ruling that blocked a statewide vote recount,[8] George W. Bush won Florida by a mere 537 votes of 11.1 million ballots cast, a stunning 0.009 percent margin. Bush would go on to serve two terms. When Nader considered another run four years later, the once Libertarian host of *Real Time with Bill Maher* and progressive activist and documentary filmmaker Michael Moore each got on their knees, begging Nader to reconsider.[9]

As Nader waged his 2000 campaign to Gore's left, defeated nativist Republican primary candidate Pat Buchanan waged a third-party campaign to Bush's right. Buchanan didn't come close to Nader's electoral success. And yet in Florida, which turned the election, Buchanan played a decisive role. Palm Beach County, on Florida's gulf coast, was largely Democratic. Democratic Supervisor of Elections Theresa LePore introduced an unusual ballot hoping to help the county's elderly voters. It listed the candidates for president and vice president in oversized font to the left and right along opposing pages. Holes punched down the center corresponded to the candidates, with several parties alternating along the sides of each page. Studies have shown that rather than benefiting the elderly residents, at least 2,000 voters—nearly four times Bush's margin of victory in Florida—found the butterfly design so confusing that they mistakenly voted for archconservative Buchanan instead of Al Gore.[10] If Nader's 2000 campaign didn't cost Gore the presidency, due to the butterfly ballot Buchanan's third-party candidacy certainly did.

The 1992 election pitted incumbent Republican President George H. W. Bush against Democratic nominee Bill Clinton. Ross Perot, a businessman with a populist bent, waged a third-party campaign. Perot gained sufficient support to be invited to join the two major party candidates in each of the three presidential debates. Perot's centerpiece issue was the North American Free Trade Agreement (NAFTA), a treaty among the United States, Canada, and Mexico. Perot urged voters to listen for a "giant sucking sound," which, he claimed, represented their manufacturing jobs moving south to Mexico.[11] Although studies show that Perot probably didn't pull more votes from Bush than Clinton, the Perot campaign posed risks for both candidates.[12] Bill Clinton captured the first term of his two-term presidency with just 43 percent of the popular vote, making George H. W. Bush a one-term president.

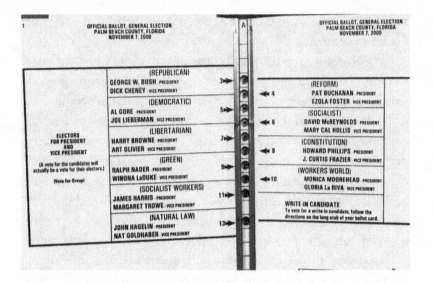

Butterfly Ballot from the 2000 US Presidential Election,
from Palm Beach County, Florida. Public domain,
Wikimedia Commons

After an unsuccessful Republican primary, John Anderson waged a third-party campaign in the 1980 election. The election pitted incumbent Democratic President Jimmy Carter against the hard-right Republican nominee Ronald Reagan. In the first of two scheduled debates, Carter refused to debate Anderson, leaving Anderson and Reagan alone on the stage. Many commentators regarded this as a sign of weakness, an impression Carter struggled to overcome in the remaining debate. When Carter accused Reagan of opposing Medicare, thereby depriving seniors of health care, Reagan retorted, "There you go again," explaining that he preferred an alternative bill advancing similar objectives.[13] In another gaffe, Carter recounted that his thirteen-year-old daughter, Amy, had told him nuclear proliferation was the nation's greatest challenge.[14] The damage Anderson's candidacy posed for Carter remains uncertain. By some accounts, Anderson siphoned more Republican than Democratic votes.[15] Regardless, Reagan trounced Carter, going on to serve two terms.

Although each presidential campaign is unique, political scientists and constitutional scholars discern important patterns.[16] The 1980, 1992, and 2000 presidential elections were affected in potentially decisive ways by third-party candidates, none of whom had a chance of winning or of sparking a viable three-party system.

Spoilers and Randomizers

Third-party presidential campaigns have a fraught history in US politics, and yet, the lure of third parties remains strong. This isn't surprising. Whatever one thinks of her politics, Ocasio-Cortez's claim is largely true. In many democracies, voters embracing AOC's Democratic Socialist agenda wouldn't join their nation's counterpart to Joe Biden's center-left Democratic Party. Likewise, many traditional conservatives, including voters who helped Trump defeat Hillary Clinton in 2016 and produced a closer 2020 outcome than pollsters predicted, would resist joining their nation's counterpart to Trump's nationalist GOP. This is true more generally for members of the Tea Party and Libertarians who often vote Republican and for Democratic Socialists and Green Party members who often vote Democratic.

Third-party presidential candidates who siphon votes from the closer major party candidate, throwing outcomes to the more ideologically distant major party candidate, are called spoilers. The most obvious spoilers wage campaigns to the left of the Democratic nominee or to the right of the Republican nominee. In the 2000 presidential election, Ralph Nader was a spoiler for Gore, and but for the peculiar butterfly ballot, Buchanan threatened to be a spoiler for Bush. Third-party candidates who occupy a crossover position, such as John Anderson in 1980 or Ross Perot in 1992, are randomizers. Such candidates play a less certain role as they risk pulling votes from each major party candidate. In doing so, these candidates also risk rendering the choice of president, the leader of the free world, a matter of chance.

Trump's 2016 Republican Takeover

Donald Trump has emerged as the most divisive figure in our national politics. He is the most divisive politician to win the presidency in modern history and quite possibly our nation's entire history. From his initial 2015 trip down the Trump Tower escalator to announce his 2016 Republican candidacy through his ultimate electoral defeat in 2020 by Joe Biden, the Trump administration wrought tremendous pain. Viewed through the lens of his opponents, Trump at least covertly aligned with white supremacists and neo-Nazis; denigrated Mexican immigrants; split refugee families; insulted and sought to ban Muslims; infiltrated local law enforcement; abrogated long-standing relationships with allies; coddled petty dictators; and engaged in remarkable machinations, including helping to foment a violent break-in at the US Capitol to undermine the legitimacy of his successor. That insurrection resulted in at least four immediate deaths, two later deaths by suicide, and more than 140 serious injuries to police officers. In addition, Trump treated COVID as the basis for a culture war, insisting upon calling it the "China virus" and consistently undermined lifesaving measures, which may well have cost hundreds of thousands of lives.

Donald Trump became the first president to thwart the peaceful transition of power, priming his supporters to believe that he could only be defeated by fraud. Trumpism pitted children against parents and spouses against each other. It pushed decades-long friendships past the breaking point. And yet, despite the anger and frustration Trump fomented, including in his own party,[17] without serious constitutional reform, designs on a viable third party were no more likely to succeed in the aftermath of the Trump presidency than they had been in the past.

Each primary campaign cycle involves an ongoing tug and pull. Many voters firmly commit to single issues, such as race, immigration, crime, abortion, climate, guns, religious freedom, or health care. Other voters commit to an ideology that major party leaders regard skeptically, such as libertarianism or democratic socialism. Whether principally committed to a singular cause or a broader set of ideals, such voters work toward nudging the nomination for the major party they ultimately support ever closer to their preferred ideological position. Each general election cycle reverses the dynamic, with the party's committed members begging frustrated voters to overcome their differences and embrace the nominee, however grudgingly.

In the two most recent presidential elections, 2016 and 2020, these all-too-familiar dynamics produced unprecedented levels of anger and frustration. After Trump lost in 2020, he persuaded his most ardent supporters that the election had been stolen. Some went so far as to attack the US Capitol on January 6, 2021 and to physically threaten Democratic and Republican leaders. This included Vice President Mike Pence, whom they viewed as a traitor for ultimately, if reluctantly, certifying the election result.[18]

As this book goes to press, several events are playing out in real-time, including the aftermath of a House investigation into the January 6 events and four sets of indictments against Donald Trump, two federal and two state.[19] The federal charges include allegedly instigating the January 6 attack on the US Capitol building and concealing classified documents at his Mar-a-Lago home in Florida.[20] The state charges include allegedly concealing payoffs to Stormy Daniels, a former porn star with whom he had a sexual encounter, and to former Playboy model Karen McDougal, with whom he had a longer relationship, in a scheme to defraud voters; and exerting pressure on a state official to change the outcome of the Georgia vote count in the 2016 election. In a civil suit, Trump was found liable for a forced sexual encounter in late 1995 or early 1996, with a plaintiff's verdict of five million dollars.[21]

Every US election presents its own unique personalities, salient issues, and complex political landscape. Although each presidential election includes some candidates running third party, those campaigns are often symbolic. Unlike the 1980, 1992, and

2000 presidential elections, the 2016 and 2020 elections did not include third-party candidates likely to pull sufficient votes from the two major parties to affect the outcome. And yet, the dynamics affecting all these elections are rooted in our two-party system. This is true whether or not a threatening third-party candidate enters a particular presidential race.

Frustrated voters routinely lament the absence of meaningful choice, wishing for a third party that captures their values. The sentiment is visceral and understandable. But consider the confounding nature of this instinctive response. If the goal is to prevail in high-stakes elections with the hope of exerting a benign influence on public policy and administration, the more compelling strategy is to crack the opposing alliance, never one's own. Holding out for influence while ensuring electoral defeat is Pyrrhic.

The third-party dilemma isn't universal. The political options we face arise from institutional structures, not the intensity of our desires. In the lead-up to the 2022 midterms, 2020 Democratic presidential hopeful Andrew Yang, joined by former Republican New Jersey Governor Christine Todd Whitman and David Jolly, a former Republican congressman from Florida, announced the Forward Party, claiming that two-thirds of voters are frustrated with the two-party system.[22] But frustration can't forge meaningful third parties. For that we need structural reform.

Democracy is the ultimate high-stakes game. Different nations play by different rules. Alternative institutions produce better incentives and invite more meaningful choices. Parliamentary systems let voters support third parties that help form the government and influence policy. Turning the third-party dilemma into a multiparty solution requires radical change both to our electoral rules and to our system of executive accountability.

In 2016, Donald Trump and Mike Pence prevailed in the Electoral College despite losing the popular vote by nearly 3 million of approximately 129 million votes cast.[23] In 2020, Joe Biden and Kamala Harris flipped Trump's 2016 Electoral College mar-

THE THIRD-PARTY DILEMMA 43

gin and captured a 7 million vote lead of approximately 159 million votes cast.[24] In these election cycles, traditional conservatives, meaning voters who are skeptical of governmental regulation, committed to longstanding social norms, and reluctant to embrace progressive—what some dismissively label as "woke"—causes, faced a wrenching choice. On the Republican ticket, they could support a candidate widely regarded as the least qualified and most personally vile in modern history and who catered to an increasingly populist, nationalist, and neofascist base. On the Democratic ticket, they could support a candidate who, although center-left, was distant from their views on wide-ranging policies and who, especially in 2020, risked increasingly strident progressive pressures.[25]

On the other side, progressives and Democratic Socialists who previously supported Bernie Sanders or Elizabeth Warren faced constant pleading to support the center-left Democratic nominees, Hillary Clinton in 2016 and Joe Biden in 2020. Clinton and Biden each sought to form and maintain a coalition capable of averting what they regarded as an existential threat. For them, defeating Trump and Trumpism was more important than embracing, beyond what was necessary to win, an ambitious policy agenda committed to nationalizing health care; relaxing immigration constraints; neutralizing carbon emissions; reconfiguring, if not actually abolishing, police departments; publicly funding community college; and alleviating student debt.[26]

In these elections, the trade-offs differed for progressives and conservatives. Progressives were pushed to support a party that had nominated mainstream candidates, even as those candidates tacked further left. Conservatives were pushed to support a threatening, uninformed, and incurious nationalist selected in 2016 against a vast field of experienced candidates who themselves tacked harder right. Despite these differences, the dynamics confronting these two opposing constituencies shared a root pathology. Regardless of the frustration such voters faced, viable third parties didn't exist and couldn't simply be willed into being.

As the 1980, 1992, and 2000 elections demonstrate, however intense it might be, voter frustration can't produce third parties that play a role other than spoiler, helping a more distant major party candidate, or randomizer, pulling votes from both sides and rendering outcomes as between the two major party candidates a roll of the dice. Unless we change our electoral system, efforts to create a new conservative party from the remnants of Trump's GOP or a crossover party that pulls in disaffected Republican and Democratic voters will suffer the same fate.

The number of viable parties in a democracy is a function of its systems of voting and executive accountability. In most democracies, those systems emerge from choices made when the constitution was written and adopted, or as products of long-standing tradition. Even when a constitution doesn't mention political parties, the number of parties and the functions they serve are features of constitutional design.

Party Games: Rock, Paper, Scissors Reconsidered

To understand what's wrong with how our major parties function, we must first understand what's right. Even troublesome systems once emerged to solve a problem. The difficulty is that solving one problem often creates others. When this happens, we either keep tinkering at the edges, hoping the problems get smaller and more manageable, or if they don't, face the need to revisit choices made long ago. Our two-party system is like that. It solved a problem, but it's past time to tinker. So, what did the two-party system accomplish?

The answer returns us to the childhood game from chapter 1. For now, let's stick with the original version: rock defeats scissors (by crushing), scissors defeat paper (by cutting), and paper defeats rock (by covering). As we've seen, no matter which option one child selects, another child's selection might defeat or be defeated by it. Now imagine that an overeager teacher—the kind of adult who takes all joy out of childhood games—tells the children they can't play with scissors. Of course, the children protest that two fingers can't cut anything, but the teacher remains undeterred, leaving them to play Rock Paper. There's no more cycle. By the rules of the game, paper always wins. Time to play something else!

Our two-party system does just that. It's like the teacher removing an option and breaking the cycle. To see why, we have to simplify things quite a bit, envisioning a different game, producing a different problem that our electoral rules solve.

Let's reimagine the 2016 election under an alternative set of rules. The election takes place all in one round based on polling giving each of three candidates sufficient national recognition to run and with the outcome determined by the national popular vote rather than the Electoral College. Recall that in the actual election, Hillary Clinton received 3 million more votes than Donald Trump of 129 million votes cast.

Assume these three candidates: Donald Trump, John Kasich, and Hillary Clinton. Donald Trump is a Republican nationalist who seeks to *Make America Great Again.* John Kasich is a traditional Republican who believes Trump's catchy slogan is a thinly veiled cover for something much darker and who also disagrees with the progressive pull of the Clinton candidacy. Hillary Clinton is a center-left Democrat who believes Trump represents an existential threat to the United States and who generally rejects Kasich's conservative economic policies.

Imagine three voters, Alex, Bonnie, and Carol, each representing about one-third of the electorate. Alex is a traditional conservative. He's concerned by the threat Trump represents but is more troubled by the progressive pull of the Clinton candidacy. Alex ranks the candidates Kasich, Trump, Clinton. Bonnie is a moderate Democrat. She prefers Clinton's center-left policies to Kasich's economic conservatism, and she's most fearful of a Trump presidency. She ranks the candidates Clinton, Kasich, Trump. Carol was part of her state's Tea Party movement and is now a devoted member of Trump's antiestablishment and nationalist base. She regards the Republican and Democratic major party establishments as indistinguishable, Tweedledee and Tweedledum, and perceives herself threatened by immigrants and others who she believes seek to upend the traditional American way of life. Although she disdains Clinton, she believes a Kasich presidency will prevent the once-in-a-lifetime opportunity that Trump presents for genuine change. By contrast, she believes a Clinton presidency might just anger traditional Republicans enough to produce a 2018 midterm upset, giving Trump a better shot in 2020 if he fails in 2016. Carol's preference ranking is Trump, Clinton, Kasich.

Alex: Kasich, Trump, Clinton
Bonnie: Clinton, Kasich, Trump
Carol: Trump, Clinton, Kasich

In this election, no candidate wins a majority. If we used ranked-choice voting, as some reform advocates propose, these voters end up playing the electoral version of Rock, Paper, Scissors: Kasich defeats Trump (Alex and Bonnie), Trump defeats Clinton (Alex and Carol), and Clinton defeats Kasich (Bonnie and Carol).

Our two-party system, first and foremost, breaks cycles. It ensures that for the highest office in the land, a candidate is virtually certain to win. Each party narrows the field to a single nominee, even if a candidate who lost in the primary might have had a better shot than the chosen nominee at defeating the other party's selected candidate. Like the teacher banning scissors, the parties effectively remove all options but two. And like children frustrated by the revised game—Rock Paper—many voters just walk away.

In the actual 2016 race, Donald Trump defeated Kasich in a primary field of sixteen candidates and went on to defeat Clinton in the general election based on the Electoral College. Even so, Trump was one of only five US presidents who won that office despite losing the national popular vote.[27] We'll never know how an alternative Republican candidate such as Jeb Bush, Marco Rubio, or John Kasich might have fared against Clinton in the general election. It's possible such a candidate would have defeated Clinton without producing an upside-down outcome, winning the Electoral College while losing the national popular vote.

Clinton was also widely regarded as high valence, but for her, this was almost exclusively negative. Unlike Trump, she lacked enthusiastic base support. She was largely viewed as a necessary accommodation in the battle against Trump.[28] A less divisive Republican nominee would likely have avoided the anxiety that Trump's candidacy provoked. While Trump defeated Kasich in the Republican primary and while Clinton got more votes than Trump in the general election, in a contest between Kasich and Clinton, Kasich, or another more mainstream Republican nominee, might have secured more popular votes.

Due to our two-party system, we can only speculate about how such alternatives might have played out. Indeed one function the two-party system serves is preventing us from knowing whether a candidate who lost in the initial round might have won in the general election. Eliminating other candidates in the field not only breaks a cycle; it also gives the appearance that the winner won by a majority even if another candidate might have changed the result or performed better by preventing an upside-down outcome. The system we have enhances the winning candidate's appearance of legitimacy, possibly masking an underlying Rock, Paper, Scissors game that leaves upwards of two-thirds of voters frustrated.

Games Parties Play

To better understand how an outlier candidate who might perform less well in a general election could win a major party nomination, let's consider a popular, yet obviously oversimplified, framing of our politics. The framing consists of a single line from left, for liberal, to right, for conservative. Imagine two

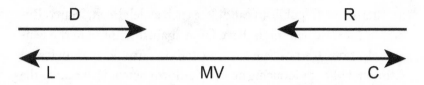

Candidate Ideological Convergence along a Single Dimension.
C = conservative; D = Democrat;
L = liberal; MV = median voter; R = Republican.

candidates each starting at opposite ends. Assume voters only care about which candidate's policies they prefer, and the candidates care only about winning.

In this game, each candidate will move closer and closer to the center, assuming that by doing so, he or she will capture more voters. Those who are frustrated to the left of the liberal candidate or to the right of the conservative one will continue supporting the closer candidate provided the two candidates don't cross paths. The game predicts that the two candidates will crash at the center on what political scientists call the median voter.

Recall that in the 2000 election, Ralph Nader claimed the choice of George W. Bush or Al Gore was Tweedledee or Tweedledum. The claim was absurd by any measure. And yet, in this simple game, that's just the result we'd observe. It might not be surprising that economist Anthony Downs popularized this game in his book *An Economic Theory of Democracy*[29] published in 1957. That was shortly after the American Political Science Association faulted the two major parties for being largely indistinguishable and just five years after both the Democrats and Republicans courted Dwight D. Eisenhower to be their presidential nominee.[30] Even if the candidates don't entirely converge on the median voter, this simple game helps explain how the major parties themselves eliminate the necessary space for third parties to thrive.

And yet, since the mid-twentieth century, our politics have dramatically changed. The parties have become increasingly distinct, so much so that the divisions between them make it exceedingly difficult for either party to govern effectively, especially when a single party doesn't control the White House and both houses of Congress. This didn't happen overnight. Despite Nader claiming otherwise, in the 2000 election, George W. Bush and Al Gore were widely divergent, more so than Richard Nixon and John F. Kennedy, who ran against each other in 1960, yet far less so than Donald Trump and Hillary Clinton in 2016 or Trump and Biden in 2020.[31] There is a troublesome pattern, with the parties once closely overlapping and then growing increasingly distant. The trend lines have been well-documented by the Pew Research

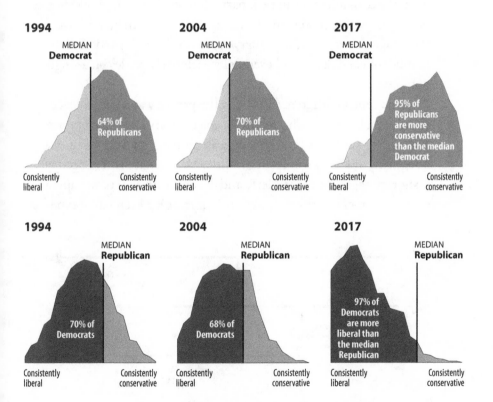

Less Overlap in the Political Values of Republicans and Democrats Than in the Past (survey conducted June 8–18, 2017). Modified from Pew Research Center, *The Partisan Divide on Political Values Grows Even Wider*, October 17, 2017, p. 13

Center, which showed that from 1994 until now, the modes, or ideological centers, of the parties have grown increasingly far apart.

Rather than a normal distribution of voters centered around a mean—the driver of the Downsian model—since the early 1990s, we have experienced an increasingly bimodal voter distribution. This partly results from better sorting, with fewer conservatives registered as Democrats and fewer liberals registered as Republicans. Today's parties are better grouped ideologically.[32] But the larger story involves two parties with modes that continue to grow increasingly distant over time.

With a few tweaks, this simple one-line framing helps to explain the dynamics within each party. Rather than a single election pitting three (or more) candidates against each other, we have a two-stage election. In the primary/caucus cycle, each party vets any number of candidates, and eventually each party settles on a single nominee.

The central difference between the primary and general elections is that those voting for either major party's nominee represent only a subset of the electorate. Each party's voters comprise a segment of the longer left-right line. Democratic voters occupy a shorter segment to the left, and Republican voters occupy a shorter segment to the right. We might imagine each party expe-

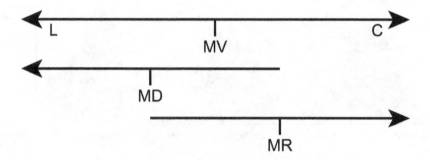

Truncated Party-Line Segments as Compared
with General Voter Distribution.
C = conservative; L = liberal; MD = median Democrat;
MR = median Republican; MV = median voter.

riencing the dynamic that Anthony Downs captured, with Democratic and Republican candidates converging on each party's median voter. That would explain some divergence between the parties in the general election, avoiding Ralph Nader's Tweedledee or Tweedledum. But there's more to the story, and this is where valence comes into play.

The Seesaw Game

Let's return to the playground but this time where we find preschoolers. Remember the seesaw, also called a teeter-totter. It's a long narrow board with handles at each end, balanced on a fulcrum at the center. As a child on one side rides up, the other rides down, and vice versa. This simple ride explains something quite important. In a two-party system, Newton's third law of motion—for every action there is an equal and opposite reaction—becomes the first law of politics. The two parties are locked into a battle, and changes in the position on one side necessarily elicit an equal and opposite response on the other.

Single Ideological Dimension Cast as a Seesaw.

Political scientist Lee Drutman, among others, has demonstrated that a single line, even as modified to allow for primaries, fails to capture something essential in our politics.[33] We can explain this with the seesaw. Drutman's alternative framing depicts a four-quadrant box divided both horizontally and vertically. The horizontal line captures liberal economic policy to the left and conservative economic policy to the right. The vertical line captures conservative culture or identity politics to the top and liberal culture or identity politics to the bottom.

Let's start in the upper-right quadrant and move counterclock-
wise. The upper right, conservative on culture and economic policy, captures traditional Republicans. The upper left, liberal on
economic policy and conservative on cultural issues, captures what
many commentators call populism or nationalism. The lower left,
liberal both on economic and social policy, captures traditional
Democrats. And finally, the lower right, liberal on culture/identity
and conservative on economics/policy, captures libertarianism.

Now let's revisit the playground. Before anyone gets on, the
seesaw is perfectly balanced. This corresponds to the horizontal
line, right versus left on policy, that separates the two top quadrants from the two bottom quadrants. Now let's replace the preschoolers with Trump and Clinton, placing them on opposite
ends. Recall that in Professor Downs's framing, the candidates are
expected to converge on the center, depicted here as the fulcrum

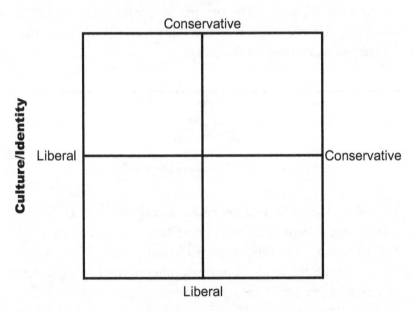

Four-Box Matrix Capturing Economics/Policy
and Culture/Identity Political Dimensions.

itself, which represents the median voter. As the Pew data demonstrate, however, the modern voting distribution is bimodal. This requires the candidates to make an important strategic choice. They can campaign hard to the base, hoping to motivate turnout, or they can signal moderation and try to capture less ideologically committed voters, including possible crossovers from the other party. Commentators debate which strategy is more effective.[34]

But that's not the only strategic choice. A second strategic decision involves trying to enlarge the base coalition by appealing to culture or identity politics. Trump ran his primary and general election campaigns playing to a nationalist base, a pattern he continued as president by opposing immigration, denigrating Muslims, zealously advocating for law enforcement (except on January 6, 2021), insisting upon calling COVID the "China virus," and failing to condemn neo-Nazis shouting "Jews will not replace us" at a rally protesting the removal of statues of Confederate generals, instead declaring "very fine people on both sides."[35]

Trump didn't embrace liberal economic policies. He ran a culture/identity campaign rather than an economics/policy campaign, and he did so for good reason. To run a policy campaign, you must understand policy. By all accounts, Trump couldn't be bothered with mastery, even to the point of failing to attend daily foreign policy briefings. He proclaimed himself his own most trusted advisor and declared only he could fix the economy.[36] A nationalist identity campaign requires little by way of expertise; it simply requires unapologetically embracing MAGA rhetoric, not sophistication or subtlety.

In our two-party system, voters face a binary choice, and what happens with one candidacy directly affects the other—in equal and opposite fashion. It is not surprising that as Trump rode the seesaw upward toward nationalism, Clinton, and later Biden, experienced downward pressure on the other end of the seesaw to embrace strong anti-nationalist, pro-immigrant policies that would appeal to the increasingly angry progressive base of the Democratic party.

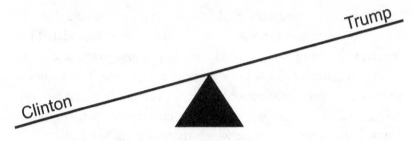

Adjusted Seesaw with Effect of Trump Campaign
and Clinton Ideological Location.

On the seesaw ride, Trump transformed our political landscape, capturing more and more of the populist base. In doing so,
he foisted a set of daunting choices on traditional conservatives.
Although once-moderate Republicans would have preferred a candidate to the right of the original horizontal economics/policy line,
they were ultimately forced to choose between Trump, who rode
the seesaw upward toward nationalist culture/identity, or Clinton,
who was pressured to ride in the opposite direction.

Our two-party system doesn't eliminate voting cycles. It sup-
presses them. We can still imagine Alex, Bonnie, and Carol cycling over Kasich, Trump, and Clinton. But with Kasich out and
two high-valence candidates remaining, anything can happen—
even Trump winning the presidency despite Clinton capturing 3
million more votes.

Better Party Games

Let's imagine a fancier playground. This one has several seesaws
all lined up in a row. If you crouch down just right, several ful-
crums stand in line behind the closest one. Now you can watch
multiple seesaws moving up and down as if fixed in the center at
a singular point.

We might imagine Trump going up on one seesaw, but another seesaw staying flat. Clinton might decide not to embrace

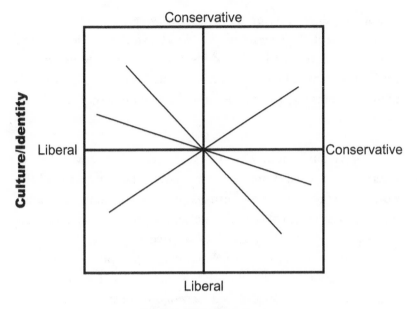

Conservative

Culture/Identity

Liberal   Conservative

Liberal

Policy/Economics

Multiple Perfectly Aligned Seesaws Occupying
Myriad Locations within a Four-Box Matrix.

substantially more liberal cultural positions, but Bernie Sanders
for the Democratic Socialists might press down as Trump moves
up. With the seesaw's length extended past the outer right and
left edges of the four-box frame, we can imagine candidates taking a ride that lands anywhere within those boxes. Candidates can
thus position themselves in a manner that represents any set of
combined choices on economics/policy and culture/identity. In
this game, voters aren't forced to commit to a binary choice of two
extreme candidates, neither of whom matches their ideology or
policy preferences.

The fancier playground isn't a fantasy. It's how politics is
played out in multiparty parliamentary democracies around the
world. In those systems, voters enjoy a menu of options across all
four boxes. Rather than being admonished—election cycle after
election cycle—to vote strategically for either of two major-party

candidates, despite liking neither, voters vote for candidates who truly represent their views of the world. And after the election, in proportion to which parties' visions prove most appealing to voters, the party leaders negotiate a governing coalition. Through these negotiations, the third-party dilemma emerges the third-party solution.

To improve our system, citizens must understand how we got to where we are, what more satisfying systems look like around the world and why, and how we can adapt our institutions to create a system that is more cohesive and better functioning. Chapter 3 explains the historical foundations of our two-party system and how it went off the rails in the information age. Chapter 4 provides a parallel account of media, including social media. Together, these chapters provide an unvarnished view of our constitutional system and the problems it has created for our politics and culture.

CHAPTER 3

Constitutional Gridlock

HOW A SYSTEM WE MANAGED FOR TWO CENTURIES SUDDENLY WENT OFF THE RAILS

Under the Articles of Confederation, Thomas Jefferson and John Adams represented the new nation in Paris and London, respectively. The senior Adams brought along his son, young John Quincy, for part of his time abroad, and the widower Jefferson brought along his daughter, Martha. At various times, the statesmen and their children met together. In one diary entry, John Quincy noted that he and his father joined Jefferson and Martha for dinner.[1] At the dinner table sat three future presidents whose political fortunes would solidify and entrench our two-party system.

Adams and Jefferson went on to lead opposing political parties. Adams, the Federalist heir to George Washington, defeated Jefferson in the nation's first contested presidential election in 1796. In a rematch four years later, then–Vice President Jefferson defeated Adams, making him a one-term president. Jefferson served two terms. The political contest produced a rift between two friends, which physician Dr. Benjamin Rush managed to successfully mend after the former presidents retired from public life. The restored friendship produced a half-century of invaluable correspondence until both men died, remarkably, on July 4, 1826, precisely fifty years after the signing of the Declaration of Independence.[2] For the former presidents, political discord yielded to restored affection. Our two-party system fared less well. This chapter tells that story.

The story of our elections is symphonic, four movements with connected themes. First, I will explain how, despite the Framers' intention to avoid parties, three presidential elections and one midterm election embedded the Democratic and Republican parties into our electoral system. Second, I will explore the complex interrelationship between our parties and our nation's tragic history of race, a feature deeply infused into our culture and central to our politics. Third, I will discuss the changing roles parties played in moving from coordinating local political activity and vetting candidates to servicing candidates who reached constituents directly with the help of technology. Lastly, I will describe hyper-partisan gerrymandering, the electoral mapping process that lets controlling state parties gain disproportionate representation as compared with the state's demographics, producing egregious distortions and other problematic consequences even beyond the capacity of those responsible to control.

In chapter 4, I will present the closely parallel history of media. Together, the chapters reveal an inversion: rather than voters and readers choosing representatives and media, representatives and media now choose voters and readers.

Emerging Parties

The United States isn't just home to the world's oldest operating constitution; it's also home to the two longest continuing political parties.[3] The Democratic Party was formed by supporters of

Andrew Jackson leading up to the election of 1828. After being defeated by John Quincy Adams in 1824, Jackson was elected in a rematch four years later. John Quincy Adams, like his father, served only one term, and he was the first of five presidents to serve despite losing the national popular vote.[4] The Republican Party was formed in 1854 by members of the former Whig Party and remnants of other parties, including the Free Soil Party and antislavery Democrats angered that the Kansas-Nebraska Act allowed slavery to expand into emerging western states.

Abraham Lincoln's 1860 presidential victory both eviscerated the Whigs and instigated Southern secession. Four years later, under the ephemeral National Unity Party, Lincoln was reelected with a different vice president, having replaced Hannibal Hamlin with Southern Democrat Andrew Johnson. Although enduring rivals, the Democratic and Republican parties have long shared a symbiotic relationship that transformed our governing institutions and ultimately wreaked havoc with our politics and culture.

In chapter 2, I illustrated the third-party dilemma with one midterm election, 2018, and three presidential elections, 2000, 1992, and 1980. In this chapter, I also introduce three presidential elections, 1800, 1824, and 1860, and one midterm election, 1842. These elections help to explain how our two-party system became an entrenched and deeply problematic feature of our electoral politics, ultimately threatening our nation's ability to continue as a thriving democracy.

From Anointed to Contested

In the first two presidential elections, President George Washington and Vice President John Adams ran largely unopposed.[5] Washington limited himself to two terms, from 1789 to 1797. Although Adams, a Federalist, defeated Jefferson in 1796 and served as president from 1797 to 1801, Jefferson, Adams's Democratic-Republican vice president, defeated Adams in 1800 and went on to serve two terms. This seemingly unimaginable result—a vice president from a different party defeating his own president—arose from a peculiarity in the original Constitution. The feature reflected the Framers' mistaken belief that they had devised a system that avoided what they called factions and we call parties.

In the original presidential election system, each elector to the Electoral College cast two ballots with the understanding that one was for president and the other for vice president, although the Constitution drew no such distinction. Formally, the scheme treated the two ballots as if both were for president. The majority candidate would be president, and the second-place winner would be vice president. The early parties developed an informal arrangement to avoid a mishap. One designated elector would throw a vote originally intended to support the party's vice-presidential candidate instead to an alternative candidate. This ensured that the party's presidential candidate received one more vote and thus emerged the winner.

The 1800 election was complicated because no candidate received a majority of Electoral College votes. Under the Constitution's fallback provision, the House of Representatives was tasked with choosing among the top three candidates—Adams, Jefferson, and Aaron Burr—with each state receiving one vote. Although Burr was intended as Jefferson's Democratic-Republican running mate, Burr took the failed Electoral College as an opportunity to press his advantage and seek the top office.

Alexander Hamilton, a Federalist who profoundly disagreed with Jefferson on the proper scope of federal power (for example, by creating a national bank), nonetheless helped Jefferson get elected, undermining Burr after an astounding thirty-six House ballots. Hamilton is claimed to have stated that he preferred a man with the wrong convictions to a man with none.[6] These events played out center stage in Lin Manuel Miranda's *Hamilton*, where after the 1800 presidential election, Burr assured Jefferson of his loyalty. Jefferson dismissed Burr, saying he'd get the Constitution fixed so that such a thing never happened again. And he did. Although the Twelfth Amendment doesn't mention parties, it lets candidates for president and vice president run together on party slates. For the first time, the Constitution implicitly recognized the central role parties had already come to play. For Burr, Hamilton's betrayal was sufficient to trigger the duel ending his life. As Burr proclaimed in the musical, "I'm the damned fool who shot him!"[7]

The Twelfth Amendment reveals a rarely understood feature of the original Constitution. By mistakenly assuming they had avoided political parties, the Framers invited a 1796 election anomaly that seems unimaginable today: Adams, a Federalist president, alongside Jefferson, a Democratic-Republican vice president. Before the Twelfth Amendment, nothing prevented candidates from different parties from occupying those offices. As a result, in the original constitutional scheme, before the Twelfth Amendment, a successful impeachment could remove the president and potentially change the party controlling the government. To that extent, the scheme was more analogous to a parliamentary no confidence vote, which can end a failing government, albeit with a lower standard than our impossible-to-satisfy impeachment clause, which requires "Treason, Bribery, or other high Crimes and Misdemeanors."[8]

Under the Twelfth Amendment, with the president and vice president running as a party slate, removing the president following impeachment generally elevates the president's chosen successor and party loyalist.[9] Even aside from impeachment's extraordinarily high bar, this changed dynamic has effectively gutted the clause. In nearly a quarter millennium, it has never been used to forcibly remove a sitting president.[10]

The 1824 Election, Andrew Jackson's Democratic Party, and Fusion Ticketing as Primitive Ranked-Choice Voting

After the 1800 presidential election, the only other presidential contest resolved in the House of Representatives featured John Adams's son, John Quincy. In 1824, four Democratic-Republican candidates ran for president and three for vice president. Through a practice known as fusion ticketing, the listed party candidates varied by state to appeal to voters in different regions.[11] John Quincy Adams appealed to the Northeast, he and Andrew Jackson split the Mid-Atlantic, Henry Clay dominated in the West, and Jackson and William Crawford split the South.

Later, in the mid- to late-nineteenth century, fusion tickets evolved, letting smaller parties list major party candidates at the top of the ticket with their own candidates down-ballot.[12] The parties provided preprinted ballots listing these preferred candidates, which voters submitted. Australian ballots, or blanket ballots, listing all candidates for voters to select from weren't introduced in the United States until after 1888.

Fusion tickets are a primitive form of ranked-choice voting. A voter could support a minor party and still endorse a major presidential candidate without wasting a vote. Not surprisingly, the two major parties came to disapprove of the practice, ultimately having it banned. In the 1997 case *Timmons v. Twin Cities Area New Party*, the Supreme Court sustained the ban against a First Amendment challenge,[13] with two dissenters stressing that the ban entrenched the two major parties, preventing third parties from negotiating platform issues.[14]

Fusion ticketing in the 1824 election took a different form, with major parties listing different candidates at the top of ballots deployed in varying regions of the country to appeal to alternative cross sections of voters. Andrew Jackson won a plurality of both the popular and Electoral College votes but not a majority. While John Calhoun, listed as running mate for both Adams and Jackson, easily won that office, the presidential contest wound up in the House of Representatives. Following Twelfth Amendment protocol, the House voted among the top three candidates, excluding Henry Clay who came in fourth, with each state casting one vote.

Many politicians anticipated that, as plurality winner, Jackson would be chosen. Instead, Henry Clay threw his support to John

Quincy Adams, who won. Adams appointed Clay as secretary of state, a position widely viewed as a launching pad to the presidency. Jackson and his supporters cried foul, claiming a corrupt bargain.

The 1824 election had an unanticipated effect on our electoral system, with continuing influence two centuries later. New York Senator Martin Van Buren, a Jackson loyalist who would become our eighth president, took the upset as motivation to solidify the emerging Democratic Party. A gifted strategist, Van Buren insistently avoided ideological commitments on slavery and was largely opposed to what Henry Clay had called the "American System," which favored central regulatory powers to improve the economy. Van Buren instead favored decentralized governance and broader electoral participation, including immigrants, albeit limited to white males.[15] Van Buren forged the first national party, with constituents north and south, by emphasizing local concerns and patronage, providing jobs to party loyalists before the civil service was professionalized.

Even by modern standards, the 1828 rematch between Jackson and Adams was salacious. In addition to leveling personal accusations against Jackson, the "Hero of New Orleans," for the unauthorized execution of militia deserters, Adams supporters claimed Jackson's wife of four decades, Rachel, was an adulteress. Although Rachel's divorce from a prior marriage hadn't been finalized when she initially wed Jackson, the couple had soon remedied that with a second ceremony. Tragically, Rachel died of a heart attack following the 1828 election before Jackson took office, possibly from the strain on her personal reputation. For their part, Jackson's supporters leveled dubious accusations against Adams of having procured prostitutes for the Czar when Adams served as Russian minister.[16]

Jackson, a populist whose presidency featured the tragic Trail of Tears, defeated Adams, limiting him to a single term. Jackson went on to serve two terms. His loyal supporter, Martin Van Buren, who served Jackson first as secretary of state and then as vice president, was elected as president for one term, from 1837 to 1841, after which he was defeated.

The 1842 Midterm and Two Sides of At-Large Congressional Voting

The second two-party system, following the Federalists and Democratic-Republicans, pitted the Democrats against the Whigs. Like the Democrats, the Whigs were also a national party that eschewed firm policy commitments that risked alienating a major part of the electorate. For example, Northern Whigs were less tolerant of slavery than both Southern Democrats and Southern Whigs.

The 1840 election pitted William Henry Harrison, a Whig, and John Tyler, a nominal Whig and former Southern Democrat, against Van Buren, who ran without a running mate. Harrison won but died after just one month in office and before succession rules were clarified. The original Constitution didn't specify what happened upon a president's death, and some called upon Tyler to take the title Acting President. Tyler declined. Tyler's detractors, including former President John Quincy Adams, then a Whig congressman, referred to the new administration as "His Accidency." The Twenty-Fifth Amendment, ratified in 1967, resolved the line of succession with a vice president becoming president upon the premature end of a term.

In the late 1830s and early 1840s, the Democrats held majorities in several states, including in the South. Georgia, Mississippi, Missouri, and New Hampshire selected their House delegations with at-large voting. This placed the Whigs at a disadvantage as bloc voting—Democratic majorities voting for their party's candidates across the board—could cost even a large Whig minority a state's entire congressional delegation. The concern wasn't theoretical. With the accidental Tyler administration, the Whigs set about ending at-large voting in the 1842 Apportionment Act, instead requiring single-member geographical districts.

Even following a ban on at-large House elections, in the 1842 Georgia election, which still followed the practice, the Whigs failed to win a single House seat despite capturing 48.5 percent of the vote.[17]

Although he supported Henry Clay's presidential candidacy in the Whig Party convention, Tyler was more sympathetic to states' rights than the Whigs, who were generally more tolerant of centralized power. Tyler didn't like the Apportionment Act, which ended a longstanding state practice, but he signed it into law to clarify the rules governing the upcoming 1842 midterm election. In a presidential signing statement, Tyler questioned the constitutionality of the single-member district mandate, giving Georgia some cover in failing to follow it.

The 1842 statute didn't conclusively settle the ban on at-large voting, and Congress variously banned or condoned the practice until as late as 1967. Ninety years after the 1842 act, the Supreme Court held in the 1932 *Wood v. Broom* decision that federal apportionment statutes only governed elections until the following apportionment statute took effect.[18] Even so, the expectation of single-member geographical districts became dominant despite occasional statutory lapses and failures to enforce rules prohibiting at-large schemes. In a 1967 statute, Congress finally banned at-large voting outright, insisting upon single-member congressional districts.[19]

Although at-large voting initially benefited Democrats and harmed Whigs, when the Democrats and Republicans became dominant, single-member districts benefited both major parties. The practice rendered majoritarian elections in congressional districts inevitable, effectively blocking third parties. For some periods of our history, two parties came to dominate a region but not the country as a whole. The most notable example is the Farmer-Labor Parties, which dominated in western states and elected members of Congress.[20]

By 1967, when Congress permanently banned at-large voting, only Hawaii and New Mexico still used it. Hawaii, which had been admitted as a state in 1959 and which had two House members, expressed little objection despite its unusual geography posing districting challenges.

Politically, at-large voting within multimember districts is generally a two-edged sword.[21] Although such processes, coupled with a non-majority allocation method, potentially lower the bar for electing third-party candidates, as seen in the 1842 Georgia election a controlling party can game the system to entrench its power.

The 1860 Election

Transitional periods may introduce additional parties as we shift from one stable two-party system to another. We saw this in the shift from the first party system, with Federalists and Democratic-Republicans, to the second, with Democrats and Whigs. Although other parties have emerged or receded over time, when the system stabilized, two parties dominated. Shifts across systems might arise from unforeseen events or long-simmering problems that eventually boiled over. Political scientist John Aldrich refers to such results as "punctuated equilibria,"[22] meaning that although different historical events may have produced a different combination of parties, once the dust settles, we end up with two. The transition from the second to third systems, from Democrats and Whigs to Democrats and Republicans, is a punctuated equilibrium.

The Whigs primarily emerged from the National Republican Party and were joined by members of the Anti-Masonic Party and former Democrats who opposed Jackson's populist presidency.[23] Whigs represented a more educated and professional class than the Democrats. Like the Democrats, the Whigs tended to avoid clear commitments on slavery, but they generally accepted stronger centralized powers. Over time, the fault lines among Whigs intensified, with Northern Whigs less tolerant of slavery and Southern and Western Whigs more accommodating.

The Whigs' fate began to seal after the divisive 1854 Kansas-Nebraska Act and as the Republican Party grew dominant in the North. The Act repealed the Missouri Compromise, which had disallowed slavery's expansion into the western territories. The later statute let territories set their own slavery policies, thereby failing to resolve the issue nationally or to limit slavery to existing jurisdictions.

The fractures among Northern antislavery Whigs and more accommodating Southern and Western Whigs became acute in the 1856 presidential election. Zachary Taylor, a Whig, had been elected president in 1848 but died two years later and was replaced by Vice President Millard Filmore. In 1852, Filmore lost the Whig nomination to Winfield Scott. Filmore ran on behalf of the Know Nothing Party, and John R. Frémont ran as a Republican. With the Whig alliance split, Democrat Franklin Pierce prevailed despite capturing only 45.3 percent of the popular vote.

Although accommodating different approaches to the issue, the ascendent Republican Party was uniform in opposing slavery. The dominant position sought to cabin slavery and prevent expansions into new territories, with some Northern Republicans embracing a staunch abolitionist view. The 1860 Republican Party convention divided, with New York Senator William Seward expecting to receive the nomination having secured a plurality of votes. The one-term Whig congressman from Illinois, Abraham Lincoln, had emerged as a national figure through a well-timed biography and speaking tour. This followed the famed Lincoln-Douglas debates in the 1858 Illinois race for the US Senate and a well-received speech Lincoln gave in New York, Seward's home state. Other hopefuls further divided the field. Lincoln's supporters brilliantly strategized to ensure that among those for whom he was not a first choice, Lincoln would be the second.[24] Lincoln defeated Seward and, with other candidates dropping away, secured the nomination on the third ballot.

In the general election, Lincoln defeated Democratic Senator Stephen Douglas in what became a nationwide rematch of the

1858 Illinois Senate election. Lincoln also defeated John Breck-
enridge, the sitting vice president and Southern Democratic nominee, and John Bell of the Constitutional Union Party. Lincoln's
victory, perceived in the South as a commitment to end slavery,
motivated Southern states to secede. Along with the Supreme
Court's infamous 1857 *Dred Scott v. Sandford* decision,[25] which
held that persons of African descent could not be US citizens and
which, by striking down the Missouri Compromise, foreclosed
political compromise on slavery, the 1860 election precipitated the
Civil War. Southern secession challenged the premise that We the
People, a higher sovereign than the states, had conferred vital attributes of state sovereignty to the federal government. Although
the Civil War vindicated that premise, had it turned out otherwise, drawing that conclusion wouldn't be so tidy. Despite the
Union's victory, little about the second constitutional crisis—
sometimes called the Second Founding—is neat. And its disor-
derly nature informs the crisis we face today.

Near the end of the Civil War, with over 600,000 soldiers
dying, Lincoln was reelected on the ephemeral National Unity
Ticket alongside Andrew Johnson, a Southern-sympathizing former Democrat. Lincoln's assassination elevated Johnson to the
oval office and produced major setbacks in ensuring the freedom
of formerly enslaved people. As depicted in the 2012 movie *Lincoln*, with Daniel Day-Lewis brilliantly portraying the sixteenth
president, Lincoln masterfully maneuvered Congress, sending the
Thirteenth Amendment, formally ending slavery, through for
state ratification. Along with so much else, Lincoln's assassination limited that amendment's force.

Ultimately, the second constitutional crisis produced two more
constitutional amendments, totaling three. The Fourteenth
Amendment overturned *Dred Scott* and ensured that African
Americans would be both citizens of the states in which they were
domiciled and of the United States. It provided all persons due
process and equal protection of the law and ensured citizens would
not be denied privileges or immunities. The Fifteenth Amend-

ment ensured African American men could not be denied the right to vote due to their race.

These amendments likewise were severely limited in their practical scope to the point of taking nearly a century to give them effect, and even now, they have yet to be given full effect. Lincoln's January 1, 1863, Emancipation Proclamation didn't end slavery, nor did the Reconstruction Amendments enacted from 1865 to 1870. Ultimately, enslaved persons were freed when Northern troops invaded Southern states and territories, which in some instances occurred as late as 1865. President Joe Biden recognized this in declaring Juneteenth a national holiday.[26] The true anniversary of American freedom is celebrated fifteen days earlier and commemorates events eighty-nine years later than the Fourth of July.

The Fourteenth and Fifteenth Amendments fell short of their aspirational text. The compromise of 1876 elected Republican Rutherford B. Hayes president instead of Democrat Samuel Tilden on the condition of Northern troop withdrawal, reversing the considerable gains in the eight-year Ulysses Grant administration and ending Reconstruction.[27] Southern states enacted impossible-to-satisfy voting requirements, once more disenfranchising African American men. More broadly, a regime of Black Codes kept freedmen second-class citizens. African Americans were routinely brutalized by thinly veiled efforts of government officials who treated the Ku Klux Klan as private, despite condoning and sometimes joining it outright.

Negative Rights and the Problem of Race

Even aside from its systems of elections and executive accountability, our Constitution differs from most modern constitutions across the globe. It's founded upon late-eighteenth-century conceptions of rights. Modern constitutions express positive rights to which citizens, or persons generally, are affirmatively entitled. Instead of expressing obligations to citizens or persons for the

government to fulfill, our Constitution sets limitations, or negative rights, that people may assert against the government. Both
framings are problematic but in different ways. Positive rights
constitutions create a disjuncture between promises made and
kept. Consider, for example, the jarring contrast between the South
African Constitution's promise of food and housing and the extensive shantytowns in such cities as Cape Town and Johannesburg.[28]
Expressing a constitutional obligation to provide even basic min-
imums does not of its own force ensure the significant political
and financial commitments required to bring such promises to
fruition.

The negative rights conception creates serious problems of a
different sort. The Fifteenth Amendment prevents states from de-
nying the right to vote based on race. But states seeking to deny
African Americans access to voting have found endless creative
alternatives. And although the methods have evolved, the problem isn't limited to the period following Reconstruction. It per-
sists today, and it played a role in the 2020 presidential election
between Donald Trump and Joe Biden. The Republican Party has
become expert at exploiting the Constitution to support pretextual laws depriving minorities, most notably African Americans,
of voting rights, knowing that they overwhelmingly support
Democratic candidates. Along with partisan gerrymandering, this
has become a principal strategy by which the modern Republican
Party, with its shrinking electoral base, assumes disproportionate
power relative to demographics.

Examples of Southern Democratic restrictions that historically disenfranchised African Americans without expressly mentioning race include grandfather clauses, property ownership
requirements, literacy tests, and poll taxes.[29] The Twenty-Fourth
Amendment, ratified in 1964, prohibited poll taxes, but with so
many other available tricks, that hardly mattered. Southern states
easily found alternative strategies. More recent Republican strategies adversely affecting turnout among African Americans and
other disadvantaged communities have included government-

issued voter identification requirements, limiting polling locations, banning third-party ballot collectors, restricting mail-in voting, and even banning giving water to voters waiting in long lines in the heat during the COVID-19 pandemic.

Dissenting in the 2013 Supreme Court decision, *Shelby County v. Holder*, Justice Ruth Bader Ginsburg evocatively captured the resulting dynamic: "Early attempts to cope with this vile infection [of suppressing the Black vote] resembled battling the Hydra. Whenever one form of voting discrimination was identified and prohibited, others sprang up in its place."[30] The *Shelby County* majority invalidated the continuing application of Section 4 of the Voting Rights Act of 1965, which subjected states with a history of express racial discrimination in voting to a process of administrative review under Section 5 designed to ensure new laws would not limit voting rights. The Supreme Court held that it was unfair to continue a regulatory regime premised on practices invalidated half a century before.

The Voting Rights Act extended voting rights beyond the poll tax ban. Section 2 ensured non-retrogression of minority voting rights, meaning it protected African Americans against laws reducing their voting power. Section 5 imposed the process of administrative review in covered jurisdictions. That meant the Attorney General or a federal district court would review changes in voting laws in states with a history of express racial discrimination to ensure newer policies would not reduce effective minority representation. As newer variations of pretextual state laws evaded the act's effectiveness, at least for a time, Congress fought back.

Amendments enacted in 1982 extended the Voting Rights Act for twenty-five years and prohibited laws that effectively diminished voting rights without requiring proof of discriminatory intent.[31] The amendments overturned a 1980 case that rejected a challenge to at-large voting in the city council of Mobile, Alabama.[32] As happened with the Democrats and Whigs surrounding the 1842 Apportionment Act, the problem was bloc voting.

This time, however, the voting bloc was racial.[33] A white majority voting bloc ensured no Blacks were elected, leaving the substantial African American minority, like the 1842 Georgia Whigs, unrepresented.

Some members of Congress who opposed the 1982 Amendments expressed concern about lawsuits challenging racially restrictive voting laws based on disproportionate impact without proof of discriminatory intent. Opponents argued the change might be interpreted to require proportional representation, aligning electoral outcomes with each party's percentage of the vote. The amendments passed after Republican Kansas Senator Bob Dole assured his colleagues the revision wouldn't have that effect.[34]

Like so much involving race, the legacy of the Voting Rights Act is complicated. At least with respect to districting, the act sometimes united African Americans and Republicans against the interests of Southern Democrats. In the longer history of the two major parties, the Democrats have assumed the mantle of African American civil rights, and the Republican party ultimately absorbed the last remnants of the Southern Democrats, also called Dixiecrats. Today, African Americans are the Democratic Party's most reliable constituency.[35] And yet, the historical relationship between the African American community and the Democratic Party has often been fraught. African Americans have long faced a trade-off between broader influence as a minority in more geographical districts versus greater concentration in fewer districts, with majority power to elect representatives of their own race. The Republican Party has benefited from, and ingeniously exploited, this trade-off as part of its electoral strategy.[36]

In effect the Voting Rights Act lets Republicans gain more House seats by packing African Americans into racially dense districts that lower overall Democratic voting strength. In our winner-take-all districted voting system, the odd marriage between African American voters and Republicans has generally been resolved in favor of more African American seats but with the minority representatives having less power to effectuate policies designed to benefit their communities. A system of proportional representation—precisely what Senator Dole disclaimed—would counter the peculiar dynamic of enhancing African American voting rights at the expense of the party with which the vast majority of such voters are more closely aligned.

Changing Parties and Parties Changing

Throughout our history, political candidates and parties have shared a reciprocal relationship. In exchange for access to party structures and networks used to contact and organize constituents, aspiring politicians have long ceded nomination vetting processes to party elites. This relationship evolved along with mid-twentieth-century technologies. High valence candidates and officeholders gained access to increasingly powerful channels of direct-to-constituent communications such as talk radio, cable television, and social media. Elite party vetting processes increasingly played a subordinate role to processes driven more directly by communications among high valence candidates and their voting constituents.[37]

Provided the candidates expressed the core ideology, or values, of their respective parties, the shifting emphasis in functions could be reconciled with the party's primary mission of gaining power to further desired policy objectives. For example, neither President Franklin Delano Roosevelt's fireside chats nor John F. Kennedy's 1960 televised debate performances, first against Hubert Humphrey in the primary and then against Vice President Richard Nixon in the general election, created a fundamental transformation of Democratic Party ideology. On policy, Kennedy was not terribly distant by modern standards from either his primary or general election opponents, although he was more charismatic. Greater challenges arise when high valence candidates evade elites to press policies or other objectives that challenge the party's central values.

No election exemplified this changed dynamic more power-fully than the 2016 Republican primary. Throughout a campaign against fifteen candidates, most with considerable political experience, Donald Trump vilified Republican Party leaders. This included 2008 Republican presidential nominee and war hero Senator John McCain (Trump preferred soldiers who don't get caught). It also included several once-leading primary contenders: Senator Marco Rubio (calling him short), Governor Jeb Bush (decrying his lack of energy), and Carly Fiorina (criticizing her physical appearance). In one debate, Jeb Bush proclaimed that Trump couldn't insult his way to the presidency.[38] Bush was wrong.

In a campaign marked by ignorance, inconsistency, and incuriosity, Trump's defining attribute was his taste for derision of party leaders and opponents. For a time, such leaders as Speaker of the House Paul Ryan and 2012 Republican presidential nominee Senator Mitt Romney sought to distance themselves from the wreckage. But especially for Republicans, once selected, the party serves the candidate, not the other way around.

The transformation didn't happen overnight, and the changed relationships weren't symmetrical between the Republican and Democratic parties. In the 1980s, conservative talk radio provided Republican candidates a largely unfiltered and unbalanced medium for direct constituent communication to base party voters. In 1987, the Federal Communications Commission abandoned the Fairness Doctrine, which had required the presentation of competing political views. This coincided with the emergence of *The Rush Limbaugh Show*. Launched in Sacramento, California, the longstanding broadcast conveyed the host's singular conservative take on nearly every political and social issue.

Democrats struggled for a counterpart, largely because the two parties operate so differently. As a general matter, at least historically, Republicans have coalesced around commitments to free markets, small government, decentralized decision-making, traditional values, and distrust of social mandates for change. The Democrats aren't so neatly aligned on a defining set of core principles. As Will Rogers famously stated, "I am not a member of any organized political party. I am a Democrat."[39] Democrats are an amalgam of disparate interests that must unify again and again, brushing over tensions that compete for priority. The core constituent groups today include advocates for racial justice, gender equality, reproductive rights, LGBTQ+ rights, progressive tax and social welfare policies, market reforms, and climate reform. The challenge for the anti-Limbaugh, and later the anti–Sean Hannity, another prominent and controversial talk radio host, is that what is most critical to one Democratic constituency isn't necessarily motivating to another. There's a difference between sympathizing with a cause and rallying for it.

Within the Republican Party, talk radio contributed to an emerging wedge separating once mainstream, or center-right, constituents from a hard-line, anti-elite, and populist base. Some candidates were able to navigate the competing factions, benefiting from the medium while also playing well with party elites.[40] The wedge intensified in the social media age. Trump exploited this to full advantage, entrenching the Republican Party's candidate-service role.

Although the parties are not entirely symmetrical in this regard, the Democratic Party has experienced similar dynamics with a growing wedge emerging between party elites and candidates who appealed to an increasingly strident base. In the 2016 Democratic primary, for example, tensions arose concerning superdelegates, Democratic officeholders and elites who generally favored Hillary Clinton over the insurgent Bernie Sanders. Sanders regarded himself as unfairly treated and threw his support behind Clinton late and somewhat grudgingly. Two years later, Alexandria Ocasio-Cortez unseated ten-term Congressman Jim Crowley and, joined by the Squad, campaigned against the party's moderate elite wing.

Although the parties evolved from vetting to supporting candidates, the transition isn't absolute. High valence candidates for major offices reach out directly to voters; lower level candidates continue to rely upon party structures for support. And even at the highest level, the presidency, the Democratic system of super-delegates has allowed, even recently, those with insider status to press against newcomers who might appeal to a populist base.

On both sides, these dynamics are exacerbated by party rules that disallow open primaries, meaning those in which voters of either party can participate, pulling the party toward the center.[41] And Republican gerrymanders have empowered the party base to largely eliminate moderates.[42] This trend marks the final movement in our discordant symphony.

Partisan Gerrymandering and *Ratf**king* Our Democracy

Gerrymandering isn't new. The term dates to Elbridge Gerry, who worked a redistricting to benefit Democratic-Republicans at the expense of Federalists in an 1812 Massachusetts election. Originally an Anti-Federalist, and later diplomat to France under John Adams, Gerry came to support the Constitution after ratification. In 1789, he was elected governor of Massachusetts, and two years later, he signed a bill that produced a salamander-shaped district splitting up what had been a Federalist stranglehold over five districts and letting Democratic-Republicans claim three.[43]

There's some dispute as to who coined the portmanteau combining *Gerry* and Sala*mander,* but it stuck, even though the surname Gerry, unlike gerrymander, was pronounced with a hard G. As used today, gerrymander describes far more sophisticated, often bizarre, efforts to draw electoral lines, enhancing the political power of the controlling party. For House gerrymandering, what matters most is which party controls the state legislature. States take a variety of approaches as to how to draw district lines, a process that typically takes place following the decennial census. State legislatures dominate, and in all but four states, which use independent commissions, the process provides the party in power considerable control.[44]

The Original Gerry-Mander.
The Gerry-mander, newspaper cartoon from 1812,
by Elkanah Tisdale (1771–1835).
Public domain, Wikimedia Commons

Political parties have drawn bizarre lines to advance their objectives, and doing so has sometimes implicated racial considerations under the Voting Rights Act of 1965. In the famous 1992
case *Shaw v. Reno*, Justice Sandra Day O'Connor compared North
Carolina House District 12 (labeled in the figure) to a Rorschach
inkblot or a bug splattered on the windshield of a car traveling at
high speed.[45] By comparison, the original gerrymander looks
quaint, and today, even District 12 no longer seems so stark. In a

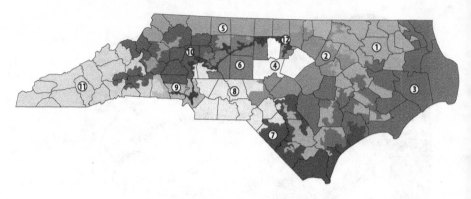

North Carolina District 12 Map, 1993.
North Carolina District 12 Map, Shaw v. Reno,
509 U.S. 630, app. 1 (1993). Public domain

dissenting opinion in a racial gerrymandering case, Justice Stevens
pointed out the irony that against a sea of bizarrely drawn districts, a district bearing a normal shape looks odd.[46]

Historically, districting reflected a complex combination of
factors, including grouping communities of interest; providing
special protections to underrepresented constituencies such as
farming or rural voters; and protecting actual or functional incumbents, meaning representatives whose districts were redrawn following a decennial census. Apportionment statutes emphasize
contiguity and compactness, but absent an equal protection violation, this is rarely enforced.

Beginning in the 1960s, the Supreme Court struck down districts with egregiously unequal apportionment.[47] To the extent
practicable, each district is expected to have an equal number of
voters. This might have encouraged a reversion to at-large voting,
as that scheme, eminently familiar to the Framers, ensures equally
weighted voting across all districts. But our electoral system has
yielded to dominance by two major parties. Both parties benefit
from winner-take-all single-member districts, which fence out
third parties. Once more, our electoral scheme hasn't played
out as the Framers envisioned.

The parties aren't symmetrically situated on gerrymandering. Republicans greatly benefit by compressing African American voters, a core Democratic constituency, as supermajorities in what are now called minority-majority districts. The statutory protection of such districts tends to disadvantage Democrats, sometimes disallowing strategies that would increase their aggregate representation. Even so, Democrats blinked on gerrymandering.

Over the past thirty-five years, the Supreme Court has flirted with, then dropped, holding state legislatures to account for extreme partisan gerrymanders. In the 1986 case *Davis v. Bandemer*, the Supreme Court rejected an equal protection challenge to a partisan gerrymander that gave Republicans greater districting results than was reflected in overall votes cast or party registrations.[48] In a later series of cases, Justice Kennedy, the swing vote, held out the possibility of finding a future instance of extreme hyper-partisan gerrymandering impermissible.[49]

Donald Trump persuaded Kennedy to retire, having appointed his former clerk Neil Gorsuch to replace Justice Scalia, and with the promise of another former Kennedy clerk, Brett Kavanaugh, poised to take Kennedy's seat. With the new appointment, the Supreme Court ended any flirtation with ending extreme partisan gerrymanders at the earliest opportunity. In the 2019 case *Rucho v. Common Cause*, the Supreme Court finally resolved that challenges to such practices weren't suitable for judicial resolution. *Rucho* gave the green light to practices that, immediately following Barack Obama's 2008 presidential election, ensured that Republican mapping would block democratic and Democratic—small *d* and large *D*—voting from having a meaningful impact on House representation for at least a decade.[50]

The Supreme Court never struck down a districting scheme based on partisan gerrymandering despite suggestions over several decades, by Justice White and then by Justice Kennedy, that it might. Whatever else one might say about Donald Trump, in stroking Kennedy's ego to gently nudge him off the Supreme Court, Trump revealed himself as an insightful strategist. For

Kennedy, the ego stroking of appointing two former clerks to the Supreme Court came at a price that *Salon* editor David Daley aptly, if unceremoniously, described as "Ratf**king" our democracy.

In *Ratf**ked: Why Your Vote Doesn't Count*, Daley recounts the remarkable history of REDMAP, the Republican 2010 post-decennial census state mapping strategy.[51] The term "Ratf**king" dates to the 1920s when Edmund Wilson used it to describe a "dirty deed done dirt cheap."[52] Woodward and Bernstein used it to describe Watergate, and Daley used it to characterize the steroidal state gerrymanders following the 2010 decennial census, a scheme so airtight that its creator was confident it would likely take until the 2030 census to undo.

The most notable part of the strategy was the decision to focus on below-the-radar races, meaning state legislative districts that few beyond local communities cared about. Relatively small financial contributions in select state electoral races had a huge payoff—pennies on the dollar. And since the states control congressional districting maps, this let Republicans draw maps that spread the wealth of Republican voters across a maximum number of districts, consolidating Democratic, including minority, voters as supermajorities in as few districts as possible.

Some of the stories Daley recounts are astonishing in their audacity. Until the 2010 plan, Democrats and Republicans gerrymandered when in power to gain an edge; in 2010, Republican operatives gained a laser-like capacity to draw district lines to maximal effect, distorting electoral outcomes in an unprecedented manner and entrenching those outcomes so that Democrats would need consistent supermajorities to begin reversing course.

Donald Trump lost the House to the Democrats in the 2018 midterm, and Joe Biden lost the House to the Republicans in the 2022 midterm. Although the Democrats gained the House well before the estimated target year 2030, the REDMAP strategy was still a remarkable success that in many ways exceeded the expectations of those who devised it. Indeed, those who created the methodology became concerned about having created a Frankenstein monster they couldn't control. The scheme produced such hyper-partisan House districts for both parties that only a minuscule number of districts remained competitive in the sense that either party could plausibly win. The genuine political threat facing Republican House incumbents is no longer a Democratic challenger; instead, it is being primaried by a more extreme Republican partisan.

Overall, the REDMAP scheme exacerbated Congress's governance challenges. The scheme ultimately compelled considerable numbers of elected Republicans publicly to embrace demonstrably false claims concerning the January 6, 2021, insurrection, despite having witnessed it in real time. This has had spillover effects on constituents more generally, with the effect of also throwing the once more tepid Senate into its increasingly partisan dysfunction.

From the start, our systems of elections and executive accountability thwarted the Framers' expectations. In the information age, it has spun out of control. We no longer play Rock, Paper, Scissors, a game marked by robust checks and balances, institutional jealousies, and layered sovereignty. Instead, the presidency threatens to be the rock that crushes, with no *Federalist Paper* available for cover.

CHAPTER 4

The End of Trust

EXPERTS, THE GOVERNMENT, AND THE MEDIA

In the lead-up to the 2020 election, vast segments of the American public insisted the COVID-19 pandemic was exaggerated; that social distancing, masking, and vaccinations were attempts at governmental control, even tracking, of citizens; that then-President Trump couldn't lose absent voter fraud; and that preventing mail-in, drop-off, or online ballots was essential to election integrity.[1] Each of these claims was countered by overwhelming, publicly available evidence reported by experts and reliable media sources.[2] After the election, large numbers of voters insisted that by certifying the Electoral College vote count for Joe Biden and Kamala Harris, then–Vice President Mike Pence would be abdicating his constitutional responsibility and undermining our democratic institutions. Misinformation may have cost hundreds of thousands of avoidable deaths to COVID, as well as the lives of several police officers (some by suicide) in an attempted US Capitol insurrection.

Problems of biased reporting and insistently clinging to misinformation aren't unique to the hard right. Left-leaning bias
beginning in the Trump era has included overly zealous claims
concerning coordination with Russian officials, certainty respecting unverified claims reported in the Steele Dossier, more conclu-
sive claims regarding the Mueller Report than were supported in
its ambivalent presentation, and imprecise coverage of Trump
statements concerning a Unite the Right rally in Charlottesville,
Virginia.[3] It has also included a premature willingness to embrace
reports of racist incidents that don't always bear up to scrutiny.[4]
Still, it would be naïve to claim that the threats to our democracy
by such reporting are uniform across the political spectrum.

The immediate claim is simpler: both sides of our electorate
assimilate news and news-like information more easily when it
corresponds to their worldview. Each of us holds conceptions—
cultural, historical, religious, socioeconomic, racial, and yes,
political—with which we frame the complex landscapes of the
world in which we live. We rely on anchors, conceptual landmarks,
or heuristics that fit information into framings conducive to
claiming a logical sense of how the world works and our place in
it. Indeed, studies demonstrate that presenting contrary information causes large segments of the public to remain even more
strongly committed to their prior disproven views.[5]

Individuals vary in their capacity to assimilate challenging
new information, and few have the time to independently investigate even a small fraction of the stories they encounter. Stories
that fit our ideological views comfortably are easily accommo-
dated. Stories that challenge our conceptions of the world force a
harder choice: either investigate more closely, risking further challenges to suppositions informing our worldviews, or reject them
as false, confident that somewhere out there lies a source, perhaps
several, confirming nearly every story or labeling it a bogus lie.

This chapter focuses on the role of media in creating or enhancing our cultural and political divides. The chapter explores
two parallels: first, between the history of parties (see chapter 3)

and the media, and second, between dynamics affecting media in the information age and in earlier periods. Although the information age has compressed developments that in earlier periods took decades or even centuries to unfold, exploring these parallels is essential to properly understanding the role of today's media in widening the wedge that has contributed to our growing cultural divides and constitutional dysfunction.

This chapter will reveal several features of media in the information age reflected in earlier press periods, including concerns about foreign interference with news coverage; changing norms in distributing news and news-like information as a function of developing technologies; inverting the relationship between readers and advertisers, making readers products, not consumers; and growing reliance on hyper-partisan delivery of news, with sometimes dubious pricing strategies, to increase readership and advertising revenues. The parallels between the developing press and political parties include early reliance upon and financial support of media party elites; broadening access to gain credibility, with corresponding changes in coverage; and a push toward greater professionalism and partisan detachment, producing a populist pushback demanding alternative sources for news and news-like information.

Conservative talk radio in the 1980s formed a wedge between elites and base voters within the Republican Party that broadened in the cable news ecosystem and became ripe for exploitation in the age of social media. Information age technology allowed conservative social media to exploit this wedge, altering the dimensionality of politics. The effect was to press upward within a two-dimensional ideological space, emphasizing culture and identity over economics and policy.[6] In our two-party system, what I've called Newton's First Law of Politics takes hold: for every political action, there is an equal and opposite political reaction.[7] When a valent major party candidate such as Donald Trump rides up or down on a teeter-totter, the candidate running against him necessarily rides down or up. The modern media landscape created a loop that both exploited and benefited by these dynamics, widening our cultural and political chasm.

This chapter proceeds in three parts: Part I reviews three historical periods—the party press, the penny press, and the era of press professionalization. It describes the role of conservative talk radio in forging a nagging wedge between Republican Party elites and an increasingly frustrated base. Part II presents the emergence of news media conduits. With a special emphasis on Facebook, now Meta, this part explains how new venues for news and news-like information exacerbate hyper-partisan divides and undermine cultural cohesion. Part III introduces news rating systems, with a special emphasis on the Ad Fontes Media Bias Chart. The chart helps explain how incentives for generating and disseminating news and news-like content changed in the information age. The chapter concludes by explaining how news in the information age exposed the raw nerve of our culture and identity politics, compromising societal cohesion and constitutional norms.

Along with chapter 3, this chapter demonstrates that information age technology has transformed systems that once let elites vet candidates and news sources into one that, by democratizing access, has undermined control across the board. This includes a loss of control for news consumers and creators as well as for candidates and voters. Information age technology empowers high valence politicians to choose their constituencies, and it lets divisive and unreliable news sources select readers. Both our politics and media have been inverted, limiting the agency of readers and voters alike, the very actors these systems nominally seek to empower.

The way out of the loop is to change the political incentives that generate it. This demands radical reform, changing the incentives in our two-party system defined by ever-growing divisions between two increasingly hostile and distrustful tribes.

The Partisan, Penny, and Professional Press

The eighteenth-century lexicographer Samuel Johnson famously said, "No man but a blockhead ever wrote except for money."[8] Whether for money, prestige, power, or influence, it is certainly true that writing must be motivated. Writing is costly, and conveying writing to readers is even more so. Just as classical composers demanded sponsorship in the royal courts, writers have always needed sustenance.[9] In our nation's earliest history, political writing, casting events in a favorable or problematic partisan light, was supported by parties.

The colonial period produced several newspapers, which split over favoring or opposing independence from Great Britain. Had rebellion failed, several leading publishers would have faced conviction under British sedition laws.[10] In the period that followed independence and that threatened national collapse under the Articles of Confederation, the press divided over supporting or opposing the Federalist project of genuine national unity.

The *Federalist Papers*, eighty-five essays authored by James Madison, Alexander Hamilton, and John Jay, collectively writing under the pseudonym Publius, played a central role in the demise of the Articles of Confederation and in advocating for the Constitution. The essays were initially published from October 1787 through May 1788 in two New York newspapers, the *New York Packet* and the *Independent Journal*.[11] The rival *Anti-Federalist Papers*, authored with pseudonyms Brutus, Cato, Centinel, and the Federal Farmer, were published most prominently in the *New York Journal*. Although the *Federalist Papers* are widely regarded as a classic contribution to American political theory, they were published as advocacy pieces shortly before the period associated with the partisan press, from 1790 to 1830. Had history turned out differently, Publius would be a footnote, and the authors behind Brutus (Robert Yates), Cato (George Clinton), Centinel (Samuel Bryan), and the Federal Farmer (Melancton Smith or Richard Henry Lee) household names.[12]

Despite the Framers imagining no political parties, or factions, following ratification of the Constitution, George Washington and John Adams controlled the presidency for the first three four-year terms as Federalists. The Anti-Federalists emerged as the Democratic-Republican Party, with Thomas Jefferson as its leader and James Madison joining its ranks. Despite remaining a committed Federalist, Alexander Hamilton endorsed Thomas Jefferson for president against Aaron Burr.

The Washington and Adams Administrations relied on several newspapers for support, including the *Columbian Centinel*, *Massachusetts Spy*, the *Connecticut Courant*, *Minerva* (later named *Commercial Advertiser*), and *Gazette of the United States*. Alexander Hamilton played a significant role in bringing *Minerva* to New York. In the Adams Administration, the *National Gazette* and *Aurora National Advertiser* emerged as the principal newspapers supporting the opposition, with the *National Intelligencer and Washington Advertiser* playing a singular role in Jefferson's 1800 electoral victory.[13]

In the partisan press period, newspapers were unapologetic voices of sponsoring political parties. They were unafraid to employ colorful, even scurrilous language in portraying the opposition, as famously shown in the lead-up to the 1828 contest between John Quincy Adams and Andrew Jackson. Presentations were often slanted to support candidates or to advance specific political objectives.[14] Early on, press divisions correlated with geography, with the Federalist press favored in the North; the Democratic-Republican press favored in the South; and Pennsylvania, the keystone state, holding the balance.

Earlier in this period, partisan papers emerged as such vicious political tools that the senior John Adams had enacted the Sedition Act, criminalizing partisan attacks leveled by Jefferson-supported newspapers—ultimately successfully—against his administration.[15] The Adams administration also enacted the Alien Enemies Act to avert foreign interference against the administration. Unlike with British sedition laws, there was little doubt that criminalizing the press for even brutal political speech violated the express terms of the First Amendment, which ensured not only freedom of speech and religion but also freedom of the press. Indeed, the press is the only private institution given express constitutional protection.

Recall from chapter 3 that John Adams, Thomas Jefferson, and John Quincy Adams played a decisive role in the ascendent two-party system. Their elections also played a major role in the history of the press. The partisan press helped Thomas Jefferson defeat John Adams, making Adams the first one-term president.

Following the 1824 election, with John Quincy Adams defeating Andrew Jackson despite securing fewer popular votes, Martin Van Buren set about forming the first truly national party. As part of the Albany Regency, a group of New York state officeholders who became a centerpiece of the later Democratic Party, and with support from emerging newspapers, the party set about electing its nominees and defeating the opposition. By 1828, the strategy succeeded, with Jackson ousting John Quincy Adams, making him the second one-term president. The Democratic Party, which avoided strong commitments on divisive issues, including most notably slavery, emerged as the first of two major parties. It was later joined by the Republicans, and these two parties have continued into the modern era.

Historical periods are rarely as discrete as in textbook presentations. Vicious media attacks on candidates didn't newly emerge in the partisan press era or go away with the penny press or even the later period of press professionalization. These aspects of media overlapped, and yet, specific attributes came to characterize specific historical periods. As in other domains, developments in the press have always been affected by developing technology and financing. With high-speed presses emerging in the 1830s, new press technologies allowed newspapers to produce more attractive products at lower cost.[16]

The partisan era was marked by heavy emphasis on opinion and advocacy. The papers, typically four pages long, cobbled together materials from other sources, sometimes with mismatched appearances as needed to fit the page. The penny press, led by such figures as James Gordon Bennett Sr., Samuel Bowles, Horace Greeley, and Henry J. Raymond, allowed for greater consistency, with upwards of eight pages rather than four, and a lower price— hence the name. Improved printing technology avoided the earlier period's unattractive features, with intermingled blocks from myriad sources and inconsistent typeset and quality. The penny press offered twice the length at a small fraction of the earlier pricing at six cents.

The penny press introduced intense media competition and alternative business models, with newsboys hawking papers on street corners to widen distribution. The pricing scheme increased reliance upon advertisers, as opposed to partisan sponsors, to fund production and distribution. The period was marked by broader distributions, with unofficial sharing of papers to market enhanced readership to advertisers. The democratization of media access went beyond party detachment and encouraged a broader scope. This included coverage designed to appeal specifically to women, emphasizing culture and society, not simply politics. While we associate personal ads with back pages of local city papers or swiping left or right on a cell phone, the origins reside in the penny press, as young women and men moved to urban centers and sought potential suitors.

Beginning in the 1850s, a prominent group of editors, including Horace Greeley, William Randolph Hearst, and Joseph Pulitzer, emphasized that independence from partisan influence was the benchmark for quality reporting and editorial coverage.[17] Whereas earlier writers employed pseudonyms when expressing strong opinions on the matters of the day, this period marked the emergence of the modern editorial form—speaking with the authoritative voice of the paper. Despite inevitable bias, the era presented more dispassionate presentations of current events and opinions, which emerged as hallmarks of quality and prestige. This period later benefited by Linotype, a superior press technology introduced in the 1880s.

Although no press period was devoid of bias or political objectives, the professionalization era was notable for its shift in tone and quality. More newspapers also became national, with local papers emerging in major cities and in western states and territories. Throughout this period, and even earlier, given the limited availability of reliable information, it wasn't uncommon to read multiple papers each day.

The process of a growing national press benefitted from emerging wire services, such as the Associated Press and United Press International, which provided greater access nationwide to coverage well beyond the local news.[18] Throughout the professional press period, many cities offered competing newspapers, with a major paper published in morning and evening editions and a second paper appealing to a distinct demographic. The *New York Times* was juxtaposed with the *New York Post* and the *Boston Globe* with the *Boston Herald*. Generally, one paper was regarded as more elite, catering to a white-collar readership and advertisers, with the other, often in tabloid form, catering to a working-class or blue-collar readership. Wire services let smaller papers focus on investigating local news while still offering general national coverage. Over time, coinciding with the emergence of talk radio, the market for tabloid papers and second daily editions began to taper.

Conservative Talk Radio and the Shock Jock

Throughout the professional press period, a dominant attribute of news media, like political parties, was control by elites. Not surprisingly, a market emerged for alternative sources of coverage that appealed to those pushing back against such control and a perception that institutional arrangements tended to benefit elites of both parties at their expense. Populism is characterized by pushback against elites and transcends ideologies too often simplified as left or right. Recall that within the four box matrix, populism combines liberal economic policies with conservative culture or identity politics (see chapter 2). The policy dimension can also emphasize exclusionary measures that benefit core constituencies who perceive themselves as threatened by competition over jobs and wages by immigrant or minority groups.

Conservative talk radio emerged as an increasingly powerful force in the late 1980s, coinciding with syndication, letting dominant personalities reach broader national audiences.[19] The most notable early figure was Rush Limbaugh, whose program was syndicated in 1988. Other key figures include Sean Hannity, Michael Medved, Glenn Beck, and G. Gordon Liddy, famous for his role in Watergate.

This period also marked the ascendence of shock jocks, such as Howard Stern (*The Howard Stern Show*), Don Geronimo and Mike O'Meara (*The Don and Mike Show*), Don Imus (Imus in the Morning), and Greg "Opie" Hughes and Anthony Cumia (*Opie and Anthony*). Conservative talk radio and shock jock radio overlap. Some sources count Rush Limbaugh, early in his career, as a shock jock who later took a political turn. By contrast, Howard Stern, although occasionally delving into political issues and once considering running for governor of New York, largely gained fame or notoriety for more salacious content.[20]

Radio hasn't always been the realm of conservative hosts or shock jocks. Franklin Delano Roosevelt used fireside chats to connect with the electorate through radio, just as other high-valence politicians from John F. Kennedy to Donald Trump used television to communicate directly with voters. But beginning in the 1980s, the conservative talk radio format was ascendent, offering up counternarratives that increasingly appealed to the Republican base.

The talk radio format let listeners tune in on their daily commutes, listening as the host lambasted political and media elites as failing to meet the concerns of regular people. Talk radio benefited from technologies that made radio music formats less profitable.[21] Conservative hosts deliberately blended entertainment, news, and opinion, never demarcating, as in the professional print media, any boundary lines. While its fair to criticize these radio personalities for often being fast and loose with facts, it's important to acknowledge their talents. They remained entertaining and provocative for hours on end, appealing to a base of listeners who often regarded themselves as disenfranchised, at least in a figurative sense.

Talk radio didn't merely appeal to a narrow group, however. Given our two-party system, these personalities contributed to forming an increasingly essential bloc within the Republican Party that, over time, elites could not ignore. In effect, talk radio provided an early version of a feedback loop that nudged Republican politicians toward their increasingly conservative base.[22] And as cable television came to dominate network coverage, Rupert Murdoch's Fox Media landscape, only partly counterbalanced by CNN and later MSNBC, helped solidify these emerging divisions.[23] In some instances, these media shifted from being fast and loose with the facts to peddling outright lies. In April 2023, Fox News agreed to pay a reported $787.5 million to settle a lawsuit by Dominion Voting Systems based on evidence allegedly demonstrating that several prominent hosts, despite lacking any factual basis, repeatedly conveyed Donald Trump's lie that the 2020 presidential election had been stolen from him.[24]

The media landscape didn't simply sow ideological divides among viewers or listeners; it increasingly affected elections and public policy. As early as the 1990s, the strengthened conservative base of the Republican Party invited Newt Gingrich to become Speaker of the House. His "Contract with America," written with Representative Dick Armey, established commitments that spoke to Republican base voters.[25] The party abandoned one notable commitment, term limits, upon gaining power.

The emerging wedge between Republican base voters and party elites was exploited, in far more strident form, in the age of social media. A critical feature of the two-party system is the inability to relinquish a key constituency without the risk of losing power. Conservative talk radio and cable news helped instigate a process that over time foisted difficult choices on Republican Party elites.

News Media Conduits

Although technology always played an important role in conveying news, it was transformative in the information age. Suddenly and for the first time, literally anyone with a computer and an internet connection could generate content and convey it to anyone in the world with access to the same technology. This was a first step in changing the landscape of how news is generated, conveyed, and received. But internet technology itself is of little value without entrepreneurs who develop platforms that are accessible to a broad base of users.

Sitting in his Harvard University dormitory was an undergraduate freshman named Mark Zuckerberg. Among other places, Zuckerberg's story was told, with admitted liberties, in *The Social Network*, featuring Jesse Eisenberg.[26] Zuckerberg, hailing from New Jersey, was a computer programming genius whose talents landed him in trouble when he devised *Facemash* in 2003, a sexist game inviting Harvard students to rank the physical appearance of classmates.[27] The socially awkward freshman was approached by twin brothers, Cameron and Tyler Winklevoss, aspiring Olympic rowers and entrepreneurs, who hoped to create a platform for young men and women to connect socially, and perhaps professionally, over the internet.

After agreeing to be their programmer, Zuckerberg realized the remarkable potential of what he had devised. Rather than play a secondary role in the Winklevoss venture, he guarded his innovation and started his own business. In February 2004, in his sophomore year, Zuckerberg launched The Facebook to

Harvard students, and by June 2004, the business expanded to reach students in over thirty universities.

Although the accounts are not always consistent, the Zuckerberg story is widely known. Here are a few of the story's most notable features. Zuckerberg, joined by roommate Dustin Moskovitz, a programmer from Florida, and other Harvard students then in their sophomore year, took leave from Harvard to move to Menlo Park, California. Facebook disengaged with Harvard classmate and early investor Eduardo Saverin. And the company enlisted Sean Parker, of Napster, a music-sharing platform that was forcibly shut down, to serve as its first president prior to Parker resigning due to a cocaine scandal. In addition to securing early funding, Parker renamed The Facebook simply Facebook.[28] Despite several lawsuits and early missteps, Facebook, now called Meta, emerged as the most successful social media venture ever. In doing so, Facebook shaped world history.

After opening to all users over seventeen years old, not just students, in 2006, Facebook created an altogether new medium connecting creators of news and news-like information with receptive audiences, without providers having to create independent distribution channels. For users, Facebook is free. If social media has a mantra, it's this: if you aren't paying, you aren't the consumer; you're the product. So it is with Facebook. Users are products sought by producers of news and news-like information who need increasingly broad audiences to lure in advertisers. In the brave new social media world, advertisers play the financial role political parties played in the partisan press and that royalty played in sponsoring classical musicians. And as in the penny press, the true coin of the realm was never the list price; it was always the vast user base that advertisers demand.

Nearly simultaneous with Facebook's 2006 launch, Twitter launched its alternative platform. Tweets were limited to 140 characters, raised to 280 characters in 2017, and today users can convey longer content through multipart threads, including embedded links to various media sources. Twitter played an outsized role in the ascent of Donald Trump's 2016 Republican Party takeover, even as the relationship with his preferred social media network proved fickle. On January 8, 2021, Twitter permanently banned Trump for a campaign of misinformation concerning the claimed stolen 2020 election and the potential risk of inciting violence, one day following Facebook's more limited two-year ban.[29]

In late 2022, mercurial entrepreneur Elon Musk acquired Twitter. Musk soon faced serious challenges for claiming to embrace First Amendment absolutism despite Twitter's status as a private company. This included restoring access to Donald Trump, Marjorie Taylor Green, Ye, and other banned users. This in turn led several high profile users, including Shonda Rhimes, Sara Bareilles, and Whoopi Goldberg, to abandon the platform.[30]

With the benefit of these and other news media conduits, for the first time in history, regardless of education level, professional training, grasp of nuance or complexity, or even basic writing skills, anyone wishing to do so has instant access to a costless infrastructure with which to broadcast content globally. Until the bans, and now with Twitter access restored, Donald Trump used these platforms, especially Twitter, to connect directly with voters while avoiding—or disparaging—professionally vetted sources.

Universal access fundamentally transformed the market for news and news-like information. Immediate access to limitless sources is somewhat like taking a final exam with open access to the Library of Congress. The challenge in sorting potentially limitless sources is no less intimidating—and no more helpful—than a closed-book exam. Although Facebook and Twitter sort content based on user input, the algorithms are largely indifferent to qualitative assessments of source content. Instead, the algorithms channel content in ways that simultaneously maintain the presence of users while dividing them into competing camps.

In recent years, commentators have complained about the increasingly hostile political and cultural discourse on these forums. Although this includes users who often announce an intent to leave, it also includes Facebook's first president Sean Parker. In an

Axios interview, Parker expressed regret that Facebook "exploit[s] a vulnerability in human psychology by creating a social-validation feedback loop."[31] Individuals planning to leave for other venues routinely find themselves reengaging.

In many respects, social media alternatives to Facebook and Twitter resemble third parties trying to compete with Republicans and Democrats. Just as individual politicians or voters can't generate meaningful third parties out of sheer frustration with the two-party system, Facebook or Twitter users cannot escape from social media's deeply troubling dynamics. As one example, the social media platform MeWe's millions of users pale in comparison with Facebook's and Twitter's vastly larger number of users who engage more regularly and who aren't defined by specific interests or a common ideology. Efforts to replicate Twitter in the aftermath of the Musk takeover by platforms such as Mastodon, Plurk, and Minds have faced similar challenges. The problem with alternative outlets is appealing to like-minded people. Facebook and Twitter draw in people hailing from across ideological divides and across the globe. Simply wishing for better options, whether third parties or preferable social media venues, won't bring them about.

Metcalfe's Law

A helpful starting point in explaining Facebook's social media dominance is Metcalfe's law. The law states that the value of a network rises as a function of its users. A social network of two is as valuable as children's walkie-talkies, although over a longer distance. A social network of three to six might resemble early party-telephone lines. As a network grows from one thousand to one million to one billion, it becomes so significant in reach that it becomes virtually impossible to displace. Even a superior alternative is unlikely to succeed unless users become so dissatisfied that they are not only motivated to leave en masse but to do so for a singular alternative. Splitting over multiple alternative forums is self-defeating, not unlike voting third party in the United States today.

As established technologies invite new entrants with differentiated products, accomplishing a mass exodus for a singular alternative becomes nearly impossible. Most alternatives appeal to specific groups, with some inviting users to create groups of their own. One such forum, which is no longer operating, called itself "tribe." But Facebook isn't a party line. And as an alternative to Facebook, tribe's very name seemed to miss the point.

Metcalfe's law establishes that over large numbers the value of a network grows for all users with each new added user. The dynamic closely resembles what economists call natural monopoly.[32] That term describes utilities or other businesses with very high start-up costs. Common examples are gas lines or electricity connected to homes and hub-and-spoke distribution systems, such as the US Postal Service. Others include theme parks, airplanes, and transit systems. All of these require sufficient scope and scale, appealing to vast numbers of consumers to make the investments sustainable. These industries can be economical because as more and more consumers use them, causing the business to get larger and larger, the cost per user declines. The problem is that the dynamic makes it nearly impossible, at least for a long time, for competitors to enter the market.

Many commentators have faulted Mark Zuckerberg for being insufficiently zealous in safeguarding users from misinformation, foreign interference, and other problematic networking behaviors. Zuckerberg maintains that the company's commitment to freedom of speech counsels against intruding into platform content.[33] At best, this claim is misleading. Zuckerberg rests on First Amendment values that simply don't apply to Facebook.

The difficulty begins with properly characterizing Facebook, Twitter, and other social media platforms. To the extent Facebook bears features of a natural monopoly, this would justify governmental regulation, as with utilities, to ensure that providers with the power to block competitors nonetheless serve the public. But unlike utilities, the difficulty isn't Facebook's pricing strategy. Users subscribe without paying a fee. Instead, Facebook relies on algorithms that target users, often with problematic content, to keep them actively engaged and where advertisers can find them. Remember, if you aren't paying, you're the product.

The First Amendment justification for avoiding content-based interference disregards that Facebook, Twitter, and other social media platforms are privately owned businesses serving as venues for other content providers. They aren't content providers themselves.

In 2019, comedian Sasha Baron Cohen, a.k.a. Borat, gave a deadly serious speech in which, likely unintentionally, he exposed the irony of casting these venues as content providers. On one side, Cohen recognized the grave harm of allowing conspirators and anti-Semites who deny the Holocaust to use the forum, but on the other side, he admonished treating Facebook as a publisher.[34] Doing so might extricate Facebook from specific protections under Section 230 of the Communications Decency Act, which shields platforms from liability for content generated by users.[35] But treating news media conduits as news content creators would also provide Facebook and Twitter the stronger shield of First Amendment protection.

In two cases decided in May 2023, the Supreme Court ruled against family members of US citizens killed in attacks by ISIS (Islamic State of Iraq and Syria) who challenged the status of Twitter and Google's YouTube and the scope of these platforms' protections under Section 230. The Twitter suit challenged the shield from liability for content posted by independent sources allegedly engaged in terroristic activity. The YouTube suit more narrowly questioned whether the platform's user-channeling mechanisms designed to encourage engagement transform the platform into a content provider.[36] Justice Thomas, writing for a unanimous Court in the Twitter case, and a per curiam opinion in the Google case, both determined that claimants had failed to state the necessary elements of their legal claims. As a result the Court avoided reaching the scope of Section 230, leaving for another day whether the statute continues to shield such platforms from liability regardless of the nature of independently sourced content and whether social media algorithms for channeling content render such platforms content providers.

Facebook, or Meta, isn't a literal monopoly, a term that's widely misunderstood. Examples of single businesses providing all goods or services in any given market sector are rare. More generally, firms hold varying degrees of power within markets, which they gain by distinguishing their goods or services from those that others provide. Brand loyalty gives firms market power, letting them set prices in a way that operates to the detriment of consumers as compared with an ideal of perfect competition. In the real world, pure competition is as elusive as pure monopoly. Most markets fall between simplistic elementary economics textbook models.

As compared with Facebook, Twitter is a differentiated product. In some respects, Facebook and Twitter differ in much the same way persons prone to obsessive-compulsive behaviors differ from persons prone to attention-deficit disorders. In the realm of political discourse, Twitter is hit and run; Facebook is stay and fight. Twitter's 280-character limit, even allowing for multiple-thread tweets, is rarely conducive to extended one-on-one conversation or debate. By contrast, Facebook facilitates never-ending embedded dialogues in comment threads and sub-threads, sometimes enduring for weeks or months on end.

As is generally true for differentiated products, neither Facebook nor Twitter is "better" other than by the lights of individual users with varied tastes and predilections. But the differences affect how users convey or consume news and news-like information. Absent the ban, a populist candidate such as Donald Trump could use Twitter—his preferred medium—to instantly reach millions of followers. He could avoid lengthy discourse about policy or historical events without getting caught in any weeds. The attacks from the other side emboldened his followers, who dismissed them as products of out-of-touch elites.

From a political perspective, Twitter often emerges more powerful. From a news dissemination perspective, Facebook has taken over the world. Media sources well understand that in the information age, users gain access not by direct subscription, but by indirect Facebook hits targeting them based on undisclosed algorithms, or what Professor Frank Pasquale has aptly labeled the "Black Box."[37]

Forums like Facebook and Twitter aren't content creators, and they aren't the government. They're a novel vehicle that has fundamentally and radically changed the market for news production and dissemination. These news media conduits are forums that allow publishers to connect through complex algorithms with wide readerships. Once we recognize that Facebook's consumers are publishers and advertisers, not the users, who are the product, we gain a better understanding of how Metcalfe's law provides Facebook with tremendous market power despite not being a pure monopoly. True news content providers have limited venues that reach a broad base of readers. In the social media world, Facebook holds singular power to make or break publishers, whose choices are often more constrained by resources than by the ideological commitments of their creators.

The Media Bias Chart

News conduit users rarely subscribe independently to the vast array of content providers whose materials routinely land in their feeds. And the occasional linked paywall is far more likely to encourage users to embrace the poster's characterization than to invite a new paid subscription. There are few checks on the quality, or reliability, of the sources users typically encounter. Many individuals have sought to evaluate the proliferation of information-age media sources. Some rankings systems, such as AllSides, cast media along the dimension of left versus right.[38] Others seek to discern the accuracy of specific stories.[39] Both strategies are important but also problematic. Any left-right categorization is necessarily incomplete. And ascertaining the veracity of stories runs up against questions of reliability of the fact-checkers.

In 2016, Vanessa Otero, a Colorado patent attorney, experimented with a different approach. At first, this was her informal attempt to make sense of a complex media landscape for family and friends, recognizing that a left-right analysis failed to provide a complete account.[40] Instead, she cast a limited number of media sources along two dimensions, which in more recent iterations she has labeled ideological bias (graded from left to right) and reliability (graded from top to bottom). Over the years, and now several iterations later, the resulting graphics have assumed a shape roughly corresponding to a Gaussian curve.[41] The shape doesn't result from population densities, but rather it emerges as a set of equilibrium points over the chart's two dimensions.

The initial iteration of her chart surprised Otero by going viral, producing millions of hits. In the intervening years, she fleshed out and refined the graphic and methodology, now with a professional staff of analysts who follow her rankings criteria. For each assessment, Otero ensures three reviewers, at least one of whom is ideologically distant from the other two. No longer practicing law, Otero is the chief executive officer of Ad Fontes Media, a Colorado public benefit corporation devoted to improving the media landscape and educating the public concerning the reliability and bias of news and news-like information.[42] In full disclosure, I personally serve on the Board of Advisors for Ad Fontes Media.

The Media Bias Chart's two dimensions expose an inverse relationship between reliability (on the vertical axis) and bias (on the horizontal axis). The curve is continuous, or nearly so, beginning in the lower left toward the upper center and back down toward the lower right. Some versions have been skewed, with sources cast more deeply in the direction of extreme bias and low

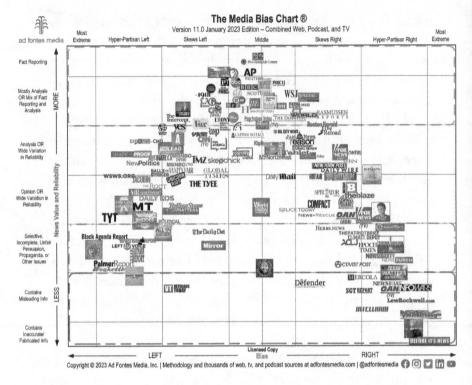

The Media Bias Chart.
Version 11.0, January 2023 edition © 2023 Ad Fontes Media

reliability on the far right than far left. Today's multiple charts rank not only hundreds of news media sources, such as newspapers and their online counterparts, but also magazines, blogs, televised news reporting, and online-only content providers.

Virtually everyone reviewing the chart will find something to disagree with, even strongly. Yet in some respects, disagreements across the spectrum tend to strengthen rather than undermine the project's own claim to reliability. Disagreements generally take two forms: first, scaling, with those on the right claiming that the treatment of the left is too generous and should be pressed deeper into the liberal-bias tail, and those on the left making an opposing claim; and second, source-specific placements, with each side claiming some sources are treated too harshly or leniently along either dimension. Even the analysts contributing to the chart are apt to disagree on these matters as is invariably true when individuals separately contribute to a combined product.

What's harder to contest is the observation of a set of media distributed over a range of positions with stronger ideological positioning correlating to lower overall reliability and with the ideological center correlating to greater reliability. Reliable reporting is not systematically likely to favor either side of the political spectrum over the long term. The greater the reliability, the more centrist the sources are apt to emerge when assessed along a conventional left-right ideological scaling.

We can roughly divide the chart into three discrete segments:

First, at the top center are sources that in earlier periods corresponded to widely distributed and respected print media. These sources were the hallmark of the long era of press professionalization. Such sources as the *New York Times, Washington Post,* and *Wall Street Journal* placed reporters around the globe, invested in costly distribution channels, engaged in careful content editing, and segregated opinion from news and analysis, often with a literal wall. Production was daily and expensive, with subscription fees signaling a largely educated, generally higher income readership, thus of considerable value to advertisers. These investments created barriers to entry and provided a quality-commitment bond. And these sources thus tended to eschew the quick hits of salacious or highly biased coverage that risked dissipating the carefully cultivated asset of reliability.

Second, at the lower edges, corresponding to hyper-partisan bias and low reliability, are news sources that lack the historical investment costs associated with the print medium era—reporters around the globe, staffing, editorial expertise, and distribution channels—that serve as quality-commitment bonds. Media sources lacking bonding criteria can gain broader readership by delving into strongly partisan and heavily biased, sometimes salacious coverage, opinion, or analysis of events reported initially by other sources, including wire services. At the extreme, these sources engage in highly slanted presentations that bend facts or disregard them altogether, including entering the realm of conspiratorial accounts.

Third, connecting these extremes are the points along the descending sides of the Gaussian-shaped curve. Along the diverging sides are media sources committed, in varying degrees, to careful analysis of original reporting by others coupled with opinions grounded in defensible factual predicates rather than hyper-partisan extremes. Media sources meeting these criteria will inevitably be biased in either direction but will seek to avoid the extreme bias that risks sacrificing reputations for carefully grounded analysis and commentary.

Combining these groupings—high reliability/low bias, low reliability/high bias, and intermediate reliability/intermediate bias—gives the Media Bias Chart its shape. The resulting curve represents a set of maximizing, or equilibria, points for entrants into the media marketplace, with each seeking as broad and valued a set of readers as possible, viewed from an advertiser-revenue perspective and subject to resource constraints and editorial biases.

Readers who increasingly rely upon news media conduits such as Facebook and Twitter rather than independent sourcing face the challenge of navigating the reliability of sources targeting them in their daily feeds without helpful benchmarks. It's naïve to envision an ideal and dispassionate press, professionally edited and invariably factual, as the benchmark against which all feeds should be compared. There are no sources that, like Sergeant Joe Friday in the 1950s TV series, *Dragnet*, seek "just the facts, ma'am." That even includes Joe Friday, who never said that in the original show, as opposed to Dan Akroyd, who did while playing Friday in a *Saturday Night Live* sketch.[43] The history of the press recounted in this chapter tells a more complicated story. All writing is costly and motivated. Even so, absent conventional barriers to entry arising from staffing, editorial, and distribution costs, for many Facebook and Twitter users, there is no discernible distinction between a vetted article in the *New York Times* or *Wall Street Journal*, on one side, versus a hyper-partisan post produced by any number of dubious sources, on the other.

The business model of news media conduits exacerbates these challenges to the detriment of our democracy and culture. News media conduits aren't content creators; they're venues connecting news and news-like content providers (the consumers) with users (the product). And news media conduits aren't neutral in this connecting endeavor. Their revenues depend upon ongoing active-user engagement. The longer users remain engaged, the more value news media conduits can extract.

These social media venues have developed sophisticated algorithms that target readers with news and news-like content designed to ensure users remain glued to the screen. This is evident not merely by the frequency of visits but even more so by active indicators of involvement that include clicks, comments, shares, likes, and other reactions. The triggers to engagement bear no correlation to quality, or when they do, the correlation is likely inverse, as revealed in the Media Bias Chart.

Consider two seemingly opposing means of promoting engagement—presenting materials with which users are viscerally inclined to agree and perhaps share, or presenting stories that provoke visceral disagreement, even anger, eliciting negative user responses. These opposing triggers share something in common. Both correlate with content providers occupying the extremes on the Media Bias Chart, rather than top center. A central lesson in the never-ending battle for democracy is the threat of extremes on all sides and the challenge of vigorously pursuing moderation. This is as true of media as it is of political parties and candidates.

Studies demonstrate that when presented with contrary information, individuals are prone not to reconceiving their early understandings, or what statisticians call "Bayesian priors."[44] Instead, they are more apt to dismiss the information as false, fitting the data to their preconceived notions rather than changing their perceptions to accommodate newly available information.

Oppositional presentations are often as effective in promoting user engagement as coverage consistent with the tribal views of users. Careful, nuanced, up-the-middle analysis, on the other hand, is not.

Elected officials are no less prone to the influence of social media than other members of society. Indeed, they may be more so. After all, their careers depend upon satisfying constituencies residing in our social media world. Because of hyper-partisan gerrymandering, as revealed in David Daley's *Ratf**ked*, aspiring or elected officials increasingly face a highly partisan electorate embracing a common, rather than probing or balanced, conception of the salient issues of the day.

With news media conduits, partisan gerrymandering now takes two forms. News consumers are gerrymandered through targeting algorithms that entrench readers based on content, and voters are gerrymandered with districting lines. Both dynamics exacerbate hyper-partisanship. Those responsible for creating these dynamics can no longer control the effects. As one example, in a postpresidential event, Donald Trump was roundly booed for announcing he had been vaccinated and given a booster as he confronted an audience that took his anti-COVID-precaution views to such extremes that they couldn't commend his responsible behavior.[45]

We've emerged from the media history described in this chapter as two societies fed juxtaposed accounts of reality respecting nearly every salient news story and increasingly respecting fundamental cultural values. Our system of news reporting has reified the worst features of the early partisan and penny presses, and it has solidified the entrenchment of our ever-widening and increasingly dysfunctional two-party system.

It doesn't have to be this way.

PART II

The World Tour

CHAPTER 5

The European
Tour

ENGLAND, FRANCE, AND GERMANY

What We Can Learn from Other Democracies

We are now ready to begin the virtual world tour. Thus far, with
the benefit of familiar games, we've considered the third constitutional crisis and the third-party dilemma, and we've explored the
parallel histories of our nation's two-party system and the press.
Together these stories help explain the difficult choices voters face
and our growing constitutional and societal dysfunction.

I ended the last chapter observing that it doesn't have to be
this way. But to avert the crisis we face, we must be open-minded
enough to learn from the experience of other democracies around
the globe. We must understand how other nations conceive democracy across two complementary axes: first, how they elect the
lower legislative chamber, and second, how they structure executive accountability. And we must compare other democracies' most
defining attributes—both good and bad—against our own. Only
then can we make informed choices about how best to improve
our system.

As we begin our journey, it will help to have a sense of why I've arranged this trip as I have, touring seven nations in the next two chapters. We begin in Europe, touring England, France, and Germany; in chapter 6 we travel to Israel, Taiwan, Brazil, and Venezuela.

We'll start in London, the original source of so many American legal customs and norms. English common law continues to drive our legal system a quarter millennium after we broke away from the motherland. Although the Framers rejected a monarch, Alexander Hamilton might have happily anointed George Washington king (this detail didn't make the musical). Many Americans remain fascinated with the British monarchy, including the passing of Queen Elizabeth II, England's longest serving monarch, and the coronation of King Charles III; the tragedy of Princess Diana; and the global media attention surrounding Meghan Markle and Prince Harry, the "Spare," who together stepped away from their royal duties, moving to the United States.[1]

Looking at England from America can seem like facing a carnival mirror—striking differences overwhelm glimmers of similarity. The United States is a presidential republic; the United Kingdom, composed of England, Scotland, Wales, and Northern Ireland, is a parliamentary monarchy. The United States has the oldest continuing written constitution; England's "constitution" embraces longstanding unwritten traditions. Here's one: After the general election, the reigning monarch, who has no policymaking role and serves as a ceremonial head of state, invites the leader of the party holding the most seats in the House of Commons, the lower of the two houses of Parliament, to form the government. In general, parliamentary coalitions form after the general election, whereas in our presidential system, coalitions form at the primary/caucus stage.

Our next stop is Paris. France has strongly influenced American politics for centuries. For instance, the French philosopher Montesquieu helped shape the Framers' understanding of separation of powers. Both the Federalists and the Anti-Federalists relied on Montesquieu, despite holding opposing views on the US Constitution.[2] You may recall that the Frenchman Maurice Duverger speculated as to why some nations, such as the United States and England, tend toward two dominant parties. As explained in chapter 2, Duverger's insight is more a general observation than a law. Although he didn't coin the term, Duverger also popularized "semi-presidentialism" to describe the French Fifth Republic, established by Charles de Gaulle in 1958.[3] Semi-presidentialism blends features of presidentialism with parliamentary democracy. France elects its president and parliament separately. Unlike the United States and England, France's system has produced upwards of twenty parties.

Our last European stop is Berlin. It's impossible to appreciate modern Germany's parliamentary system without relating it to the tragic history of Nazi Germany. The German system reflects a resolve never again to let a fascist party gain power.[4] Germany's ingenious defense mechanism, called mixed-member proportionality (MMP), blends districted and party-based seats, with voters each casting two ballots and with party proportionality controlling the entire chamber.

After visiting Israel, Taiwan, Brazil, and Venezuela, chapter 6 concludes with a three-by-three matrix that captures several key insights from the entire world tour. (Although we'll tour seven nations, including the US and a brief Israeli period operating on a different system fills all nine boxes.) The tour reveals inevitable trade-offs along two democratic axes. The first axis includes three general categories of executive accountability: presidential, hybrid (including semi-presidential and semi-parliamentary), and parliamentary. The second axis includes three general methods of electing a nation's lower (sometimes exclusive) legislative chamber: districted, hybrid (including MMP and a related system called mixed-member majoritarian, or MMM), and proportional. All democratic systems inevitably confront choices across both axes.

Let's begin.

London: Driving the Double-Decker

John Nash, a Nobel laureate in economics featured in Sylvia Nasar's book *A Beautiful Mind* (and a movie starring Russell Crowe), explained how individuals making independent decisions effect a combined outcome, or sometimes a set of outcomes, in helpful or harmful ways.[5] Game theorists identify such an outcome as a Nash equilibrium, sometimes a "pure Nash" equilibrium. A pure Nash equilibrium arises when all parties behave rationally, expect others to do the same, and produce a result or set of results that none can improve upon on their own.[6] Nash's insight is so profound that it helps explain phenomena as varied as traffic patterns, pricing strategies, the Cold War, and voting systems. While radically simplified, Professor Anthony Downs's account of mid-twentieth century US politics helps explain how our two-party system emerged as a pure Nash equilibrium.[7]

Another pure Nash equilibrium is visible when we board one of London's famous double-decker buses: people here drive on the left side with steering wheels on the right. The United States is opposite. It's fine if everyone drives on the right or left side of the road, so long as they're consistent. Problems arise only if we don't achieve either pure Nash outcome; if some drive left and others right, the results are deadly. Alternative driving regimes, each requiring coordination, is a helpful metaphor in designing a constitutional democracy.

Winston Churchill famously said: "Democracy is the worst form of Government except for all those other forms that have been tried."[8] Another Nobel laureate in economics, Kenneth Arrow, proved that it's impossible to create a perfect democratic system, or at least one satisfying a set of conditions that he thought were basic in a democracy.[9] Arrow's intuition is connected in important ways to the sorts of cycling dynamics explored in part I (see chapters 1 and 2), and to the inevitable challenges that arise in seeking to avoid them. Despite their different perspectives, Churchill and Arrow reached the same troubling conclusion: All democratic systems are problematic in some way. I'll go one step further—all democracies are anti-democratic in some way.

I find that conclusion more liberating than troubling. We know up front that we aren't going to find a perfect democratic system on our trip. It doesn't exist. As with driving, there's more than one way to do things. This lets us look at actual systems critically. We can think about their differing strengths and weaknesses and consider which system's features are most helpful in overcoming the challenges we face.

In 1770, Voltaire, another famous Frenchman, wrote: "Perfect is the enemy of good."[10] On our tour, let's look for the good and consider how to make our own troubled democracy better.

The Palace of Westminster

The Palace of Westminster is sometimes called the House of Parliament. Both the House of Lords and the House of Commons meet here. Today's magnificent Gothic Revival building, designed by Charles Barry and Augustus Pugin, replaced the original, which stood on the site beginning in the eleventh century until it burned down in 1834.

Voters in the United Kingdom elect members of the House of Commons, the lower house, in geographically districted winner-take-all elections. The upper house, the House of Lords, is appointed. Although the Parliament is bicameral, the House of Commons has a much greater policymaking role than the House of Lords, including the power to send certain legislation directly to the monarch. The monarch, who nominally holds power to reject legislation, last did so in 1708.[11] Today's monarch plays no policy role beyond whatever insights he offers in private weekly audiences with the prime minister.

Although England, Scotland, Wales, and Northern Ireland, together comprising the United Kingdom, have differing voting systems for their separate national legislative bodies, House of Commons elections are based on single-member districts that are winner-take-all, meaning a plurality winner prevails. The House of Commons includes smaller parties, but one of the two major parties typically secures a majority of seats, thus avoiding the need to form a multiparty coalition. By protocol the reigning monarch, now King Charles III, invites the leader of the party with a majority of seats to form the government. If no party wins a majority, the King invites the leader of the party with a plurality to do so.

In the modern era, power has volleyed back and forth between the Labour and Conservative parties. Consider this sequence of prime ministers since 1979: Margaret Thatcher, 1979–1990 (Conservative); John Major, 1990–1997 (Conservative); Tony Blair 1997–2007, (Labour); Gordon Brown, 2007–2010 (Labour); David Cameron, 2010–2016 (Conservative); Theresa May, 2016–2019 (Conservative); Boris Johnson, 2019–2022 (Conservative); Liz Truss, 2022 (Conservative); Rishi Sunak, 2022–present (Conservative).

This electoral pendulum somewhat resembles recent US pendulum swings: Bill Clinton, 1993–2001 (Democrat), George W. Bush, 2001–2009 (Republican); Barack Obama, 2009–2017 (Democrat); Donald Trump, 2017–2021 (Republican); Joe Biden, 2021–present (Democrat). The British experience appears somewhat muted, with fewer swings and with the dominant parties controlling for more extended periods, although the recent experience, post-Brexit, has produced considerable leadership turnover within the Conservative Party.

By statute, the House of Commons sits for five years, although the prime minister can suspend it earlier. The House of Commons can vote "no confidence" in the prime minister, and the prime minister can call a vote of confidence to ensure continued support. Given the two-party system, no confidence voting is rarely successful, at least formally. The last successful example was in March 1979, when by a single vote, 311–310, Prime Minister Jim Callaghan (Labour) was voted from office.[12] Before that, it hadn't happened since 1924.

The two-party system creates a zero-sum power struggle—a party is either in power or in opposition. When democratic politics succeed, policy arguments take center stage. But lurking beneath sometimes polite, often divisive, policy discourse lies a genuine struggle over power—how to get it, hold it, and control who gets it next. These attributes of politics become acute, and disturbing, when democratic institutions erode. In the United Kingdom's two-party system and in ours, processes to end a government—no confidence and impeachment, respectively—present special challenges. Our systems divide politicians and voters into two major camps. More generally, the two-party system has produced systemic threats not only in the United States, but also in the United Kingdom.

Lessons from Brexit

On June 23, 2016, the United Kingdom sent shockwaves through the world by voting in a pre-legislative referendum to leave the European Union after forty-seven years.[13] Until the mid-twentieth century, the United Kingdom disallowed referendums as a violation of legislative supremacy, and they remain rare, requiring pre-approval by Parliament.

The Brexit referendum asked a simple question: "Should the United Kingdom remain a member of the European Union or leave the European Union?" The day of the referendum, a poll predicted 52 percent to remain and 48 percent to leave. The result was almost precisely opposite, with 51.89 percent voting to leave and 48.11 percent voting to stay.[14] England (including Gibraltar) had the strongest leave margin, 53.38 percent to 46.62 percent, followed by Wales at 52.53 percent to 47.47 percent, with Northern Ireland and Scotland favoring remain by 55.78 percent and 62 percent, respectively. After Brexit's narrow approval, there was evidence of buyer's regret, but pleas for a revote failed.[15]

How did the United Kingdom find itself in this troubling circumstance? In 2010, David Cameron's Conservative Party came up short of a majority in Parliament. It was a rare election when, despite two dominant parties, the UK's parliamentary system produced an unexpected alliance. Cameron formed a majority coalition with the Liberal Democrats based on their shared desire to take down Labour Prime Minister Gordon Brown. The coalition was so strange that a Stanford political scientist dubbed it "the Odd Couple."[16] It left Cameron in a tenuous position. In 2013, he acceded to demands for a Brexit referendum to avert the risk of Conservative Party hardliners defecting for the far-right United Kingdom Independence Party (UKIP).[17] Cameron staked his success on sending Brexit to voters, hoping it would fail. It didn't, forcing Cameron to resign.

Following Theresa May's relatively brief service as prime minister, from 2016–2019, Boris Johnson, who served only slightly longer, began working toward Brexit's implementation from 2020 until 2022. Both May and Johnson survived no confidence votes of 37 percent and 41 percent respectively, but both were sufficiently weakened that each ultimately was forced to resign.[18] For May, the challenge was implementing Brexit. For Johnson, a series of scandals surrounding cabinet members ended in broad resignations and widening distrust in his leadership. Johnson's major achievement was helping to effectuate Brexit. Queen Elizabeth II then appointed Conservative Liz Truss as her last official act, just two days prior to passing away on September 8, 2022.[19]

Queen Elizabeth II ascended the throne in 1953 at age twenty-five, with Winston Churchill serving as prime minister. Remarkably, the Queen's last official act as the United Kingdom's longest serving monarch was to appoint its shortest serving prime minister. Ms. Truss announced her resignation in just six weeks.[20] Truss, the Queen's fifteenth prime minister, was also her last. Rishi Sunak was appointed prime minister on October 25, 2022, becoming Britain's first prime minister of color and the first appointed by King Charles III.[21]

Analysts have identified demographic similarities between UK constituencies supporting Brexit and US constituencies supporting Donald Trump.[22] In both the Cameron and Trump elections, nationalists within a dominant conservative party held sufficient leverage to foist a disturbing choice upon party elites—either join them along a dangerous path or relinquish power. Despite Cameron's odd coupling, the lack of a robust multiparty system prevented more fluid party combinations to avert the threat. Without genuine multiparty democracy, conservative elites in both instances lacked the means to let discordant members splinter off, joining another party or forming their own.

Intuitively, direct democracy might appear to be the most democratic system of all: put a question directly to voters and let them decide. But this is deceiving.[23] Legislative referendums such as Brexit demand an up or down vote, with large numbers making a tie virtually impossible. Direct democracy, whether citizen ballot initiatives or legislative referendums, disallows the give-and-take of often-messy legislative negotiation and compromise, and it enables legislators to lay the blame for hard policy choices on the electorate. The jury's still out on Brexit's full implications, but the remarkable turnover of Conservative Party leadership—all achieved without a general election—demonstrates the dangers of a faction within a single party in a two-party system assuming the reins of power.

The London Eye

One of London's fun attractions is the London Eye, a massive Ferris wheel with rotating gondolas that offer spectacular city views.[24] As with the double-decker, it's also a helpful metaphor for political systems.

Returning to Downs, the simplest framing of our two-party system is a line, with the right representing conservatives and the left representing liberals. Imagining that line as a children's seesaw adds some nuance. Sitting on either end and balanced on a fulcrum, as one child or candidate rides up or down, the other rides down or up. In chapter 2, we saw that aligning several figurative seesaws depicts candidates sorting across the two political dimensions of economics/policy and culture/identity, rather than forcing them onto an oversimplified right-left divide.

A two-party system risks extreme elements within one party forcing it to move up or down, elevating identity politics and subordinating policy, while forcing the other party, like a child on a seesaw, to respond in kind. In the United States, we experienced this full force in the 2016 and 2020 elections. The dynamic can leave centrist voters in either party feeling politically homeless.

Imagine replacing the fulcrum with an axle, allowing the riders to rotate completely, 360 degrees. That's dangerous for children, like a swing set that swings too high. But it's perfectly safe on the London Eye! Riders travel full circle in gondolas, capturing amazing views. Now imagine that the Eye offers passengers two options. For the more adventurous, gondolas sit at the outermost edge, rotating far right and left, and soaring to great heights. For more timid riders, gondolas closer in provide a lovely ride, but one that veers less far in all directions.

Two sets of gondolas forming an inner and outer loop evoke a hardboiled egg cut in half, with the yolk forming an inner circle, or core, and the white forming an outer circle. Political scientists Norman Schofield and Itai Sened explain that whether a democracy has two parties or many, the underlying politics embed dynamics we can compare with a sliced egg, and now with the London Eye.[25]

In most democracies, voters typically experience some degree of risk aversion. Some prefer freer markets and smaller government; others prefer regulation and distributive justice. But most aren't ideologues demanding either unfettered markets or extreme distributive policies. Some voters are concerned about a loss of cultural identity; others more openly embrace multiculturalism and historical remediation. But few insist either on walling off borders and "othering" foreigners, or on abolishing borders and abandoning any sense of national identity.

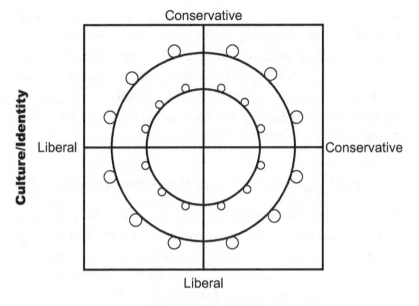

The London Eye as a Metaphor for Ideological Locations
within a Four-Box Matrix.

The yolk, or inner loop, corresponds to a nation's core voters who, although invariably leaning left or right and pressing up or down, eschew extremism and ever-widening policy swings in favor of incremental adjustments and varying degrees of accommodation. The egg white, or outer loop, represents voters who more aggressively seek to occupy extreme positions that push away from the electorate's core with respect to economics and policy, national identity and culture, or both.

In the United States, the Democratic and Republican parties' mid-twentieth century convergence seems increasingly remote (see chapter 2). When electoral systems foist upon voters increasingly stark choices, voters sort themselves across available options. A political system with genuine third parties, those promising a meaningful role in forming the government, offers more choices

and lets politicians and voters sort more productively. Some parties will ride the outer loop, spinning into the white, but the dynamic process of multiparty bargaining lets new parties emerge
and enables established parties to avoid having hardliners hijack
them onto a threatening path. Although no system is perfect, over
time genuine multiparty democracy encourages more politicians
and voters to find their way to the core.

Buckingham Palace and Ten Downing Street

Some scholars have suggested that although the United Kingdom
and the United States share two-party systems, the British monarchy offers a protection we lack. The monarchy helps blunt hard-
right populism. Conservatives tend to align with the monarch,
who benefits from institutional stability.[26]

Economist Mancur Olson described monarchy as a "stationary bandit."[27] He claimed that royal banditry is beneficial as
compared with anarchy's roving thievery. That may seem extreme, yet consider the open grandeur not only of Buckingham
Palace, with its endless staffing and changing of the guards, but
also the royal family's many other elaborate homes. Although
Brexit offers a counterexample, the natural alliance of conservatives with monarchy makes it harder for those on the right to upend basic institutional structures. A stationary bandit needs a stable society to be left alone. Despite this benefit, in seeking practical
solutions to America's own political challenges, I'm certain our
response to Lin-Manuel Miranda's spitting King George III, or
now King Charles III, is still "No, we won't be back!"[28] We need
another solution.

Before leaving London, here's a fun fact about Ten Downing
Street, home to the prime minister and often compared with the
White House. Ten Downing is black, but beneath that black fa-
cade is yellow brick. Over the decades, soot darkened the exte-
rior, and eventually the decision was made just to paint black over
the original bricks: a very pragmatic, very British way to manage

a problematic original design. As for us, we'll need more than a face-lift. Ensuring a thriving democracy demands radical reform.

Paris: The Champs-Élysées and the Palais Bourbon

The Palais Bourbon, home to the French National Assembly and about a ten-minute ride from the Champs-Élysées, is the focus of our tour. Other famous Parisian sites include the Eiffel Tower, the Louvre, the Arc de Triomphe, and the Notre Dame Cathedral. The Palais Bourbon was originally a private palace built for the Duchess of Bourbon, the legitimated daughter of Louis XIV and Françoise-Athénaïs.[29] It was nationalized during the French Revolution. During the First Republic, the lower house, the ancestor to today's National Assembly, met there. The original country house faced the River Seine, and over the centuries the structure expanded. Today it boasts a vast collection of art and a rich combination of architectural styles.

The French Fifth Republic, established in 1958, produced a power-sharing arrangement with a popularly elected president, serving a five-year term, and a prime minister whom the president formally appoints. In 2000, France modified its earlier seven-year presidential term to five years, aligning the terms of the presidency with those of the National Assembly *députés*, or delegates.[30] Because the National Assembly is empowered to dismiss the prime minister, for practical reasons the president's appointments generally reflect the body's majority backing. The prime minister chooses the cabinet ministers, who ultimately answer to the prime minister rather than directly to the president, thereby forging the power-sharing in a system called premier-presidentialism. In practice, following Charles de Gaulle's claim that state power resides ultimately in the president, the French model has developed into a strong version of semi-presidentialism.[31]

Voters directly elect the president in a two-stage process. France sets a relatively low bar to run for president in the initial balloting: at least 500 *parrainages*, from no fewer than thirty different departments, and with no more than one-tenth coming from a single department or collectivity. *Parrainage* means patron or sponsor. Departments are administrative or territorial divisions. The presidential contest includes multiple candidates, none of whom typically receives a majority. Two weeks after the first round, assuming no majority winner, the top two candidates run off. Unlike the United States, with our primary/caucus cycle, the combined initial round in France can produce a runoff between two candidates having relatively lower levels of initial support.

From its inception, the Fifth Republic has elected presidents representing four separate coalitions, each comprising several parties: Gaullist (Conservative), Centrist, Liberal-Centrist, and Socialist. Here's the chronology: Charles de Gaulle, 1959–1969 (Conservative); Georges Pompidou, 1969–1975 (Gaullist Conservative); Valéry Giscard d'Estaing, 1974–1981 (Liberal-Centrist); François Mitterrand, 1981–1995 (Socialist); Jacques Chirac, 1995–2007 (Gaullist Conservative); Nicolas Sarkozy, 2007–2012 (Gaullist Conservative); François Hollande, 2012–2017 (Socialist); Emmanuel Macron, 2017–present (Liberal-Centrist). The broader range of presidential coalitions in France, as opposed to the volley between two major parties in the United States, arises from the different electoral structures in the initial election round.

In the United States, third-party candidates risk being a spoiler, benefiting a voter's least favored major party candidate, or a randomizer, making the choice between the major candidates a roll of the dice (see chapter 2). Because France has multiple initial entrants in the presidential election, with the top two candidates running off, a candidate can win the second round even with relatively low initial electoral support. The resulting governance challenge is exacerbated by the large number of parties represented in France's parliament.[32]

Think back to the London Eye and the sliced egg. In France, the ultimate winner risks pushing the outer limits of the core. The potential for instability is reflected in the considerable variance in duration in office of the prime minister. In the Fifth Republic, the duration for this office has ranged from a mere 323 days for Socialist Édith Cresson (1991–1992) to 6 years and 87 days for a Union for the New Republic/Gaullist conservative coalition under Georges Pompidou (1962–1968). Over the entire Fifth Republic, although France elected eight presidents, it has had twenty-two separate prime ministers, a ratio of almost three to one.

The Challenges of Semi-presidentialism

These dynamics help to expose the challenges of semi-presidentialism, or more generally of blending presidentialism with multiparty democracy. The president of France doesn't necessarily hail from a party with a strong backing in the National Assembly as compared with the president of the United States or the prime minister of the United Kingdom, given those nations' two-party systems. Nor does France's president hold office with the support of a multiparty legislative coalition whose members' fates are necessarily tied to the president's ongoing success. The National Assembly's 577 deputies are elected subject to a simple majority rule in a first round with a minimum 25 percent registered voter turnout, as opposed to first-past-the-post. Candidates generally fail to meet this high initial threshold, producing a second-round contest among those who received support of at least 12.5 percent (one-eighth) of registered voters. Although this sometimes produces a contest with only two candidates, in the typical multicandidate race, the second-round outcome is by plurality. Because few candidates anticipate meeting the simple majority requirement in the first-round presidential and National Assembly contests, multiple candidates, some representing party coalitions, are motivated to run, thereby producing a multiparty Assembly.[33] The independently elected president thus confronts shifting parliamentary coalitions, with more rapid turnover in the office of prime minister.

Duverger claimed that the success of the French premier-presidential system resulted from its strong presidential form. The relatively frequent turnover of prime ministers demonstrates that parliament is locked into an ongoing dynamic in which it seeks to accommodate the president, with the president also accommodating shifting parliamentary coalitions, as reflected in turnover in leadership.

Presidential candidates typically represent a coalition of parties, and when the president has a parliamentary majority, it is usually the product of a broader coalition. Even so, the candidates generally represent a relatively small subset of the electorate as compared with the two-party system in the United States and United Kingdom.

Macron, Le Pen, and Frexit?

France has not been immune to the risk that an extremist party might assume power, as many feared in both its 2017 election and the 2022 rematch between Emmanuel Macron, representing the centrist party La République En Marche, and Marine Le Pen, the hard-right nominee for the National Rally Party.[34] Ultimately, Macron won both rounds, for two successive five-year terms. In the second contest, Le Pen sought to soften the edges of her earlier campaign. She abandoned her earlier call for Frexit, a possible referendum on withdrawing France from the European Union. Le Pen initially equivocated and later expressed opposition.[35]

Given the timing of the 2017 election, many feared a result echoing Donald Trump's 2016 victory in the United States and the successful Brexit referendum that same year. Although Le Pen was twice defeated, her party's parliamentary success suggests a still ongoing threat. In June 2022, just two months following her second electoral defeat, her party obtained an impressive 89 seats out of the National Assembly's 577 seats.[36] With a majority at 289 seats, the National Rally emerged as the largest opposition party and the second-largest party overall. Macron lost his earlier centrist-majority parliamentary coalition, and this unexpected result has provided the National Rally with significant legislative prerogatives. As of this writing, the National Rally has sufficient power to instigate a no confidence vote and, as an opposition party, to refer disfavored bills to the Constitutional Council, which can ban implementation upon determining a law exceeds the bounds of permissible constitutional authority.

Another development also threatens Macron's presidency as this books goes to press. Budget challenges arising from an aging population have forced Macron's government to raise the retirement and pension-eligibility age from sixty-two to sixty-four.[37] By US standards, retiring at sixty-four would seem unobjectionable, but in France this has produced massive protests. Social scientists have studied the work-leisure differences between the United States on one side, and particular European nations, including France, on the other, and whether such differences are owing to taxation, labor policies, cultural norms, or other factors.[38] Whatever the bases for these differences, in addition to ongoing French protests, some polls suggest the unrest could produce an opening for a future successful Le Pen candidacy.[39]

Overall, coalition-based presidential elections in France improve National Assembly representation despite the separate presidential elections. Even aside from the two most recent elections, the higher turnover rate among prime ministers, as compared with presidents, demonstrates the risk of instability arising from the large number of parliamentary parties. The French experience helps demonstrate that increasing the number of parties in the United States without more closely tying the presidential selection to the legislature won't ensure improved voter satisfaction or government responsiveness. More parties are necessary but insufficient. As important as the number of parties, which can be too few or too many, are the functions they serve, and specifically whether third parties play a decisive role in forming the government.

Berlin: Open Reconciliation

Unlike London and Paris, for Berlin we won't focus on governmental buildings. We'll gain more insight into the Bundestag, the lower and more important chamber in Germany's federal parliament, by considering another architectural centerpiece. The Holocaust Memorial sits across from the Reichstag building, where the Bundestag meets, and is a focal point for Berlin commuters, government officials, and tourists.

Peter Eisenman's massive memorial, featuring 2,711 uneven concrete slabs, makes the Holocaust, or Shoah—Nazi Germany's extermination of six million Jews and millions of other victims—a constant reminder of the dangers of fascism. In a controversial fundraising campaign for the memorial, a German newspaper boldly proclaimed: "The Holocaust never happened." It then continued, in smaller print, "There are still many people who make this claim. In 20 years there could be even more."[40]

In Washington, DC, visitors to the Vietnam Veterans Memorial gradually descend as the black granite walls rise, viewing their reflections against the names of thousands of veterans who died. Berlin's Holocaust Memorial isn't mirrored and doesn't bear the names of its victims. But in an important if figurative way, the Bundestag sees its reflection there.

The Bundestag

The German parliamentary system, called mixed-member proportionality (MMP), is both innovative and influential. It is also more complex than that of any of the other nations on our tour. As of this writing, Germany is in the midst of a transformation that responds to some of the challenges arising from that complexity. Germany plays an influential role in the proposed Electoral Reform Amendments. And yet, the proposed system is far simpler, and it avoids the difficulties giving rise to the changes under way in Germany.

Like the Holocaust Memorial, the German electoral system was implemented in part in response to the nation's concern about preventing future political extremism in the aftermath of the profoundly tragic and amply documented history of Nazi Germany. Adolf Hitler, leader of the Nazi Party, drafted the first volume of *Mein Kampf* while imprisoned following an attempted coup. Hitler ultimately gained power in the Weimar Republic's parliamentary system, which used proportional representation for the Reichstag, its lower house. German citizens cast a single ballot over party lists, and the chamber's size varied with the number of ballots cast. Although an improved economy prevented Hitler from gaining power in the 1925 election, the 1932 election, during the Great Depression, provided his opportunity. Intense party fragmentation and radicalization, including the growing influence of the Communist and Nazi parties, prevented a majority governing coalition from forming. In January 1933, President Paul von Hindenburg invited Hitler, as leader of the Nazi Party, which had gained a plurality of seats in the Reichstag, to assemble a coalition government.

After assuming power, Hitler relied on a constitutional provision empowering a Reichstag supermajority to amend with ordinary legislation. He used the Enabling Act to begin destroying the very institutions that brought him to power. With Hindenburg's acquiescence, Hitler declared emergency powers that the Reichstag could not override, entrenching full dictatorial powers upon Hindenburg's death in 1934.[41] Once leader of an extremist minority party, Hitler took complete control of Germany, holding the formal positions of president (head of state) and chancellor (head of government), and later adopting the singular title of Fuehrer. No governmental system can offer a complete protection against the risk of dictatorship, but the Federal Republic of Germany (FRG) was designed in part to ensure that the leader of a small extremist party could never repeat what Hitler had done.

In the FRG, the head of state is the president, a largely ceremonial office with an essential non-ceremonial role. The chief executive, the chancellor, is selected by a simple majority of the Bundestag, which meets in the Reichstag building. The Bundestag votes upon the president's nomination for chancellor without debate. Unlike the British monarch, who invites the leader of the party that won the most seats in the House of Commons to form the government, Germany's president meets with the parliamentary groups within the Bundestag and has on at least one occasion played a somewhat active consultative role, helping to ensure the Bundestag votes a successful governing coalition.[42]

Germany's legislature is bicameral, with an upper chamber, the Bundesrat, appointed at the state level.[43] Although each of Germany's sixteen states votes as a unit in the Bundesrat, state voting power is population-based. Our focus will be the lower chamber, the Bundestag, which in addition to choosing the chancellor by majority vote, plays the dominant policymaking role.

In the MMP system, each citizen casts two votes in electing the Bundestag. The first vote is for a winner-take-all constituency seat election, the equivalent of a US House district. Constituency seat conveys someone elected to represent a specific geographical district and the electoral constituency it contains. The second vote is for a party, and those elected from these ballots represent their party in the Bundestag on behalf of the state. The combined second ballot results are used to determine party proportional representation for the entire Bundestag. This includes seats awarded through the first vote, and, as I will explain, any additional required seats to make the math work.

The winner-take-all feature of constituency elections has historically led to two dominant parties, the Christian Democratic Union (CDU) and the Social Democratic Party (SPD), even though as a consequence of the list mandate voting and resulting party proportionality, neither has captured a majority of seats on its own. Since West Germany's inception in 1949, both the CDU and SPD have generally formed coalitions with the Free Democratic Party (FDP), a smaller third party. With rare exception, all chancellors have generally hailed from CDU or SPD. Here's the list since the 1980s: Helmut Kohl, 1982–1998 (CDU); Gerhard Schröder, 1998–2005 (SPD); Angela Merkel, 2005–2021 (CDU); Olaf Scholz, 2021–present (SPD).[44] Although the MMP scheme has encouraged considerable stability among parties, with neither too many nor too few, like a balloon, the Bundestag MMP produces has varied in size.

INFLATING THE BUNDESTAG

Until the March 2023 reforms, the Bundestag had a preset minimum of 598 members. Although voters cast two ballots, the combined scheme for calculating Bundestag outcomes has produced four seat categories. These include 299 Direktmandat ("direct mandate") constituency seats, which are generally awarded by majority (winner take all) on the first vote, and 299 Listenmandate ("list mandate") seats, which are filled based upon party proportionality from the second vote. Germany's sixteen states have varying representation in the Bundestag based on population, but each state has an equal number of constituency (Direkmandat) and proportional (Listenmandate) seats. Although proportional party adjustments are allocated at the state level, overall party proportionality is based on combined national results from the second ballot. The two additional seat categories are necessary to make the math work.

The first additional seat category, Überhangmandat ("overhang mandate"), ensures that those elected based on the direct mandate voting are seated even when doing so produces more seats for their party than the party earned in the state's list mandate voting. Seating the additional members of now-overrepresented parties inflates the Bundestag beyond the 598 (299 direct mandate and 299 list mandate) seats. In terms of the Bundestag's size, the larger problem is that the overhang mandate itself throws off the chamber's party proportionality.

The second additional seat category, Ausgleichsmandat ("adjustment mandate"), further inflates the Bundestag to restore overall party proportionality, ensuring that each party retains its percentage representation as reflected in the aggregate list mandate votes. As of 2021, the combined scheme produced a Bundestag with 736 members. In addition to the 299 constituency mandate seats and 299 list mandate seats, this included thirty-four overhang mandate seats and 104 adjustment mandate seats. So beyond the preset minimum of 598 seats, the Bundestag added 138 seats to make its complex scheme work.

The Bundestag's pre–March 2023 system satisfied two goals: first, it seated all constituency winners, and second, it ensured party proportionality for the Bundestag as a whole. What the scheme did not accomplish was a fixed-size Bundestag. To see why, I'll offer two versions of a state election, the first of which doesn't inflate the Bundestag, and second of which does. Then I'll explain how assessing proportionality nationally, rather than state by state, adds further complications.

THE FOUR SEATING MANDATES: DIRECT, LIST, OVERHANG, AND ADJUSTMENT

The first example involves only the first two seating mandates, direct and list. Suppose a state has ten direct mandate and ten list mandate seats for a total of twenty seats. Assume CDU receives 50 percent of a state's direct mandate seats (five) but only 25 percent of the list mandate votes. Because of the direct mandate, CDU keeps those five seats but gains no additional seats. Combining the two sets of state ballots, five seats out of twenty, precisely matches CDU's 25 percent proportional share.

Unfortunately, the math isn't always so simple. Now consider an example that, like blowing air into a balloon, first inflates the Bundestag for the overhang mandate and then inflates it further for the adjustment mandate. Assume an election in the same state, with ten constituency mandate seats and ten list mandate seats. This time the two major parties, CDU and SPD, split the constituency seats, five each. But in the state's list mandate, CDU and SPD each get 20 percent. Based on the second ballot, this entitles CDU and SPD to only four seats each out of the state's total of twenty seats. Based on the direct mandate, all constituency winners are seated. And so, CDU and SPD each keep their five seats, with one seat per party now part of the overhang mandate despite the resulting party overrepresentation as assessed by the list mandate votes.

But the math problem doesn't end there. By having CDU and SPD retain the additional seats as overhang, those parties have gained disproportionate representation as assessed by their state's list mandate votes of 20 percent per party. Other parties, for example the Greens or the merged PDS (Party of Democratic Socialism)/DIE LINKE (or Left) party, have had their proportional representation correspondingly diminished. Assume, for example, each of those smaller parties also received 20 percent of the state's list mandate vote even though they won none of the state's constituency seats. Those parties now must obtain additional seats through the adjustment mandate to ensure they receive their appropriate proportional share. As the numbers for 2021 reveal, the greater burst of air, inflating the Bundestag balloon, arises not from the overhang mandate, but from the adjustment mandate.

Even the second example fails to capture the Bundestag's complexities. The scheme is further complicated because overall party proportionality is assessed by the combined national list mandate ballots, with the seating allocated using state-level adjustments.[45] This has produced additional problems, including judicial challenges.

THE PROBLEM OF NEGATIVE WEIGHTED VOTING

Representation demands whole numbers. After all, elections are intended to seat people. And yet, proportionality routinely produces fractional results, a problem worsened by combining proportionality assessed nationally with seating adjusted at the state level. Mathematicians have demonstrated that any voting system allocating whole numbers and producing remainders, or fractions, risks anomalies when calculating seats.[46] One example is "negative weighted voting." This means a counterintuitive result that sometimes occurs when more votes cast for one party lowers that party's representation or, conversely, when not voting for a party would have enhanced that party's representation.

Intuitively, each additional vote should benefit, or at least not harm, the candidate or party for whom it is cast. We will later see that this problem is not unique to MMP, and that a related problem can arise with ranked-choice voting (see chapter 10).[47] In a 2008 case, the German Federal Constitutional Court ruled that disadvantaging a party through negative weighted voting violates the German constitution.[48] This led to further reforms designed to ensure that electoral outcomes honored strict party proportionality and that voting did not harm the party for which ballots are cast.

THE PARTY-SEATING THRESHOLD

To further stabilize political outcomes, Germany generally demands a minimum 5 percent national voting threshold for a party to be eligible for seating in the Bundestag. (An exception, described below, was repealed in the March 2023 reforms). The party-seating threshold is designed to minimize the risk of an extremist party gaining power, as occurred with the rise of Nazism in the Weimar Republic. The combined MMP scheme and the 5 percent threshold have largely succeeded in producing a stable system of multiparty coalitions. Throughout the history of the FRG, the 5 percent rule has variously produced between three and six seated parties, and for much of that history, only CDU, SPD, and FDP have been seated.

The left-wing Greens, the right-wing Alternative for Germany (AfD), and the merged PDS/DIE LINKE parties have now passed the 5 percent threshold, bringing the number of seated parties as of this writing to six. This counting follows the general convention of treating the CDU (a national party operating across fifteen states) and the Christian Social Union (CSU), a conservative counterpart operating only in Bavaria and with whom

CDU doesn't compete, as a single combined CDU/CSU parliamentary group.[49]

In a broader context, Germany's 5 percent threshold is at the higher end of proportional systems worldwide. Turkey has lowered its once-higher threshold of 10 percent to 7 percent, and the Netherlands has a low threshold at 0.66 percent (1 out of 150 votes cast).[50] In the second half of the world tour (see chapter 6), we will see that some nations have no threshold, risking governance challenges associated with hyper-fragmentation of parties. Once more we must never forget the Goldilocks principle: the goal is neither too many parties nor too few.

Before turning to the recently enacted changes to the Bundestag, it's worth noting one more stabilizing feature of the larger German governance scheme, this time involving executive accountability. For the Bundestag to end a chancellorship, it must first agree on a replacement, based on nominations by the President and voted on without debate.[51] This promotes stability by demanding continuity of governance when ending a chancellor's term prematurely, rather than risking the uncertainty of ongoing rounds of Bundestag coalition negotiations.

A New Regime on Germany's Horizon

In March 2023, Germany modified its system in a manner that abandons a key tenet of MMP. Although the new law takes immediate effect, it will be implemented in the first scheduled election in 2025.[52] The revised system no longer ensures all constituency seat winners will be seated. Instead, those winners will gain seating priority in the list mandate allocation. Although the new scheme remains to be implemented in an election, if constituency candidates generally place higher on party lists, the scheme will leave lower-ranked party candidates unseated when a state's first ballot (constituency mandate) results are more favorable to a party than the second ballot (list mandate) results.

The law also abolishes an exception to the 5 percent qualifying threshold. Prior to the March 2023 reforms, a party failing to meet the threshold could be seated provided it won at least three constituency seats. Eliminating the exception further reduces the risk of party fragmentation.[53]

The modified system is designed to avoid the twin problems of an inflating, and unpredictably sized, Bundestag along with various representational complexities, such as negative weighted voting.[54] The new Bundestag is fixed at 630 members. That number sits between the earlier 598 combined constituent and list mandate seats, on one side, and the larger 738 member body that included the overhang and adjustment mandate seats, on the other.

Returning to the balloon metaphor helps to explain why Germany's MMP system encouraged these changes and how the United States could implement a far simpler MMP system. Along with the earlier Bundestag, the MMP system itself can be likened to inflating a balloon. Squeezing one part intensifies pressure elsewhere. The MMP balloon has three pressure points: seating all elected constituency members, ensuring perfect party proportionality, and producing a fixed-size legislative body. It's impossible to ensure all three objectives are met. The history of Germany's MMP reveals that at least one of these goals must inevitably yield to the other two.

Pressing on the first two pressure points of the MMP balloon—seating constituency winners and ensuring perfect party proportionality—has put considerable stress on the Bundestag's size. Conversely, clamping down on the Bundestag's size puts stress either on seating all constituency seat winners or on ensuring proportionality. To avoid having the balloon burst, something has to give. By finally settling on a fixed-size Bundestag, Germany had to choose either to give up guaranteed constituent seating or to compromise party proportionality. It chose to keep party proportionality, thus relinquishing the overhang mandate.

Under the new scheme, when a party's state representation from the direct mandate vote exceeds its proportional seating allocation from the list mandate vote, the constituency winners are no longer assured a seat. Instead, those winners are prioritized based on the party's state candidate listing.

Germany could instead have insisted upon having a fixed-size Bundestag while taking a second-best approach to proportionality that allowed for some party-based representational distortions. This would entail capping the Bundestag at a set number, yet acknowledging that when the two sets of ballots, direct and list mandate, are combined, party-representational disparities will inevitably arise.

The scheme I propose avoids the complexities that motivated Germany's most recent change. Prior to the March 2023 reforms, Germany's MMP achieved two important goals. First, by having voters each cast two ballots, the system let voters elect specific candidates who would be seated if they prevailed in the winner-take-all constituency elections. Having each direct mandate representative accountable to a specific geographical district benefited constituent service. Second, the list mandate ballots ensured that the parties that dominated the constituency elections wouldn't independently secure a successful majority coalition. Instead, those parties would have to form coalitions with other, smaller parties. The difficulty is that combining these objectives, including insisting upon perfect party proportionality as determined nationally, continued inflating an already enlarged Bundestag. To relieve that stress and to ensure a fixed-size Bundestag, the new scheme sacrificed the first priority, seating all constituency winners, in favor of the second, ensuring strict party proportionality.

Party proportionality is certainly an important democratic principle. But as we'll see in the second half of our tour, when elevated above all remaining democratic considerations, it creates problems of its own. This includes the risk of excessive party fragmentation, which can create governance problems no less daunting than in a two-party system. It's premature to assess whether Germany's new regime, with its continuing 5 percent national party-seating threshold, will avoid that risk coming to fruition.

And as we will see when touring Israel (see chapter 6), not every change to a voting system necessarily sticks. For now, we must hope that Germany's innovation not only succeeds in avoiding the challenges motivating the change, but also that it avoids others of greater significance from arising in the future.

What America Might Learn from Germany

If the United States implements a version of MMP, as I believe it must, it can avoid the complexities that motivated Germany to abandon one of that system's two central tenets—seating all constituency seat winners. Party proportionality, while important, needs to be balanced against the risk of excessive party fragmentation. Too many parties are as dangerous in a democracy as too few.

In changing its MMP system, Germany didn't embrace presidentialism or semi-presidentialism. It also declined to adopt the superficially similar mixed-member majoritarian (MMM) system. In MMM, proportionality only governs the outcomes of the list mandate votes. There are no adjustments if the constituency mandate votes produce too many, or too few, seats for one or more parties. As we'll see in the next part of our tour (see chapter 6), despite the superficial similarity of these two voting schemes, unlike MMP, MMM tends to entrench a two-party system, and it risks enhancing the voting strength of the party in power.[55]

Path dependence captures the effect of incremental changes on systems as varied as typewriter keyboards (QWERTY over Dvorak), video cassettes (VHS over Betamax), and even developing case law.[56] Path dependence underlies political scientist John Aldrich's account of the initial ascent of the Democratic and Whig parties and the later dominance of the Democratic and Republican parties as punctuated equilibria (see chapter 3). The central lesson of path dependence is that where we end up very much depends on where we started.

Because the United States would be implementing MMP from our present two-party system, and because our case law generally requires equal representation by population, not based on party proportionality, we can strike a different balance. We can avoid the significant challenges that motivated Germany to abandon a central tenet of MMP—seating all constituency mandate winners. The United States will greatly benefit from party proportionality even if the proportionality remains imperfect as the price of meeting other objectives. This includes ensuring a fixed House size and using party votes to infuse proportionality strictly state by state, rather than as assessed nationally. From our starting point, the better path forward allows imperfect, or good enough, party proportionality, while promoting stability, both in the size of the House and in predicting the number of parties. We can gain the benefits of MMP without incurring the costs, or complexities, that motivated Germany's March 2023 reforms.

Finally, it's worth revisiting party thresholds. Until now, we haven't needed them. Unlike Germany, which experienced a once-small fascist party seizing power within a purely proportional system, culminating in Hitler's ascent, America's challenge involves breaking up the two-party stranglehold, which has produced increasingly stark divisions and widening constitutional dysfunction.

Trump's 2016 Republican Party takeover reveals the risk of a minority constituency seizing power, not as a separate party, but within a major party, and in doing so altering our right-left political landscape. This leaves moderate voters in both major parties wishing for other options, just as more timid riders prefer gondolas closer to the center of the London Eye.

Whereas Germany sought to avoid small, strident, and ascendent parties, the United States would benefit if hardline constituencies, or factions, within major parties split off, forming parties of their own. Those committed to the ideals of those newer parties could support them; those committed to riding the inner loop of the London Eye—the political core—could do so knowing that there are other options for forming a viable governing coalition that don't demand that a major party succumb to extremes. A 5 percent threshold, which in Germany has seated three to six parties, is an appropriate and cautious starting point. Including a mechanism, as the proposed Electoral Reform Amendments do, to adjust that threshold avoids the risk of failing to anticipate precisely how that starting point might play out in the United States.

Back at home, encouraging robust political competition with more fluid party combinations is essential to achieving results within the core. In the United Kingdom, this approach might have let England's Prime Minister David Cameron avoid the regretful strategy of holding his odd-couple coalition together at the price of having the European Union come apart.

The European lessons for American democracy are important, but incomplete. The United Kingdom emphasizes the dangers of a two-party system that lets a faction foist upon leaders the choice to relinquish power or acquiesce to a base. France reveals the challenges of disentangling the choice of president from legislators and of blending powers between two leaders, each responsive to differing constituencies. Despite the Fifth Republic's successes, it hasn't been immune to the risk of a populist takeover. Germany has a creative if unnecessarily complex approach, which other nations have adapted to their needs and which Germany itself continues to modify. MMP gives voters two kinds of electoral accountability, with one representative committed to concerns defined by geography, and another committed to ideals associated with a party.

In the second half of our tour (see chapter 6), we'll see variations on these systems. Taiwan embraces its own version of semi-presidentialism, and it employs MMM, strengthening its two-party system. Israel is a pure parliamentary system, with a single chamber defined by proportional representation. Israel briefly experimented with an alternative hybrid system that Duverger referred to as semi-parliamentarianism, although the label is disputed. Venezuela's presidential system also employs MMM, and we will see that it has been prone to unanticipated forms of electoral manipulation. Brazil has fallen prey to hyper-fragmentation, inviting graft and other forms of corruption. Once more, democracy can be threatened by too many parties or too few.

In closing the first half of our tour, we must always remember the impossibility of a perfect democracy. No nation should be hubristic, imagining that it has forever solved democracy's endless challenges. We must humbly learn from other nations' experiences as well as our own. Among the most critical lessons of governance is that it's easier to solve an existing problem than to foresee others that might arise. And that's okay. All constitutions are as imperfect as the humans who create them, which is why the process of constitutionality never truly ends.

CHAPTER 6

Democratic Variations

ISRAEL, TAIWAN, BRAZIL, AND VENEZUELA

To the Holy Land

We now start the second part of our world tour, looking at democracies in the Middle East, Asia, then South America. We begin with Israel.

As with Berlin, I'm not going to focus on the architecture of the Knesset building, home to Israel's legislature, or more generally on modern design. Few travel to Israel for that. Instead, they come for a deep sense of connection with a remarkable ancient land. Israel has a rich and complicated history, with Jerusalem, its capital, a center for three major Western religions—Judaism, Christianity, and Islam—and with its northern port city of Haifa home to the Bahá'í Faith. In addition to claiming ancient roots as a biblical homeland, along with Germany modern Israel has been affected in important ways by the history of the Shoah, or Holocaust.

Israel, the size of New Jersey, lives in a tough neighborhood. Since its founding in 1948, Israel has fought seven wars, faced two

Palestinian intifadas, and experienced several smaller conflicts. This tiny nation garners outsized attention on the world stage, largely owing to the perpetual conflict with the Palestinians. Many Palestinians, who claim entitlement to Israeli lands, reside either in the West Bank, previously part of neighboring Jordan, or the Gaza Strip, previously part of Egypt. In the 1967 Six-Day War, Israel seized these and other lands, including the Sinai Peninsula, which it later restored to Egypt as part of the Camp David Accords. The accords brought together Israeli Prime Minister Menachem Begin and Egyptian President Anwar Sadat, a process led by US President Jimmy Carter.

Israel's political system is purely parliamentary. Voting is exclusively by party, with no geographical districts. Unlike the European systems we have seen, or our own, the Knesset is unicameral. Inspired by *Anshe Knesset HaGedolah*, meaning "Men of the Great Assembly," a body of 120 men convened in Jerusalem during the Second Temple Period (circa 520 BCE–70 CE), the Knesset is fixed at the same number. It sits in Jerusalem, which the United States first recognized as Israel's capital in the Trump administration.

Jerusalem

Israeli geography and politics can be likened to an onion. Competing claims to Israeli lands derive from ancient and modern traditions, especially religious traditions. As we peel the outer layers, the conflicts intensify. This is especially true when we focus on Jerusalem, the capital and where we are now headed, and the West Bank, which observant Jews sometimes call Judea and Samaria. The West Bank is home to important biblical stories in the Jewish tradition and to Bethlehem, the birthplace of Jesus, in the Christian tradition. Peeling more layers, the conflicts become more acute as we enter the Old City of Jerusalem, with its many ancient sites, walls, walkways, and gates. That city divides into four quarters—Jewish, Christian, Muslim, and Armenian.

As with the Jewish people, who lost one-third of their population in the Holocaust, the Armenians suffered their own tragic genocide at the hands of the Ottoman Empire in World War I.[1] Peeling still further, now reaching the innermost layers, we come upon the site of the Second Temple, commenced by King Herod, sometimes called Herod the Great, and located on the same site as King Solomon's Temple. The temple's sole remaining wall has been a site of controversy, including its naming. During the period of Roman rule, the emperor Hadrian disallowed Jews to pray at the wall except on Tisha B'Av (literally the ninth day of the month of Av), a fast day commemorating the destruction of both the First and Second Temples. In one account, Christian onlookers adopted the name "Wailing Wall," having observed weeping Jews press their lips to the stones in prayer. This name became popular during British control of Palestine, and, although for a time the name was widely used, many Jews regard it as offensive.[2] Israel's founding in 1948 formally ended the Jewish diaspora, and with Israel taking control of Jerusalem in 1967, the wall was renamed the Western Wall. In the Jewish tradition, the raised plateau of Temple Mount, above the wall, is home to the unmarked, and not precisely located, site of the Holy of Holies, which contained the Ark of the Covenant. The site is so formidable that religious Jews will not ascend the Mount for fear of entering it.[3]

The Muslim community refers to this site as al-Buraq, based on a tradition involving the prophet Muhammad's winged steed.[4] Above the wall, high on the Temple Mount, also known as Haram esh-Sharif, sits the Al Aqsa Mosque compound. In some Muslim traditions, Muhammad journeyed here from Mecca on the Buraq during the Night Journey and ascended to heaven.[5] Muslims regard the Temple Mount's plateau as their religion's third holiest site.

The Christian quarter is home to the Church of the Holy Sepulchre and the Via Dolorosa, the route pilgrims take following the Stations of the Cross.[6] The stations begin where Jesus was sentenced to die and include several points along his path to execution, ending where his body was laid to rest before ascending in resurrection.

The religious significance of this ancient city for Jews, Muslims, and Christians is overwhelming, and it has embedded this tiny nation in a whirlwind of controversy and confusion. Opposing claims about which side caused which battle resemble, on a far grander scale and with more ancient roots, Appalachian feuding between the Hatfields and McCoys. We can't unravel these tragic conflicts, but we can consider how the dynamics have sometimes influenced Israel's parliamentary democracy.

The Knesset

Israel is a pure parliamentary democracy, meaning all members of the Knesset are selected by party-list votes. Israelis do not vote for specific candidates, and they aren't divided into electoral districts. The Knesset chooses the prime minister based on negotiations among party leaders. The prime minister, who serves as head of government and who appoints ministers who help run the government, is elected for a renewable four-year term. The Knesset also elects the president, the ceremonial head of state, by secret ballot for a single seven-year term.

Israel's president serves a notable function in helping to form the government, and on at least one documented occasion, the German president is reported to have played a similar role.[7] The Israeli president speaks with each party leader and, based on those conversations, invites the leader with the strongest support to form a coalition. Unlike in England, the leader invited to form the governing coalition in Israel might not hail from the party holding the most seats. Consulting all party leaders helps ensure that the eventual government has a broad consensus.

This method of selecting who forms the government reflects an important trade-off: Entrusting the president to determine the ordering by which parties lead coalition negotiations helps to ensure broad support, encouraging coalitions closer to the core or yolk.[8] At the same time, the process's legitimacy depends upon public confidence that in managing it, the president won't engage in partisan manipulation. Vesting the British monarch with such a non-ministerial function would risk violating royalty's apolitical non-policymaking role, explaining the protocol of invitations to form the government based on relative representation in the House of Commons. In the United Kingdom, this is simplified by the two-party system as one party typically captures a majority. If the United States embraces parliamentary democracy, as I believe it must, at least early on a system that entails some degree of judgment or discretion in the ordering process would risk undermining legitimacy. As confidence rises, however, a system affording more latitude in directing the order of party prioritization in coalition negotiations will encourage results in the core, like riding an inner loop on the London Eye.

The Israeli consultative process also reflects the considerable number of parties as compared with England or Germany, although fewer than France. Recall that Germany sets the bar for party eligibility at 5 percent, which has recently produced six parties. At Israel's founding in 1948, the threshold for party eligibility was 1 percent. The threshold has incrementally risen to 3.25 percent. The adjustments help demonstrate that some design features shouldn't be permanently fixed. It's important to devise mechanisms that let governments respond as they gain experience. Today, Israel generally has about ten seated parties, none of which captures a majority of votes. Throughout Israel's history, the government has generally included more than two parties.

The Knesset today includes Labor, a liberal party; Likud, a conservative party; and a combination of religious parties, Arab parties, and other small parties.[9] Historically, whether the government is dominated by Labor or Likud, the largest parties, Israeli coalitions have included religious parties.[10] In US politics we customarily think of the "religious right." Israel's parliamentary experience demonstrates greater fluidity. Among the religious parties' central concerns are ensuring military exemptions for constituents whose young men attend *yeshivot*, ultra-Orthodox religious schools, along with financial subsidies. Israel isn't alone in sometimes producing unconventional party alliances. In addition to Prime Minister Cameron's odd couple, in January of 2020, Ireland forged an alliance between a center-right party and a party dedicated to environmentalism, creating the novel term "Greencon."[11] In general, parliamentary systems invite greater fluidity in forming governing coalitions than presidential systems.

Back in Israel, the 2021 election, which, for a time, seemed destined to end the long and controversial stewardship of Prime Minister Benjamin Netanyahu, who had served from 1996 to 1999 and from 2009 to 2021, introduced a truly novel coalition that ultimately collapsed.[12] That government had a highly unusual arrangement: Naftali Bennett of Yamina, a right-wing party with only seven seats, would first serve as prime minister through August 27, 2023, and then cede the office to Yair Lapid, of Yesh Atid, a liberal party with seventeen Knesset seats, through November 2025.[13] It was the first coalition to include an Arab party, United Arab List, with four seats. The coalition, which quickly broke down, producing four unsuccessful elections, agreed primarily on one thing: ending the Netanyahu regime. A fifth election on November 1, 2022, ultimately restored Netanyahu to power, this time joined by Itamar Ben-Gvir, head of the Religious Zionist Party. As of this writing, the new coalition has been variously hailed and condemned as the most right-wing government Israel has yet produced.[14]

A particularly notable concern as this books goes to press arises from the efforts of the Netanyahu coalition government to abandon the established norm of judicial review. Although Israel has no written constitution, a series of basic laws have long been treated as having near constitutional status. Relying on the basic laws, the Israeli Supreme Court has assumed the power to strike down inconsistent laws enacted by the Knesset.[15] The reforms, some enacted, have prompted upwards of three-quarters of a million Israelis to engage in protests (the proportional equivalent of twenty million people in the United States) and include empowering a simple majority of the Knesset to override such Israeli Supreme Court rulings. Commentators have observed that if allowed to stand, these reforms would solidify the prime minister's influence and control over the Knesset and the judiciary, thereby compromising its status as a democracy.[16]

An earlier Israeli period witnessed a transformation of a different sort. From 1996 to 2001, Israel adopted a hybrid system, abandoning parliamentary selection of the prime minister in favor of direct election. Maurice Duverger dubbed the new system semi-parliamentary, distinguishing it from French semi-presidentialism.[17] By contrast, German political scientist Steffen Ganghof limits semi-parliamentary systems, which he advocates over presidentialism, to regimes with two legislative chambers, with one chamber having exclusive removal power over the directly elected prime minister and with both chambers having roughly equal lawmaking power. Because Israel is unicameral, Ganghof's framing excludes Israel. Regardless of label, Israel's experiment failed.

During the three elections under this regime—1996, 1999, and 2001—citizens cast two ballots, one for prime minister and one, by party, for the Knesset. Likud leader Netanyahu and Labor leader Ehud Barak claimed the direct election law was necessary to strengthen the prime minister who otherwise suffered at the hands of shifting Knesset coalitions. But the change had a near opposite effect. For prime minister, voters split ballots between the two largest parties, Labor and Likud, yet voters fractured among many smaller parties for the Knesset. No longer concerned about assembling a Knesset coalition to elect the prime minister, voters were free to support whichever parties matched their ideologies, regardless of party size. The resulting fragmentation made it even harder for the independently elected prime ministers to govern, as demonstrated by three elections in five years.[18] The failed experiment might reveal that the most serious challenge in

Israeli politics had less to do with the earlier parliamentary design than with, well, Israeli politics.

Israel's now-repealed direct election law required an absolute majority to win and provided for a runoff if no candidate succeeded in the first round. Although the Knesset parties fragmented, Israeli politicians quickly appreciated the need in prime minister elections to unite their side by supporting either of two dominant coalitions, Labor or Likud, while hoping to divide the opposition. Two-party dominance in the prime minister races was strengthened by an important feature of the direct election law—Knesset approval was not required for the appointment of ministers.[19] With both sides following the same strategy, the pure Nash equilibrium was two camps in the choice of prime minister, despite the parties those camps represented capturing no more than 44 out of 120 Knesset seats.

To Hadassah Hospital

Although our focus has been on ancient sites, let's close the Israel tour with something modern: Jerusalem's Hadassah Hospital, home to the famous Chagall Windows. Marc Chagall, an artist who conveyed biblical themes drawing influence from such movements as expressionism and surrealism, lived for a time in Russia, Berlin, and Paris. He escaped Paris for New York, anticipating the Nazi invasion. Each window represents one of the Twelve Tribes, named for the children and grandchildren of Jacob, the third Jewish patriarch.

I previously discussed the controversy in naming what is now known as the Western Wall after the founding of modern Israel and the capture of Jerusalem in 1967. These historical events ended the period marked as a Jewish diaspora, even as Jews remain dispersed throughout the world. The Chagall Windows figuratively assemble the dispersed ancient Jewish tribes who endured thousands of years across the globe into modern Israel. Israel also assumes center stage as home to other religious traditions—Islam,

Christianity, and the Bahá'í Faith. Confronting challenges other modern democracies share, yet unique on the world stage, Israel has assembled peoples with divergent religions and cultural identities, and it faces the challenge of conflicts between Jews and Palestinians, each claiming roots to these lands dating back hundreds, sometimes thousands, of years.

In Israel, the goal of democracy is finding a way for these peoples to live, and govern, peaceably together. Many modern nations struggle with lesser challenges, minus constant and intense global scrutiny. Even nations with demographics marked by greater cultural similarity must accommodate sharply differing views. We might regard Israel as in its infancy but, viewed through the longer lens of history, it's ancient. By comparison, the United States seems the troubled teenager that experienced a premature growth spurt and now struggles to find its way in the world. We too have assembled peoples from across the globe, many hoping for a better future for themselves and their children; others, defined by race, whose ancestors were forced here under truly unimaginable conditions; and still others, native to these lands, tragically displaced pursuant to calls for manifest destiny. Perhaps Israel's most significant lesson is humility. The task of democracy admits of no easy answers, save one—the constant need to improve.

Heading to Taiwan

Although larger than Israel, Taiwan is also a tiny nation. With twenty-three million people, its population places it between Florida and Illinois. To get a sense of its landmass, consider combining Massachusetts, Rhode Island, and Connecticut. Taiwan's fascinating history stems from its unique island geography where the East and South China Seas meet: southeast of mainland China, south of Korea and Japan, and north of the Philippines. In modern history, this has resulted in Taiwan's colonial status under Japan from 1895 through 1945, when Japan surrendered unconditionally in World War II, and control by mainland China through 1949.

On October 1, 1949, Chairman Mao Zedong succeeded in a communist takeover, declaring the People's Republic of China. Chiang Kai-shek, the leader of the Republic of China, retreated to Taiwan, joined by 600,000 troops and two million supporters. Today, Taiwan is referred to as the ROC (Republic of China), and mainland China is referred to as the PRC (People's Republic of China). Our tour focuses on the ROC.

The present, often tense, relationship between the ROC and PRC arises from the 1992 Consensus, an unofficial arrangement that produced two competing understandings of "one China." Although this has led to different conceptions of the extent of Taiwan's independence, it produced cross-strait agreements on trade and a basis for more official channels of continuing dialogue.[20]

Welcome to Taipei

Taiwan has emerged a democratic nation bearing a rich mix of influences. Unlike Western democracies, the Taiwanese government has five branches. The Examination Yuan and Control Yuan are primarily responsible for controlling the bureaucracy and ensuring governmental integrity. The Legislative, Executive, and Judicial Yuan more closely correspond to governmental branches in the United States and other Western nations. Taiwan's system traces its roots to Sun Yat-sen, who led the overthrow of the Qing (Manchu) Dynasty and went on to serve as China's first provisional president from 1911 to 1912 and as de facto ruler from 1923 to 1925.

Taiwan's president is directly elected. Like France, Taiwan's system is semi-presidential, although its system is called presidential-parliamentary. The label recognizes greater presidential authority, compared with France, to appoint cabinet ministers. Taiwan experienced a period of constitutional revision between 1991 and 2005. Since 2008, the Legislative Yuan has employed a system bearing a

superficial resemblance to Germany's mixed-member proportionality (MMP) called mixed-member majoritarian (MMM). The
difference is that under MMM, proportionality only affects the
party-based seats. Given the inevitable party overlap of legislators
elected by district versus party lists, unlike Germany's MMP, Taiwan's MMM substantially strengthens its two-party system.[21] Like
Israel, Taiwan is unicameral. Taiwan also adds its own special features, including the two additional governmental branches. Taiwanese citizens cast three ballots, one for the president, and for the
Legislative Yuan, one each for a districted seat and by party.

Taiwan today has two dominant parties, the Kuomintang
(KMT), sometimes known as the Chinese Nationalist Party, and
the Democratic Progressive Party (DPP), plus several smaller
seated parties. Historically, the KMT has favored stronger ties
with mainland China, and the DPP has favored stronger national
independence. For approximately fifty years the KMT controlled
Taiwan, ruling for most of that time by martial law.

The first election under the modern constitution took place
in 1996, with the KMT winning. In 2000, the DPP prevailed,
producing Taiwan's first transfer of power. The DPP was reelected
four years later in 2004. The KMT won in 2008, marking the
second transfer of power, with the KMT reelected four years later
in 2012. In 2016, the DPP again prevailed, marking the third
transfer of power, followed by a reelection in the year 2020.

As this book heads to press, Taiwan is considering further
constitutional reforms that would lower the age for voting, from
twenty to eighteen, and for some offices from twenty-three to
eighteen.[22] In addition, Taiwan has been a recent focus of US foreign policy following a visit by former Speaker of the House
Nancy Pelosi, which was criticized by mainland China. President
Biden then pledged to offer military defense assistance to Taiwan,
marking an apparent retreat from the longstanding US position
of strategic ambiguity.[23]

Given the relatively brief history of Taiwan's governmental
system, with the first election under Taiwan's modern constitu-

tional scheme in 1996, and the first use of MMM in 2008, it's wise to avoid broad generalizations. It is certainly good news that, thus far, the transitions of power between the KMT and the DPP have been peaceful. Taiwan's 2008 adoption of MMM helps explain why Taiwan has two dominant parties, as compared with France, which also has a version of semi-presidentialism.

Today, the Legislative Yuan, which is unicameral, has approximately four seated parties, along with several seated independents. The same parties have dominated both the presidential elections and those in the Legislative Yuan, with the KMT and the DPP sharing most of the districted seats and party seats. From 1996 through the 2008 election, the Legislative Yuan had 225 seats, and the 2008 reforms, which introduced MMM, also reduced the size to 113. Further distinguishing Taiwan and Germany, until its 2023 reforms, the Legislative Yuan is fixed in size, with no overhang seats. Of the 113 seats, 73 are districted, 6 are set aside for aboriginal constituents, and 34 are proportional, with votes allocated by party. The party seat allocation must have at least 50 percent women. As in Germany, Taiwan's threshold for party eligibility is 5 percent.

It's worth reflecting briefly on Taiwan's two additional branches of government: the Examination Yuan and the Control Yuan. A five-branch system seems unfamiliar given our longstanding commitment to three—legislative, executive, and judicial. And yet, that's an oversimplification. In the United States, constitutional scholars often describe the regulatory state—federal agencies independent of pure executive or legislative control—as a fourth branch. Although we lack a branch designed to police government integrity, The Ethics in Government Act of 1978, inspired by Watergate and President Richard Nixon's Saturday Night Massacre, insulated an independent prosecutor from presidential removal authority. The Supreme Court upheld the act against a separation of powers challenge, but Congress let the statute lapse in the Clinton Administration.[24]

Taiwan's legislative seating allocation method implicates an early debate between Alexander Hamilton and Thomas Jefferson concerning seat allocations in the House of Representatives. Hamilton favored largest remainders, and Jefferson favored a divisor system, also called the D'Hondt method after a mathematician who independently discovered the rule.[25] Although, in general, mathematicians have sided with Jefferson, Taiwan adopted a version of the Hamiltonian remainder system, which generally tends to benefit smaller parties.

The 2021 Democracy Index by the Economist Intelligence Unit declared Taiwan the most democratic nation in Asia, which, in addition to its several unique attributes, helps explain the importance of including Taiwan on our tour.[26] At the same time, Taiwan's brief history, especially with major reforms taking effect as recently as 2008, disallows broad generalizations about its record of success. While there are reasons to be hopeful, it remains wise to be cautious.

"How Democracies Die"

As a prelude to this final part of the trip, I'll briefly mention an important book by Harvard political scientists Steven Levitsky and Daniel Ziblatt, titled *How Democracies Die*. The authors survey failed democracies across the globe, beginning their account in Chile, with the 1973 military takeover of President Salvador Allende's regime by General Augusto Pinochet. Allende's efforts at resistance failed, and he died on the very day of the takeover. The authors add that so too did Chilean democracy.[27] Since the 1990s, Chile reemerged as a thriving democracy, albeit, like Taiwan, with a relatively brief track record and as very much a work in progress. Chilean voters recently rejected a fundamentally revised constitution, drafted over a three-year period, that was widely viewed as a basis for liberalizing the democracy with newly articulated rights and expanded electoral involvement. For now, this leaves Chile in a state of uncertainty, with a system containing elements rooted in the Pinochet period.[28]

Levitsky and Ziblatt explain that we tend to think of democracies dying "at the hands of men with guns," and the authors offer plenty of historical examples: "Argentina, Brazil, the Dominican Republic, Ghana, Greece, Guatemala, Nigeria, Pakistan, Peru, Thailand, Turkey, and Uruguay." But their book isn't about democracies that "dissolved in spectacular fashion."[29]

The other way to break a democracy isn't at the hands of generals but of elective leaders, presidents or prime ministers willing to subvert the very processes that brought them to power. The erosion of democratic norms over time is an important lesson as we think about the United States.

I began this tour by observing that we wouldn't find a perfect democratic system for the simple reason that none exists. The examples that Levitsky and Ziblatt provide run the gamut of formal democratic systems. But this doesn't mean nations aren't able to erect more effective safeguards against the erosion of democratic norms. It also doesn't mean that one size fits all. Institutional reforms are context-specific. We must understand the strengths and flaws of other systems and of our own. The challenges we face today can benefit from the experiences of other nations even as each nation remains unique.

South America: Brazil and Venezuela

The final part of the world tour focuses on Brazil and Venezuela. This part of our tour will be more targeted. Rather than focusing on geographical sites or detailed histories, I'll provide specific stories that help illustrate the lessons that Levitsky and Ziblatt convey about threats to democracy as they expose the dangers either of too many parties, such as Brazil, or too few, such as Venezuela.

There's also a more general lesson from this final leg of the tour. In politics, extremes often pose the greatest threat. We must never lose sight of the Goldilocks principle—very often the most serious challenge in devising a democracy is finding a suitable middle ground. Middle grounds can be a struggle. Finding them requires a capacity to adjust institutions over time in response to newly discovered problems, only some of which we can possibly anticipate. Calibration demands subtlety and nuance, rarely absolutes. As Alexander Hamilton observed in endorsing his political rival, Thomas Jefferson (see chapter 3), democracy's greatest foe isn't necessarily the person with wrong ideas. Instead, the greater threat to democracy is the person willing to transform any ideas, even those initially well-intended, into an uncompromising ideology.

Brasilia, Brazil

We will now look at multiparty presidentialism, a cousin of semi-presidentialism, which has been particularly influential in South America. This shouldn't be surprising. The US influence has loomed large in this part of the world. Although the United States has generally been unsuccessful in exporting its electoral model—two-party presidentialism—its system has nonetheless greatly influenced South America, with some notable modifications. Some nations, such as Brazil, have lowered the barrier to entry for legislative parties. Although introducing more parties might seem an easy fix to our nation's ever-widening divides, Brazil offers a cautionary tale.

Brazil is the largest democracy on our tour, with approximately two-thirds the US population. Brazil has twenty-six separate states, each operating as semi-sovereign, roughly comparable to our own fifty-state system. And like the United States, Brazil has a three-branch government—legislative, executive, and judicial. Its national legislature is bicameral, like ours, although each state legislature is unicameral. (In the United States, all states except Nebraska, which is unicameral, have bicameral legislatures.)

In Brazil, the upper house is elected for rotating eight-year terms and the lower house for four-year terms, along with the presidency, also elected for a four-year term. Like France, Brazil elects its president independently of the legislature, with a relatively low bar, and with the top two candidates running off if no candidate captures a majority. Also, like France, the runoff candidates can hail from parties with small shares of the electorate. In contrast with the United States, France and Brazil better align their terms of office for the presidency and for their respective legislatures.

Unlike the other nations we've visited, Brazil sets no minimal national electoral threshold for seating parties in the legislature, which is elected based on pure proportionality.[30] This has sometimes produced intense party fragmentation, making governance extraordinarily difficult for the president who seeks to ensure a majority coalition to implement policy. This phenomenon was exacerbated by a practice among parties called federations, which Brazil ended in 2020.[31] Through federations, smaller parties joined together in the election to gain an advantage, but then splintered after the election cycle was complete. The broader challenge of Brazil's party fragmentation led Political Science Professor Scott Mainwaring to observe that multiparty presidentialism, at least when characterized by hyper-fragmentation, risks inviting corruption and graft.[32]

Beginning in 2014, Brazil was home to a massive political corruption scandal now known as "Operation Car Wash" (Operação Lava Jato).[33] Originally named Petrolão, or big oil, because of the connection with a money-laundering scheme associated with the state-owned company Petrobras, the more common name Operation Car Wash refers to a location that became a focal point in the investigation. The investigation was headed by two judges, Sérgio Moro, beginning in 2014, and Luiz Antônio Bonat, starting in 2019, and it officially ended when the investigative taskforce disbanded in February 2021. For a time, the investigation was heralded as an example of the power of an independent judiciary, that is, until a news source claimed Judge Moro handled parts of

the process in a manner intended to prevent President Luiz Iná-
cio Lula da Silva's Workers' Party from succeeding in the 2018
election. Some have claimed that Lula, as he is widely known and
who was released in November 2019, had been a political prisoner.
As we'll see, Lula has since made a remarkable comeback.

The investigation, which revealed connections across multiple nations in Latin America, ultimately brought down three
former Brazilian presidents, Fernando Collor de Mello, Michel
Temer, and Lula. It also implicated considerable numbers of other
elected officials both in the upper and lower chambers and in the
petroleum sector. The complex scheme involved allegations of
bribery over government contracts and included impeachment
proceedings against a then-sitting president, Dilma Rousseff.
Rousseff was charged with reallocating funds across governmental sectors, in violation of Brazilian law. She disputed the charges
but was ultimately removed as president in August 2016. Despite
having been impeached, Rousseff succeeded in fending off a separate Senate vote that would have banned her from serving in public office for eight years.[34]

The details of Operation Car Wash, which has produced
thousands of interrogations and scores of convictions at very high
levels, are less important than recognizing its relationship to the
challenge of governing in a hyper-fragmented party system.
Hyper-fragmentation risks inviting graft as a means of assembling
a needed legislative coalition. In 2020, Brazil had upwards of forty
active political parties.[35]

Certainly, I don't wish to suggest that corruption is ever a necessary, or worse yet, justified, response to the challenges facing a
democratic system or that Operation Car Wash was exclusively
motivated by hyper-fragmentation. But we must acknowledge that
institutional structures have consequences. Intense fragmentation
can be as problematic as a two- or, worse yet, one-party system.
If coalition-building is an impossible means of accomplishing
political objectives, we can expect leaders to seek other ways,
sometimes including unlawful ways, to get things done. One of

the hardest lessons of democratic systems is the never-ending need for balance. Extremism poses the ultimate threat to democracy.

This lesson once more was also on full display in Brazil's most recent October 2022 election, which has been compared to the US 2020 election. In a race many described as pitting socialism against fascism, Lula defeated incumbent President Jair Bolsonaro by a razor-thin margin of 50.9 percent to 49.1 percent, with some observers fearing Bolsonaro would not relinquish power. Some commentators credit Brazilian Supreme Court justice and the nation's election chief, Alexandre de Moraes, with insisting upon removing fake news posts and taking additional steps that made it difficult for Bolsonaro to thwart the eventual outcome. In hindsight, such claims proved premature. On January 8, 2023, Bolsonaro supporters stormed the presidential palace, Congress, and the Supreme Court, almost precisely two years following the US attempted insurrection on January 6, 2021.[36] Bolsonaro himself condemned the rioting, which thankfully failed. While the Lula victory is certainly vital to Brazilian democracy, the extraordinarily close election, and its aftermath, offers at best limited assurance against a recurring threat.[37]

It's important to calibrate the number of parties to allow voters to express sincere preferences over meaningful choices, but not to invite so many options that it becomes impossible for groups to coalesce in the project of effective governance. On this tour we've learned that a major factor in devising a system with an optimal number of parties is the role parties play in forming the government. Disconnecting the choice of parties in the legislature from the success of the presidency invites fragmentation, sometimes in extreme form. Too many parties risks inviting excessive demands as the price of supporting the government.

When coalition members are also part of the president's party or a more tightly held governing coalition, myriad opportunities arise to mete out rewards or discipline. Loyalists can gain offices or other perks; those who obstruct can be countered in elections by party members more willing to help advance the party's overall goals. Although we should rightly condemn those willing to do whatever it takes to succeed regardless of legal or moral implications, we mustn't turn a blind eye to structures that produce incentives correlating to the problematic conduct we observe.

And Now, Caracas, Venezuela

Venezuela has volleyed from a strong impulse toward privatization, especially for the oil industry, the nation's most valued natural resource, to an equal, contrary push toward socialism. A challenge for oil-rich nations, such as Venezuela, Russia, and various Arab Middle Eastern countries, is converting a scarce resource underground into a productive, above-ground, non-oil-dependent economy. This is reflected in competing accounts of what drove the 1970s Organization of the Petroleum Exporting Countries (OPEC) oil-pricing strategies. The complication is that unless and until expected returns on aboveground investment opportunities exceed the expected growth in value of what lies beneath, effective pricing sometimes resembles otherwise difficult-to-maintain cartels.[38] Today, oil-rich nations confront yet another challenge as advanced economies seek alternate energy sources to diminish the global climate impact of fossil fuels.

Beginning in the late 1990s, Venezuela has been challenged by leftist political extremism. The socialist impulse failed to improve living standards for most citizens. And in the eyes of many observers, it deeply eroded democratic norms, ultimately supplanting democracy with dictatorship.

In the United States, we often associate populism with hard-right nationalism. But populism can align with political forces on the right or left. Viewed globally, as Professors Levitsky and Ziblatt demonstrate, there are abundant examples of populist threats to democratic norms on both sides. The true threat to democracy isn't ideologies that lean left or right. Instead, it's insisting upon ideological purity or absolute loyalty to a chosen leader. Democracy unravels when ideologues, or those blinded by the raw pursuit of power, can no longer be bothered with inconvenient democratic institutions or norms that hinder bringing their singular vision of governance to fruition.

Unlike Brazil, Venezuela had a two-party presidential system. Although the relevant history for our tour begins in 1999, it involves key players with decades-long careers. This includes Rafael Caldera, who first served as president from 1969 to 1974 and from 1994 to 1999, and Carlos Andrés Pérez, who served in that office from 1974 to 1979 and from 1989 to 1993.[39]

Pérez, who generally favored privatization and courted favor with Washington, DC, managed to survive two coup attempts. In February 1992, Socialist Hugo Chávez attempted unsuccessfully to overthrow Pérez, resulting in Chávez being imprisoned. Pérez's second term ended in 1993 when he was impeached on charges of corruption. Caldera, Pérez's successor, who originally embraced a leftist platform, released Chávez from prison. Caldera later reverted to several of the Pérez administration's privatization policies, leaving an opening for Chávez, who envisioned anti-imperialist policies in line with Fidel Castro's communist takeover in Cuba, to seek power.

Chávez ultimately succeeded, serving as president from 1999 through 2013. He died in office. Chávez had been the target of at least two coup attempts, one of which he blamed on operatives within the George W. Bush administration. Chávez headed the Fifth Republic Movement (MVR) party, which dissolved in 2007 and became part of his newly formed United Socialist Party of Venezuela (PSUV).

The MVR reforms included nationalizing industries, broadening access to public education and housing, and raising the minimum wage. Chávez also reformed the constitutional system, which had been in place since 1961.

Prior to Chávez assuming power, Venezuela had a presidential system with a bicameral legislature. Upon gaining the presidency, Chávez created a new unicameral National Assembly, gave himself policymaking power by decree, and eliminated presidential term limits. He replaced many judges with MVR loyalists. To effectuate these reforms, Chávez created the National Constituent Assembly in 1999, which he vested with all lawmaking powers, suspending the earlier Constituent Assembly until the new reforms were adopted in a voter referendum. In effect, Chávez claimed that the body called upon to propose constitutional reforms held policy-making authority until the new constitutional regime was put into place. A mega-election in 2000, which covered every elected official in Venezuela, further solidified Chávez's power.[40]

Since 1993, Venezuela employed MMP, with a 60/40 split between districted and party-based, or proportional, seats. As part of his 2009 reform package, Chávez refashioned the legislature in two important ways. He revised the ratio to 70 percent districted and 30 percent party-based, which, by reducing the impact of proportionality, strengthened his hand as leader of one of the two major parties. Chávez further modified the proportionality system in parallel with Taiwan, and also with Russia and Hungary, shifting from MMP to MMM.[41]

Once more, MMM separates the two electoral components. The key difference is that the system doesn't discount for overrepresentation by party in district elections or supplement for underrepresentation. Each part of the voting—districted and party-based—is implemented separately. Rather than ensuring proportional representation of multiple parties, MMM augments the voting strength of one of two dominant parties. Two parties dominated the districted elections, which Venezuela had increased to 70 percent of the legislature. Venezuela's modification—discounting the party-based seats and shifting to MMM—helped convert a two-party system into a system that strengthened the single party in power.

The representational distortions were enhanced by two additional strategies. The first strategy involved partisan gerrymandering, concentrating the opposition into overpacked districts and spreading favorable, thinner majorities over multiple districts. Recall that David Daley aptly described this tactic in the United States as "ratf**king" our democracy.[42] The second strategy involved at-large voting. We've also seen this at home, with Democrats using bloc voting to suppress Whigs in the mid-nineteenth century, and white voters using bloc voting to suppress Black representation in municipal city councils into the late twentieth century. In both instances, rather than inviting more parties or beneficial demographic representation, bloc voting strengthened the hand of the party or race holding power.

The overall effect of these schemes greatly strengthened Chávez's political hold despite Venezuela's nominal two-party system. The system tended to generate one truly dominant party, a smaller opposition party, and several splinter parties with small legislative representation, that is, until, following a severe economic downturn in 2015, the scheme favored the opposition.[43]

There is one more important part of the story. Venezuela's shift from MMP to MMM was designed to formalize the result of a clever trick known as *morochas*, or "twins."[44] Within MMP voting systems, disproportionate gains in the districted voting are subject to offsets in party-based voting as party proportionality from the party-list ballots controls the combined set of ballots. This includes gains that might have resulted from partisan gerrymandering, a practice observed both in Venezuela and in the United States.

In 2000, before Chávez's 2010 electoral reforms, and with MMP's proportionality offsets still in effect, opposition governor of Yaracuy State, Eduardo Lapi, masterminded an ingenious strategy. Lapi figured out that having his party campaign under one name in the district election and another name in the proportional election avoided any proportionality discounting.[45] It worked. Because the parties were nominally separate, combining the twin parties produced a legislative supermajority, entrenching Lapi's power and capacity to govern. In effect, he produced a legislature opposite Brazil's hyper-fragmentation.

In 2005, the controlling Chavista party mimicked this strategy, producing a disproportionate electoral result. The opposition's failure to participate in the election as protest only made matters worse. Although this scheme initially benefited the Chavista party, the tide eventually turned. In 2015, following a gutted economy, the same electoral scheme favored the opposition, leading to the dictatorial Nicolás Maduro regime.[46]

There are several important lessons to draw from the Venezuelan experience.

First, some of the strategies that we observe in the United States, especially gerrymandering to enhance the authority of one party at the expense of another, are not unique to us. We can learn from other nations with similar experiences. Second, although reverting to at-large multimember districts in the United States might seem an appealing way to invite more parties, the Venezuelan experience provides a cautionary tale.[47] Such schemes are as likely to unite voters behind one party as to fragment them across several. Third, the use of twin parties leading to an eventual shift toward MMM, displacing MMP, arose from Venezuelan presidentialism. In Venezuela, as in Brazil, the legislature doesn't choose the president; that position is separately elected. If the Electoral Reform Amendments are enacted, creating Parliamentary America, the twin-parties strategy would fail.

This last point is particularly important. In a system that rewards the party with the largest number of legislative seats with the first opportunity to form the government, twin parties would backfire. No party would game the system by splitting into multiple parties because doing so would risk another party with more seats forming the government at its expense.

The twin-party story remains important for another reason—as a lesson in hubris. We should never assume an ability to anticipate all possible counter strategies following electoral reform. By relying upon insights from other nations, we can make wiser judgments about which electoral reforms are likely to work or fail. Even so, we must remain humble.

A General Framing

As we finish the world tour, it's a helpful time to step back and take a broader perspective. In chapter 2, I cast our political landscape along two dimensions—culture/identity and economics/policy. I also explained that ending our constitutional crisis and the third-party dilemma requires reform along two axes, our electoral system and our system of executive accountability. It's now time to assess the seven nations we've toured along the same axes. Categorizing the seven nations, each with its own unique, intricate history and political complexities, in a single table clearly requires simplification. But simplification can be a helpful basis for focusing on salient features.

The first axis, captured vertically, involves the manner by which the head of government, whether a president or prime minister, is chosen. The second axis, captured horizontally, involves the processes through which members of the lower legislative chamber, or single chamber, are elected.

The vertical axis includes three broad categories of executive accountability: presidential, hybrid systems (semi-presidential and semi-parliamentary, including Israel from 1996 to 2001), and parliamentary. The horizontal axis includes three methods of electing the lower or exclusive legislative chamber: purely districted, hybrid (including MMP and MMM), and pure proportionality. Although Table 6.1 has nine boxes to fill, when we include the United States and Israel's brief experiment, the tour fills them all. The table includes Germany's present MMP system, not the system adopted in March 2023 and that will control the first scheduled election in 2025.

During our tour, we've witnessed the pitfalls and risks of presidentialism and hybrid executive systems. Although designed to promote separation of powers and checks and balances, these systems generally thwart expectations. The US two-party presidential system has grown increasingly partisan, raising dire challenges of executive accountability and a widening cultural chasm. Within

TABLE 6.1.

The World Tour—
Systems of Election and Executive Accountability

	PURELY DISTRICTED	HYBRID	PURELY PROPORTIONAL
PRESIDENTIAL	United States (presidential, districted)	Venezuela (presidential, MMM)	Brazil (presidential, proportional)
HYBRID	France (premier-presidential, districted)	Taiwan (presidential-parliamentary, MMM)	Israel, 1996–2001 (semi-parliamentary, proportional)
PARLIAMENTARY	United Kingdom (parliamentary, districted)	Germany (parliamentary, MMP)	Israel, 1948–96; 2001–present (parliamentary, proportional)

other presidential systems we've seen, alternative legislative election protocols have also proved problematic. Venezuela's MMM has invited significant electoral manipulability, and Brazil's presidentialism combined with pure proportionality has given rise to challenges in assembling governing coalitions and problems of corruption. Although the alternative semi-presidential systems in France and Taiwan have generally functioned effectively, France has come terribly close, now twice, to electing an outlier nationalist leader. Taiwan is a very small nation whose present system is quite recent, and the government includes two additional branches, one of which is specifically dedicated to ensuring against corruption. Israel's temporary semi-parliamentary system was just that—a system quickly abandoned as ungovernable.

Across the parliamentary systems, we've seen myriad methods of legislative election. The United Kingdom's districted House of Commons, like the United States, has tended toward two-party dominance. Also like the United States, the United Kingdom has endured a faction within one party exerting disproportionate power, with Brexit reflecting parallels to the Trump wing of the GOP. At the other end of the spectrum, Israel's pure proportionality in a single chamber has invited considerable instability in forming a governing coalition.

Once more we return to the Goldilocks principle. The greatest threat to a democracy is extremes. Once we recognize the general failings, or threats, associated with presidentialism and executive hybrids, it is clear that we must consider the alternative of parliamentary democracy. The question is which parliamentary system is most effective. MMP is a conceptual midpoint between the extremes of the United Kingdom's strictly districted approach and Israel's pure proportionality. And as we have seen with Germany's recent changes, MMP itself implicates trade-offs among the values of seating district candidates, ensuring proportionality, and having a predictable size legislature. No regime is perfect; considering constitutional reform requires wisely assessing the inevitable trade-offs that most helpfully resolve the crisis we face.

Beyond our tour, countries have selected other balances. Italy, for example, employs MMM with a 30/70 district-to-proportional ratio. Even limiting proportionality to party seats under MMM, the high proportionality ratio, at 70 percent, has produced significant instability and governance challenges. In 2022, Italy elected Giorgia Meloni of the Brothers of Italy. The party has been described as neo-fascist, with Meloni herself described as Italy's most extreme leader since Benito Mussolini.[48] It's mistaken to ascribe any electoral outcome to a single cause, but likewise we mustn't overlook institutional structures that contribute to instability, thereby giving extreme parties a possible opening in their quest for power.

More generally, each legislative voting system trades off against two electoral components, even if ultimately embracing only one. The United States and the United Kingdom strike one extreme, with 100 percent districted elections and 0 percent proportionality. Israel and Brazil strike the opposite extreme, with

0 percent districted and 100 percent proportionality. Although MMP is a relatively modern innovation, viewed from this broader perspective, it's well-grounded, striking a midpoint between two longer-standing systems, each of which fares less well. MMP strikes the balance at 50 percent districted and 50 percent proportional, while also avoiding MMM's manipulability and tendency toward two-party entrenchment.

MMP relies upon districted elections to stabilize party structures, but without having either of two parties predictably control, instead engaging third, fourth, etc., parties to form a government. A parliamentary MMP system encourages voters to vote sincerely for parties that reflect their ideological views, rather than admonishing them strategically to select the least bad of two options. MMP avoids the risk of hyper-fragmentation in a purely proportional regime, and unlike MMM systems, it blunts electoral manipulation as witnessed, for example, in Venezuela.

The part that immediately follows offers three constitutional amendments, each designed to respond to the problems we face in the United States. The amendments draw upon the rich experience of the nations we've toured. In the final part, we'll consider the politics of passing these amendments, the merits of the proposal as compared with alternatives, and how our politics and culture will improve once we succeed.

PART III

Three Amendments That Will Fix Our Broken System

CHAPTER 7

Reinventing the House of Representatives

MORE VOICES, MORE PARTIES, MORE POWER

The three Electoral Reform Amendments I propose provide the least radical means of radically repairing our broken constitutional democracy. Together, they achieve three interwoven objectives: first, reinventing the House of Representatives; second, reconceiving how the president and vice president are elected; and third, reinvigorating presidential removal. These amendments effect essential reform along two key axes: the system of House elections and the system of presidential accountability.

This part, chapters 7 through 9, presents the key elements of each amendment and explains how the combined amendments will ameliorate our constitutional crisis. Part IV, chapters 10 and 11, explains why, in contrast with other proposed reforms, these amendments can be enacted and then offers the optimistic vision that Parliamentary America holds for the future. Despite their radical ambition in reconceiving our electoral system, the Electoral

Reform Amendments rest upon the rich experience of other, more politically responsive, constitutional democracies, along with a broad theoretical foundation.

This chapter focuses on restructuring and enlarging the House of Representatives. The House will double from its present 435 members to 870 members. The First Electoral Reform Amendment introduces a novel method of congressional electoral accountability. Today's Congress has two separate modes of election. This amendment retains both, and it adds a third.

Senators are chosen in state-based elections. Except in states small enough in population to comprise a single House district, members of the House are chosen in geographically districted elections.[1] These elections are typically conducted with maps drawn or approved by state legislatures following a decennial census, although some states use nonpartisan redistricting commissions.[2]

The First Electoral Reform Amendment introduces a new cohort of House members who are politically accountable to a novel constituency—political parties. These members are not elected in geographical districts, whether state boundary lines or districting maps. Instead, based on second ballot results, these representatives are selected from party lists using proportional representation. The combined scheme, with three methods of electoral accountability—statewide voting for the Senate, geographical districting for half the House, and party lists for the other half of the House—will fundamentally transform our electoral system, improving political responsiveness and voter satisfaction.

Before proceeding, it's worth acknowledging a concern some readers might have. Doubling the size of the House might appear to make political consensus even more difficult than it is now. Additional new perspectives and differing modes of electoral accountability might worsen the seemingly insurmountable challenges of negotiation and compromise. If consensus among 435 congresspersons is difficult, how can doubling that number improve things?

Economists have identified two costs of legislative deliberations: decision costs, which increase when a lawmaking body is too large, and external costs, which increase when a lawmaking body is too small.[3] This chapter will explain how, counterintuitively, the First Electoral Reform Amendment, which doubles the House of Representatives, will lower these costs individually and in combination. Beyond that, the new method of selecting half the House membership will improve political discourse, encourage meaningful compromise, and practically eliminate incentives for extreme partisan gerrymandering.

Let's begin with the amendment's key terms.

The First Electoral Reform Amendment: Reconceiving the House of Representatives

The House will double in size (from 435, under current law, to 870), with eligible citizens entitled to cast two ballots for House members. The first ballot selects among named candidates in geographical districts, continuing longstanding practice. The transformation arises from the second ballot. Here voters select from a list of qualifying parties—those meeting an initial national 5 percent or subsequently adjusted threshold. Ballot results are tallied by state.

The scheme ensures that two criteria are met: first, ensuring that all district winners are seated; and second, ensuring party proportionality for each state's complete House delegation to the extent feasible, taking both sets of ballots into account. To achieve this, party results per state are adjusted, upward or downward, after combining the separate balloting results.

Continuing current practice, Congress determines both the size of the House (meaning the number of members) and the method of state apportionment (meaning the algorithm through which it's determined how many seats each state receives following the decennial census).[4] These features are set by legislation, not fixed in the Constitution, other than the requirement that, to the extent possible, House districts should be equally apportioned based on population. That requirement derives from the Supreme

Court's interpretation of the Fourteenth Amendment equal protection clause.[5] Rather than fixing the size of the House, the First Electoral Reform Amendment continues to let Congress set the size of the House based upon myriad considerations. These include the conflicting demands of a growing national population, which encourages more districts, on one side, and concerns of producing a legislative body so large that it becomes unwieldy, on the other. For important practical reasons, as its starting point, the amendment simply takes the existing baseline, 435 members, and doubles it. Congress retains the power to make future adjustments, upward or downward, provided that each state retains an equal number of district and party-based seats.

The First Electoral Reform Amendment gives the Senate a special new power. The Senate may lower the initial 5 percent threshold for party eligibility by simple majority vote, provided the new threshold is set no later than one biennial election prior to the congressional election in which the new threshold applies. Subject to the same timing and voting requirements, if more than eight parties qualify under the existing threshold rule in a quadrennial election cycle, the Senate may raise the qualification threshold no higher than 10 percent, provided that, based on the prior two election cycles, doing so would not limit qualifying parties to fewer than eight.

Combined with the other Electoral Reform Amendments, this amendment promises to break the two-party stranglehold on our politics while balancing the contrary concern of party hyper-fragmentation. The combined amendments achieve the Goldilocks principle—avoiding too many parties or too few—either of which can render electoral politics dysfunctional.

Unpacking the Amendment

The First Electoral Reform Amendment solves a problem that has increasingly plagued our electoral system. It lets smaller—third, fourth, or more—parties thrive despite not capturing a majority of voters or electors to the Electoral College. Additionally, it lets voters support smaller parties without being admonished each election cycle not to waste their votes.

Our majoritarian electoral system includes winner-take-all elections in the House and Senate, and direct election of the president filtered through the Electoral College. This combined scheme forces a series of binary choices on voters. The system divides voters into two opposing teams, each hoping its party gains power. By contrast, party-list voting with proportional representation lowers the threshold for electoral success. Majorities, and even pluralities, are no longer needed to gain seats, and third-party votes are no longer wasted.

With an initial 5 percent threshold, as many as twenty parties could, in theory, be seated, although studies show that the actual number of parties this threshold will produce is considerably lower.[6] As a practical matter, especially with half the seats chosen in district-based elections, the results will be less fractured, yielding fewer parties. In Germany's mixed-member proportional (MMP) system, for example, a 5 percent threshold has variously produced three to six seated parties. Despite the theoretical possibility of up to twenty parties each capturing 5 percent, there's inevitable overlap among parties of district candidates and listed parties in proportionality ballots.

The amendment also avoids the risk of excessive fragmentation by empowering the Senate to raise the threshold to no higher than 10 percent, provided doing so doesn't reduce the number of parties below eight. In both directions, lowering or raising the threshold, the amendment achieves the Goldilocks principle. The Senate gains considerable, yet cabined, discretionary power to produce an appropriate number of parties, ideally between five and eight.

In proportional systems with a minimum electoral threshold, politicians have a disincentive to stake out outlier positions that appeal to such a narrow slice of the electorate that they risk failing to meet that threshold. In any multiparty system, parties will inevitably overlap in setting out policy positions intended to appeal to voters. Some will succeed better than others. Party platforms will integrate positions along both the policy and cultural axes of our politics. And district candidates will be assessed not only for their party's platform, but also for service, a benefit more difficult to achieve in a purely at-large system, and especially important given the vast geographical reach of the United States.

It's impossible to predict precisely how many parties will qualify under the default 5 percent threshold. Given our starting point with an entrenched two-party system, the goal is to produce more parties, but not so many that we risk hyper-fragmentation. This is opposite the starting point for Germany, which sought to prevent a recurrence of the hyper-fragmentation in the Weimar Republic that ultimately led to the Nazi regime.

With multiple parties in the House, no party is ensured a majority, thus making coalition building among parties essential to effective governance. Today, compromise is all too often regarded as a sign of political weakness. Each party's base increasingly insists upon unerring adherence to its most strident ideological demands. Candidates fear alienating base constituencies upon whom their political fortunes depend. The dynamic feedback loop, reinforced by customized social media newsfeeds, might seem inevitable, but it's not. Alternative institutional structures will produce better incentives and motivate more benign behaviors among voters and politicians. Coalition building rewards cooperation, not ever-widening entrenchment.

MORE PARTIES, MORE CONSENSUS

Let's revisit the opening puzzle. Even beyond politics, adding more people to the mix introduces more perspectives and options, making consensus more difficult to achieve. Two friends selecting a restaurant is easier than three. Three is easier than five. Each new participant risks complicating considerations. A small group might focus strictly on cuisine. As the group grows, its members might have to consider vegetarian or vegan options, gluten-free or other allergens, and scheduling around babysitters. These sorts of dynamics affect nearly every context requiring a group consensus. This includes seemingly simple matters like scheduling meetings (more members, more conflicts), designating leaders (more participants, more varied opinions), and arranging a meeting venue (more participants, more conflicts over location, safety protocols, confidentiality, and remote access).

You might recall Nobel laureate Kenneth Arrow, who ascribed challenges of group decision-making to the phenomenon of cycling (see chapter 5). Now let's consider insights from two other Nobel laureates in economics, beginning with Ronald Coase.

University of Chicago law professor and economist Ronald Coase won the Nobel Prize in part for a theorem bearing his name. The Coase theorem expresses the intuition that if everyone is fully informed and if there are no impediments to bargaining, private actors can negotiate around background rules to achieve desired results. In Coase's phrasing, with complete (or costless) information and low transactions costs, resources will move to where they're valued most highly.[7] The problem, Coase claimed, was the premise: in the real world, people routinely face bargaining difficulties. Information is costly. Transacting is costly. Often prohibitively so. Coase observed that transactions and information costs inhibit transacting. These factors also help identify challenging contexts for legislative bargaining.

The first context seems simplest: one buyer and one seller. Economists call this "bilateral monopoly." They identify the seller with the familiar term "monopolist" and the buyer with the perhaps less familiar term "monopsonist." A monopolist is an exclusive seller; a monopsonist is an exclusive buyer. With only one buyer and one seller, each party risks claiming a benefit that, when the two parties started out, was almost certainly meant for the other. This might sound abstract, but I suspect you've personally experienced the problem.

Think back to a time when you hired a contractor to do work in your home or purchased something expensive, like a car, with a warranty serviced by a dealership. When you started out, you had lots of choices among contractors or dealerships. But after you made the choice, you and the service provider suddenly found yourselves locked into a bilateral monopoly.[8] If you didn't take proper care of your home or car, the service provider risked incurring extra maintenance costs, only some of which could be passed on to you. And if the service provider delivered a shoddy product or did a poor job on repairs, you were stuck having to return (or have the contractor do so) rather than simply taking your business elsewhere.

These sorts of problems seem less serious when things are going well. When both sides envision a growing pie with gains to share, they tend to be happy and thus willing to accommodate occasional mishaps. Problems arise when such relationships break down. When the pie stops growing, or worse yet starts to shrink, the parties each seek more and more of whatever remains. Sometimes the parties only end up harming themselves, making their own pie smaller, but not always. Oftentimes bilateral monopoly affects others. Our two-party system creates a political bilateral monopoly. And we all experience its burdens.

When legislating, Congress is a monopolistic seller, and the president is a monopsonistic buyer.[9] Conversely, when seeking approval of cabinet members, ambassadors, or judges, or to have treaties ratified, the president is the monopolistic seller, and the Senate is the monopsonistic buyer. The challenge becomes especially acute in periods of divided government, as was the case during the Clinton administration's 104th through 106th Congresses (1995–2001), the Obama administration's 114th Congress (2015–2017), the Trump administration's 116th Congress (2019–2021) after Democrats took control of the House, and the Biden administration following the 2022 midterm elections.

Periods of divided government can be productive, although measuring productivity is challenging. One Pew study reveals notable productivity in such periods but measures that against the de minimus benchmark of any change to existing law. More generally, divided government creates genuine difficulties in addressing the most pressing matters of public policy and in seeking judicial or other appointments.[10]

Unless both sides accommodate each other, anticipating that nothing in life or politics is permanent and that sometime in the future the parties' respective roles are almost certain to change, the nation will face the serious possibility of government deadlock.[11] In these situations, the real costs are born by the electorate, not members of Congress or even the president, who can campaign by attacking what the other side has done.

Coase's happy result, with parties negotiating around rules to achieve efficient outcomes, hits a wall with too few parties— bilateral monopoly—or too many. A challenge in constitutional design is recognizing that opposing extremes can be equally dangerous: too few parties or too many, too far left or too far right, too high or too low. Ideologues disdain middling positions and imagine compromise as a sign of weakness or a lack of principle. But the rest of us must press for moderation with even greater zeal if democracy is to survive. The question is how to achieve that sweet spot. Not too hard. Not too soft. Just right.

In legislatures, including Congress, well-positioned leaders can extract political benefits by holding back even popular legislative proposals unless and until they receive something of value in exchange for their constituents, and thus themselves.[12] The risk intensifies when parties are badly fractured (the problem of too many) or when, with two parties, leaders lack effective means of disciplining members for fear of losing a coalition and access to power (the problem of too few). Legislating is less a marathon or sprint than a hurdles race. A bill sponsor must successfully jump every hurdle to get a bill passed, whereas tripping the sponsor up just once can mean defeat. In the legislation race, either extreme can make it practically impossible to get things done.

These hurdling processes, which political scientists call "veto gates," let powerful members of Congress—the Speaker of the House, committee chairs, filibustering senators, and others—withhold legislation, confirmations, debt ceiling increases, and other vital functions unless and until they receive something in return.[13] And sometimes what the base really wants is simply holding back, obstructing the opposition.

Party fragmentation also raises bargaining costs. This can arise when the fates of legislative parties aren't meaningfully tied to that of a separately elected president or prime minister, as seen in France's more frequent turnover of prime ministers than presidents and in Israel's brief experiment with semi-parliamentarianism. Governing instability can also arise within pure or highly proportional regimes that let large numbers of parties proliferate, as experienced more generally in Israel as well as in Brazil and Italy.[14]

The Framers of the Constitution thought they had avoided such challenges. Rather than a system of factions or parties—too many or too few—the Framers envisioned a multiparty institutional game. With jealousies across three constitutionally established branches—the legislature, the executive, and the judiciary—the Framers imagined a simultaneous game of Rock, Paper, Scissors *and* Scissors, Paper, Rock. Instead, the two-party system superseded their multi-institutional game, producing the bilateral monopoly we experience today.

RECONCEIVING THE "CALCULUS OF CONSENT"

Let's now consider our third Nobel laureate, James Buchanan, whose work helps explain the importance of the First Electoral Reform Amendment in working toward repairing our broken system. Buchanan, along with lawyer and economist Gordon Tullock, coauthored *The Calculus of Consent*,[15] a title evoking how best to calibrate democracy and specifically a legislature.

Buchanan and Tullock identified two opposing dynamics that affect the process of legislating, each of which can be cast in terms of Coase's transactions costs. As the number of legislators rises, so too does the difficulty of agreeing to specific proposals—the problem of too many. This problem, called "decision costs," is like adding more people to the mix when picking a restaurant. The opposite extreme is a tiny number of policymakers. A dictator or group of oligarchs might settle on a self-serving policy that proves heartless and cruel for everyone else. These are called "external costs," or simply "externalities." For Buchanan and Tullock, the solution lay in devising an optimal size legislature, including dividing into two chambers, as with Congress, with each chamber responsive to separate constituencies, states for the Senate and electoral districts for the House.[16]

As we've seen on the world tour, however, what matters most isn't the number of legislators. And splitting Congress into two separate chambers raises bargaining costs by producing another venue, inviting the challenges of bilateral monopoly. This happens, for example, when the president of one party requires confirmations by a Senate controlled by the other party. What matters most in lowering decision costs is the number of parties and the functions they serve. The concern that a larger House, with 870 rather than 435 members, will make politics unwieldy, thereby raising decision costs, misconceives the true calculus of consent.

THE PRACTICAL BENEFITS OF AN 870-MEMBER HOUSE OVER THE CUBE-ROOT RULE

Before proceeding, it's important to emphasize that the First Electoral Reform Amendment produces an 870-member House as a starting point. A consensus among political scientists suggests that an appropriate lower legislative chamber roughly corresponds to the cube root of the electorate. With a US population of 332 million, that would be about 700 members.[17] (Seven hundred times seven hundred, with the product multiplied by seven hundred once more, yields the close figure of 343 million.)

A well-functioning Congress, which these Electoral Reform Amendments will produce, can later change the House size to 700 members, or some other figure. Although the size of House coalitions will vary based on state population, the only limitation is ensuring each state has an equal number of districted and party-based members. But the double-size House holds one key political advantage over a change grounded in what's now known as the "cube-root rule." Under the First Electoral Reform Amendment, every sitting House member remains an incumbent in the district in which he or she was elected. By contrast, producing a 700-member House, whether based on mixed-member proportionality or some other system, would require redistricting across the board. Such a scheme would threaten the incumbency status of nearly all sitting House members, making its enactment less politically viable.

The 870-member body proposed in this Electoral Reform Amendment overshoots the 700 figure. Even so, the resulting constituent-to-representative ratio remains notably greater than California's lower chamber, with the largest ratio among US states, and greater than most leading democracies across the globe.[18] The cube-root rule rests on an intuition of meaningful constituent contact, not a commitment to any absolute size, especially since size will vary under the formula based on population. And there's no obvious reason to cap the size of the lower legislative chamber based on a calculation that still leaves each legislative district too large for meaningful constituent contact.

POLITICAL PARTIES AND THE CALCULUS OF CONSENT

The number of legislators, or even the constituent-to-representative ratio, says less about the functioning of a legislative body than ensuring an appropriate number of key players who negotiate and make the body's most important decisions. That turns on the number of parties and the role they play more so than the number of rank-and-file legislators. Switching from a two-party presidential system to a multiparty parliamentary system changes the party power dynamics, with leaders who form the governing coalition exerting greater influence in developing and negotiating policy, as well as greater discipline on wayward members.[19]

In the United States, each party struggles to discipline renegades, sometimes called mavericks, because of the risk of losing members to the other side. This is a direct consequence of bilateral monopoly—the problem of too few. Calls for "big tent parties" reflect the trade-off. With Democrats and Republicans close to parity nationwide, even a minuscule number of congressional seats relinquished to the other party risks throwing away control of an entire chamber. In our two-party system, the battle for control is the ultimate zero-sum game.

At the start of the Biden administration, the Senate split 50/50, with Vice President Harris throwing the razor-thin leadership to the Democrats. A single defection, for example, West Virginia Senator Joe Manchin joining ranks with the Republicans, or an earlier defection by Arizona Senator Kyrsten Sinema, would have effected a sea change, giving Republicans control of all committees and affecting which bills pass. Our electoral scheme not only affects outcomes in individual districts; isolated races can affect which party controls each house of Congress. In our two-party system, bilateral monopoly permeates the power struggle at every level, including between the president and the House of Representatives, the president and the Senate, the two houses of Congress, opposing party leaders, and party leaders and their respective bases.

Despite early trepidation about Donald Trump's ascent, including former Speaker of the House Paul Ryan hesitating to endorse him and other Republican leaders exhibiting angst, ultimately nearly all Republican leaders joined ranks, at least outwardly providing Trump enthusiastic support.[20] Had they done otherwise, they risked ceding control of the House and Senate to Democrats and personally relinquishing power with Trump threatening primary endorsements of candidates willing to toe the new party line. Even notable media personalities, like Glenn Beck, experienced this dynamic, facing the choice to support Trump or lose their audience.[21]

As Upton Sinclair famously stated, "It is difficult to get a man to understand something, when his salary depends on his not understanding it."[22] The phenomenon of discounting the threat of

dangerous candidates or ideas isn't unique to the United States. It is
the bug-turned-feature of majoritarian electoral systems. England
experienced this dynamic with Prime Minister David Cameron
succumbing to the demands of his base, not the other way around.
A bilateral monopoly can produce outcomes favoring either side.
With narrow margins, defection by leaders or the base can derail a
government. Cameron's decision to cave to his base to avoid losing
power produced Brexit. The legislative compromise, sending Brexit
to a voter referendum, reflected legislative abdication, not citizen
power. Citizens of the United Kingdom surely weren't empowered
by a referendum that eliminated the possibility of a parliamentary
compromise that might have left more British voters happy and the
European Union intact. Using the Buchanan and Tullock framing,
bilateral monopoly produces external costs that extend well beyond
the immediate players.

Electoral extremes, whether two parties or hyper-fragmented
parties, can wreak havoc with democracy. In devising a democratic
calculus, the ultimate question isn't the number of legislators; it's
the number of parties and the role party leaders play. Even in a
very large chamber, such as the House, tight organizational controls can improve its functioning. And a smaller body, such as the
Senate, faced with two increasingly divergent parties, can lose its
grip.

THE SENATE VERSUS THE HOUSE

The Senate has one hundred members, two per state, and each
senator holds considerable power. Because of the Senate's seniority
system, the levers of power bear little or no correlation to state
population. Each of California's two senators has the same power
as those of Wyoming and West Virginia. West Virginia Senator
Joe Manchin, a conservative Democrat, has exerted tremendous
power, including blocking legislation to protect abortion rights,
expand voting rights, regulate gun access, and more. For many
years, West Virginia Senator Robert Byrd likewise wielded

immense power as chair of the Senate Finance Committee, send-ing many projects and significant federal funding home.

The filibuster is perhaps the most well-known rule empow-ering individual senators to block legislation. The practice gained popular fame in the movie *Mr. Smith Goes to Washington*.[23] As an infamous real-world example, on August 28, 1957, Southern Democrat Strom Thurmond filibustered the Civil Rights Act of 1957, taking to the Senate floor just before 9:00 p.m. and continu-ing through just past 9:00 p.m. the following day. Back then, a filibuster required actual speaking, in whatever form and however vacuous. It could even entail reading entries from a phone book. To stop a filibuster, a supermajority of sixty votes must invoke "cloture," formally ending the debate.

Today's filibuster is less dramatic but no less damaging. A sen-ator seeking to filibuster a bill notifies the relevant committee chair, and the legislation is then subject to an effective sixty-vote supermajority to pass. Given the Senate's sometimes extreme representational disparities, the filibuster exacerbates the body's inherent antidemocratic qualities. Although it comes with several exemptions, when it applies, the filibuster empowers a single sen-ator, even from a tiny state, to raise the threshold for passing a bill despite overwhelming national support.[24] And the superma-jority cloture rule lets a minority of small states block a bill en-tirely. For this reason, the First Electoral Reform Amendment exempts the Senate's power to change the party-qualification threshold from the filibuster, specifying a simple majority vote.

Individual senators hold considerable power in other ways. Committee chairs can block a bill from reaching the floor. They can also block presidential nominees for cabinet posts, ambassa-dorships, and judgeships from getting a hearing or vote. This hap-pened with Attorney General and former District of Columbia Circuit Court Judge Merrick Garland, nominated to replace Jus-tice Antonin Scalia, who died during President Obama's final year of his second term. Senator Lindsey Graham insisted he would

honor his newly crafted no-hearing-in-the-final-year-in-office
rule, although he ditched it at the first opportunity. In Trump's
final year in office, Graham crafted a newer president-and-Senate-
of-the-same-party exception.[25] Trump thus secured three Supreme Court appointments in a single four-year term. He did so
despite replacing two justices, Antonin Scalia and Ruth Bader
Ginsburg, whose deaths were separated by four years and seven
months. In a bilateral monopoly, one side often secures a benefit
that, in any fair understanding of norms, is clearly intended for
the other side.

By contrast, in the much larger House, rank-and-file members generally hold less power. The Speaker of the House holds
more power than the Senate majority leader. This includes being
second in the line of presidential succession, with the president
pro tempore of the Senate (not the majority leader) third. House
members are governed by strict rules governing how the body
functions day-to-day. Committee chairs control scheduling and
other matters, with individual members taking a less prominent
role than their Senate counterparts. There's no House equivalent
to the filibuster.

Alexandria Ocasio-Cortez and the other Squad members are
in some sense exceptional. We know them because they are unusual. Even so, the Squad found nearly all its earliest objectives
thwarted by Democratic party leaders, including seeking to unseat former Speaker Nancy Pelosi.[26] In the bilateral game between
leaders and rank and file, one side or the other must yield if the
party is to hold power. House leadership won that round.

Greater member discipline makes the House less cumbersome
to navigate than it would otherwise be given its size, although it has
grown increasingly unwieldy in the age of hyper-partisan polarization. For a long time, the Senate was regarded as the saucer on
which the worst inclinations of the less temperate House cooled.[27]
For decades, a crossover group of moderate senators from each
party, variously the Gang of Six or Eight, reached accommodations
that were intended to ensure that the growing bipartisan divisions

didn't prevent essential governmental functions. This included raising the debt ceiling to ensure fiscal operations and avoid downgrading the US bond rating.[28] Today, it's harder to distinguish the two congressional chambers based on ideological extremism. From the early-to-mid 1990s, the parties have grown increasingly divergent, and this has affected both houses of Congress.

Although the First Electoral Reform Amendment only formally changes the composition of the House, its goal, combined with the two remaining amendments, is to transform both houses. Districted elections favor two parties, but the same two parties needn't dominate in each region of the country. As the House becomes a multiparty institution, a different combination of parties will dominate differing regions and states. There is precedent for this, for example, the Farmer-Labor Party, long popular in Minnesota, produced governors and sent senators to Congress.[29] As the Senate also emerges as a multiparty institution, it too is apt to benefit from coalition politics. Its members will become more open to adjusting the House proportionality threshold as needed to achieve the Goldilocks principle—not too many parties, nor too few.

THE CALCULUS REVISITED

The Calculus of Consent captures the intuition that, all else equal, it is generally easier to make decisions when you have fewer legislators, but that having more legislators provides a greater check against problematic outcomes. As Buchanan and Tullock explained, increasing the size of a legislature raises decision costs at the same time it lowers external costs. But in designing legislatures and electoral systems, everything isn't equal. The nature of lawmaking processes and the role parties play affect decision and external costs more than just size. In the Senate, if each individual member continues to hold considerable power, adding members will raise decision costs. In the House, by contrast, empowering party leaders to negotiate a governing coalition and hammer out legislative policy with greater party discipline will reduce decision costs, even in a larger chamber.

A multiparty House also avoids the external costs associated with bilateral monopoly. This includes the problematic dynamics within each major party characterized by the tug-of-war between the leaders and a more strident base. It also includes the dynamics the political branches experience when one party controls all of Congress, or even one House, and the other controls the presidency.

As with Goldilocks, the goal of multiparty democracy is ensuring that the critical decision-makers are neither too many nor too few, but just right. Focusing on party leaders, rather than the rank and file, explains why the First Electoral Reform Amendment strikes an appropriate balance. In a parliamentary system with five to eight parties, rather than two or upwards of twenty-two, voters gain influence by facing genuine competition for support at the polls. Third, fourth, and fifth parties that promise to deliver and fail, either because they refuse to join a governing coalition despite being invited to do so or because their leaders lack the political talent or valence to shape an emerging coalition's platform in their favor, will recede into the background, leaving others better suited to the task to take their place. That, of course, is as it should be.

Putting an End to Partisan Gerrymandering Games

The First Electoral Reform Amendment's two-ballot voting system provides another critical benefit beyond greater party competition. It ends incentives for hyper-partisan gerrymandering. To see why, consider Washington State. The example is convenient because the math is simple. In 2022, Washington State had ten House representatives (seven Democratic and three Republican).

Now imagine the Electoral Reform Amendments are enacted prior to a future election, such as 2026 or 2028. Assume the state's partisan leanings haven't shifted much. To keep it simple, the voters split over four parties that satisfy the initial 5 percent national voting threshold. In this regime, both the Democratic and Republican parties splinter, with more liberal Democrats favoring the Progressive Party and a smaller group of Trump enthusiasts favoring the America First Party. We might imagine that nationwide, there are other parties, perhaps five or six in total, but that not all qualifying parties catch on in every state.

In this election, the second ballot, with party-based voting, breaks down as follows in Washington State:

- Democrats = 39 percent
- Republicans = 29 percent
- Progressives = 20 percent
- America First = 10 percent

In the first ballot, with district-based voting, less has changed. The 2022 results persist—seven seats for Democrats, three for Republicans, and none for another party. Since district voting encourages two parties competing for those seats, but more than two for the party-based seats, this result isn't surprising.

Before these amendments were adopted, Washington State had ten House seats; now it has twenty. And here is where the anti-gerrymandering features of the Electoral Reform Amendments come into play. They ensure that the allocation of the state's doubled House delegation closely matches the party-based voting split, reflecting the amendment's requirement of practically feasible, or good enough, proportionality by state. Under the First Electoral Reform Amendment, the combined ballot results will closely match the party-based proportional voting results using the following adjustments:

- Democrats get one party seat on top of their seven district seats, for a total of eight (40 percent, which is close to the 39 percent vote).
- Republicans get three party seats on top of their three district seats, for a total of six (30 percent, which is close to the 29 percent vote).

- Progressives get four party seats (20 percent, matching the party vote).
- America First gets two party seats (10 percent, matching the party vote).

The math works by treating each party's proportional vote as a percentage of Washington State's total twenty-seat delegation. This neat result isn't special to a state with simple numbers. In every state nationwide, proportional allocations largely eviscerate the benefits of partisan gerrymandering, except in rare circumstances, and even then, it greatly minimizes the impact.

Partisan gerrymandering only pays off in the unlikely event of a party securing more than double in district seating (the first ballot) what it secures in the state's proportional representation vote (the second ballot). If the Democratic Party, for example, gets 50 percent of the district seats, but 25 percent of the second ballot proportional votes, the result comes out evenly. Only if the Democrats get lower than 25 percent of the proportional vote despite getting half the district seats is the proportionality discount inadequate to prevent the Democrats from some overrepresentation from district voting as compared with proportionality voting. And even in that rare circumstance, the gerrymandering payoff is dramatically reduced by the proportionately discount when the two sets of ballots are combined. If the Democrats get 60 percent of the district seats and 25 percent of the proportional vote, they wind up with 30 percent of the delegation, rather than 25 percent. That's still just half the 60 percent under the current system, with no discount. The system now in place motivates hyper-partisan gerrymandering, a result the Supreme Court has entirely green-lighted.[30]

Although the First Electoral Reform Amendment is influenced by Germany's MMP system, it happily avoids the Bundestag's complexity and administrative quirks. Under the proposed regime, the House remains fixed in size rather than growing to adjust either for imperfections in voting proportionality or based on inevitable, if intermittent, peculiarities such as negative weighted voting. Perfect is the enemy of good, and the goal isn't to needlessly upend our institutions. Instead, it's to repair our system with the least radical—although radical—reform. The First Electoral Reform Amendment is the first step toward accomplishing that task.

As explained in chapter 3, hyper-partisan gerrymandering in the form of the 2010 REDMAP strategy for a time gave a seemingly insurmountable advantage to the Republican Party. Although Democratic nominee Joe Biden prevailed in the 2020 presidential election and the Democrats carried the House, with the Senate landing as a tie, the margins of advantage remained exceedingly close because of Republican redmapping, especially considering that Biden secured greater than seven million more votes than Donald Trump of 159 million votes cast.

MMP is the most effective means of counteracting partisan gerrymandering *provided* the aggregate state second ballot results are the basis for party negotiations over selecting the president. That is the subject of the Second Electoral Reform Amendment. Simply declaring an end to geographical districting and holding at-large elections won't have this desired effect. Instead, as seen in the history of the Democratic and Whig contests in the early nineteenth century and in the more recent history involving racial bloc voting as a prelude to the 1982 Amendments to the Voting Rights Act, at-large voting has the potential to entrench the party, or dominant group, in power.

This chapter introduced the first of three Electoral Reform Amendments that together promise to end our third constitutional crisis and the third-party dilemma. We now turn to the Second Electoral Reform Amendment, which introduces reform along the second axis—the system of presidential accountability.

CHAPTER 8

Reinventing Presidential Elections

THE ART OF COALITION POLITICS

The Second Electoral Reform Amendment is in some respects the most radical. It removes the power of individual voters, through their ballots, to determine who is chosen to serve as president and vice president. The amendment vests that power, instead, in party leaders elected to the newly expanded House of Representatives. This amendment is the first step in restructuring our system of presidential accountability.

Each Electoral Reform Amendment rests on a counterintuition. As is often true, counterintuitions become intuitive when properly explained. The first counterintuition is that doubling the House of Representatives and introducing a third mode of congressional accountability—party-based proportional ballots—will improve political responsiveness by reducing decision and external costs. The second counterintuition, explored here, is that voter satisfaction and political influence will be enhanced when we shift final authority to choose the president and vice president from individual votes processed through the Electoral College (or even a national popular vote) instead to negotiations among party leaders in the House of Representatives.

Removing the president and vice president from balloting might seem to diminish voter influence. It's understandable that citizens might hesitate. And yet, indirectly choosing the president and vice president through parliamentary selection enhances citizen power in three ways: first, by rewarding the sincere expression of political preferences; second, by offering greater input into public policy; and third, by providing a stronger voice respecting who assumes these offices.

As a preliminary reflection, let's draw a comparison. First, consider democracies that couple proportional representation and parliamentary selection of the head of government, referred to as "consensus systems." Second, consider presidentialism, which vests the power to choose the head of government in the voters, not the legislature, or a parliamentary system that effectively limits voters to a choice of two parties, referred to as "majoritarian systems." Would citizens abandon consensus systems in favor of majoritarian systems, such as those operating in the United States or the United Kingdom? Satisfaction surveys of voters across such systems strongly suggest the answer is no.[1] This chapter helps to explain why.

The Second Electoral Reform Amendment builds upon the structures established by the First Electoral Reform Amendment. That amendment doubles the House of Representatives and introduces a third mode of congressional electoral accountability beyond districted or statewide elections for the House and Senate. The third mode, party proportionality, combines the results of district and party ballots.

Lowering the electoral threshold from simple majority to proportionality will infuse third, fourth, and additional parties into our electoral process. The new electoral process makes it less likely that any single party—as in our two-party system—will emerge a majority winner on its own. Joining with other parties becomes essential to forming a governing coalition. Providing qualified parties with a decisive role in negotiating governing coalitions assures voters that such parties represent meaningful choices on the ballot. The combined amendments ensure genuine party competition, not quadrennial admonitions to pick the lesser of two evils.

The Second Electoral Reform Amendment: Reimagining the Presidency

The Second Electoral Reform Amendment determines the process by which the president and vice president are selected following quadrennial elections to the House of Representatives. Because of the transformative nature of this amendment, what follows is a bit more detailed than for the other two amendments. The amendment marks a transformation from majoritarian, based on the Electoral College, to consensus, empowering elected House party leaders to choose the president and vice president by forming a governing coalition.

Following the First Electoral Reform Amendment, each state's total House delegation is based on its district seat winners and proportionality ballots. Within forty-eight hours after each quadrennial election, meaning the election for which the president and vice president are chosen, the Senate majority and minority leaders will certify party seat totals. Over time, the Senate may modify these leadership designations to reflect the emergence of multiple parties and coalition governance.[2] These certifications dictate the ordering in which party leaders may negotiate a majority coalition. If either Senate leader declines timely certification, the other may do so alone, and coalition negotiations may begin when a majority of qualifying House party leaders, as distinguished from rank-and-file members, approve the certification. If the two designated Senate leaders fail to certify the same results, a majority of qualifying House party leaders shall vote on which certification to approve, and that result will dictate the ordering of party-led negotiations.

Although proportional representation makes it less likely that a single party will obtain a House majority, a party that does so may form a government on its own. In general, the leader of the party with a plurality of seats, meaning the largest number short of a majority, will have the first opportunity to negotiate a majority coalition with other qualifying party leaders. If the plurality party leader isn't successful, the leader of the party holding the second highest number of seats will be given the next opportunity, and so on, until a majority coalition forms or until up to five qualifying parties, in descending order of seats, fail to do so.

Once a majority coalition forms, the party leading that coalition will have its preselected slate of candidates designated to serve as president and vice president. If no party leader successfully forms a majority coalition, the preselected slate of the plurality party will serve as president and vice president. The selected slate for president and vice president will serve until the next quadrennial election unless a term otherwise concludes.

The process for negotiating governing coalitions to select the president and vice president may benefit from three adjustments to the calendar in quadrennial elections: the election, swearing in House members, and swearing in the president and vice president.[3] This amendment empowers Congress, by ordinary lawmaking processes, to adjust the calendar to accommodate the terms of this amendment. It also empowers the House of Representatives to change the date for swearing in its members for the limited purpose of negotiating governing coalitions.[4] Other than for the first quadrennial election governed by this amendment, changes in the calendar must take place before the preceding biennial (nonquadrennial) election, and any adjustments to the calendar will remain in effect until changed pursuant to this amendment.

The House may set the duration for coalition negotiations provided that each party leader is offered equal time, and no less than one week, until a coalition forms. Party leaders may cede their time to other party leaders in the course of negotiations. Absent a House resolution, each successive party, up to a maximum of five parties, shall be allowed two weeks in succession from the date at which party seat allocations are certified pursuant to this amendment. Coalition negotiations end when a majority coalition forms or if none of up to five qualifying party leaders successfully negotiate a majority coalition. Upon forming a governing coalition, the leaders of all joining parties shall certify the governing coalition to the sitting vice president.

The amendment leaves existing rules governing presidential succession in place. Other than the vice president, who is first in the line of succession, those rules remain statutory. The amendment doesn't address internal party discipline beyond empowering designated party leaders to negotiate governing coalitions on behalf of their membership.

Political parties possess a First Amendment right of association. Each party may determine the processes through which it chooses its slate of candidates for president and vice president, candidates for the Senate and districted House elections, party lists from which members may be selected based on each state's proportionality vote, and designated leaders for coalition negotiations.

Unpacking the Amendment

The Second Electoral Reform Amendment transforms critical aspects of our electoral process and our system of executive accountability. Although only formally changing how the president and vice president are chosen, the amendment's effects will reverberate more broadly. This includes producing an eventual multiparty system in the Senate and among states, extending coalition governance beyond the House of Representatives and the presidency. These changes are essential to ending the third-party dilemma and the third constitutional crisis.

ENDING THE THIRD-PARTY DILEMMA

The amendment changes how the president and vice president are selected and ensures meaningful third parties. It specifies important aspects of the process by which party leaders negotiate to form governing coalitions. Some details might strike readers as minutiae, such as the calendar for setting quadrennial elections and swearing in elected House members, the process for determining the order of parties empowered to negotiate majority coalitions, the duration of successive party negotiations, and the manner in which a successful majority coalition is certified. A central feature of the amendment is providing detail where it matters while minimizing or avoiding constitutional rules in favor of facilitating helpful practices informed by experience.

The amendment sets out the essential features of having up to five party leaders, following a quadrennial election, attempt to negotiate a majority coalition in succession. To the extent practical, the amendment eliminates partisan influence on prioritizing party negotiations by giving this largely ministerial task jointly to the Senate's majority and minority leadership.

This feature differs from how party prioritization works in some constitutional democracies encountered on the world tour. In England, the monarch invites the leader of the party that secured the largest number of seats in the House of Commons to form a government. Because England has a two-party system, that leader typically represents a party holding a majority of seats. In Israel, the president, who fills a largely ceremonial role, meets with qualifying party leaders and, based on those conversations, determines which party is most likely to succeed in forming a majority coalition. Germany's president generally nominates the candidate with majority support based on coalition negotiations to serve as chancellor to the Bundestag, but after failed negotiations in 2017, President Frank-Walter Steinmeier took a more active role, consulting various party heads to help facilitate a coalition.[5]

We have no monarch, and our heads of government and state are merged in the presidency. Given our intensely divided political climate, entrusting a government official with the discretion to determine how or by whom coalitions are formed would risk undermining the legitimacy of the process by which the House selects the president and vice president. Vesting a degree of discretion in a largely ceremonial presidency or other official has much to commend it, but doing so requires widespread trust in such an officeholder to serve as an honest broker. Imagine, for example, a determination, following a process of consulting party leaders, that the plurality winner is so removed from the core that the next in line based on party seats should lead the first round of negotiations. This would risk enraging voters who supported the larger party.

The amendment anticipates that a designated Senate leader might delay certifying the results strategically for partisan gain. Should this occur, the amendment lets a majority of House party leaders approve certification by the other Senate leader and commence negotiations. This provision avoids a worst-case scenario, which one hopes will never arise, of a single party obstructing or delaying the negotiation process.

The amendment acknowledges the possibility of one party winning a majority of seats, thereby forming the government on its own, but treats that as a special case. More generally, the process begins with negotiations by the plurality winner and works its way down for up to five parties. The amendment limits negotiations to five parties, not an unlimited number. The fifth most successful party is apt to have a relatively small percentage of seats, and any smaller qualifying parties will almost certainly have been involved in negotiations.

The First Electoral Reform Amendment empowers the Senate to adjust the party-qualification threshold and creates the possibility of more than five qualifying parties being seated. Parties with fewer seats than the fifth-ranked party may still form part of a governing coalition, but they may not lead negotiations or have their slates serve as president and vice president. This rule limits the time for negotiations, encouraging parties to move

toward the core to gain sufficient support to lead coalition negotiations. This feature dampens the present tendency of our two
major parties increasingly to campaign toward their ever-diverging
bases, further dividing the electorate into opposing camps.

THE PLURALITY FALLBACK PROVISION

The amendment specifies that if up to five qualifying parties fail
to form a majority coalition, the plurality party shall form the government. This fallback provision might seem troublesome, especially since the plurality party had the first opportunity to form a
coalition and failed. Should this occur, the plurality party likely
falls outside the core, or more simply, is an outlier or extremist
party. For this provision to kick in, up to four other efforts to form
a coalition, likely including attempts to exclude the plurality party,
must fail.

An important aspect of constitutional design is recognizing
that not all possible outcomes will arise. Setting out a fallback
provision that is unlikely to be triggered helps motivate benign
behavior. This provision balances two competing concerns: the
threat of an outlier party controlling the presidency versus
the threat of failing to form a governing coalition. Parliamentary systems sometimes fail to produce controlling coalitions,
with multiple unsuccessful rounds of negotiations leading to repeat elections. In some systems, such as in Israel, the president
will call a subsequent election, and failing a successful coalition
in that later round will do so again and again. In Germany, the
president may dissolve the Bundestag, terminate the chancellor,
and call a new election.[6]

The possibility that no government will form is generally
problematic, but those problems are substantially enhanced in the
United States, the world's dominant superpower and largest economy. The fallback provision—a government led by an unpopu-
lar, even deeply problematic, party—is helpful precisely because
it signals a threat that can be avoided with accommodation and
compromise. The possibility of endless rounds of negotiation

poses the greater risk because it fails to put the party leaders' feet to the fire, letting them avoid the hard decisions required to form a government. Providing a backstop—specifying an outcome if up to five attempted negotiations fail—ensures that party leaders and rank-and-file members understand the stakes of failing to work toward a majority coalition, thereby devising a solution in the core.

PRESIDENTIAL SUCCESSION AND DURATION

The amendment leaves other important rules concerning the presidency in place. Unlike in a pure parliamentary system, it continues existing quadrennial presidential terms on a fixed calendar, including the two-term limit. Parliamentary systems vary in whether they have fixed election calendars, but in general, the head of government, usually called a prime minister, may serve for however long the governing coalition remains intact.[7]

This amendment retains existing presidential terms for two reasons. First, doing so provides greater predictability, both domestically and internationally, regarding the duration of an administration. Second, limiting each term of office to four years and the presidency to two terms infuses a greater commitment to parties as fonts of competing policy ideas than as venues for high-valence politicians whose central goal is to persist in power. Per Beyoncé, no political actor, no matter how gifted, is irreplaceable.[8] A term-limited presidency helps avoid constructed crises to perpetuate power, a phenomenon all too common among once-democratic nations that turned autocratic.[9]

The amendment neither changes existing succession rules nor gives them constitutional status. Other than the vice president, succession rules are dictated by the Presidential Succession Act.[10] In this regime, the vice president is next in line, followed by the Speaker of the House, the president pro tempore of the Senate, the secretary of state, and then a continuing line of cabinet officers. For at least two years, the only officeholder in this line of succession plausibly unaligned with the governing coalition party is the president pro tempore of the Senate, third in line. That office is typically given to the senior-most senator in the majority, which might not align with the party controlling the presidency and House of Representatives. The Speaker will be a highly ranked member of a coalition party, most likely the dominant party, and cabinet officials, some of whom may be appointed pursuant to coalition negotiations, are presidential appointees, subject to Senate advice and consent.[11]

In the midterm election, the coalition controlling the House might change, with a newly designated Speaker emerging as an opposition leader high up in the line of succession. In a hyperpartisan political climate, we might imagine the new House leadership seeking to deploy its electoral advantage for strategic gain. Rather than seeking to displace the president based on maladministration, the Speaker might seek to become president.

In combination, the three proposed amendments offer several protections against this scenario. The vice president, from the same party as the president, remains first in the line of succession. Of course, House leadership could seek to remove both the president and vice president, placing the Speaker next in line. The Third Electoral Reform Amendment (see chapter 9) sets out a 60 percent threshold for removing the president based on a no confidence vote and is specifically designed to address this concern.

Recall that the Framers envisioned a regime without parties and that the Twelfth Amendment, for the first time, implicitly recognized parties by letting candidates for the top two offices run on a slate. Before the Twelfth Amendment, removing the president by the only lawful means—impeachment—potentially changed the party in power. This might have occurred, for example, had President John Adams, a Federalist, been impeached and replaced by Democratic-Republican Vice President Thomas Jefferson. With the ill-fated exception of Abraham Lincoln, a Republican, and Andrew Johnson, a Southern Democrat, elected under the National Union Party, after the Twelfth Amendment, having a president and vice president of different parties became implausible. The proposed amendments continue this aspect of our current practice along with the stability it provides as compared with many parliamentary regimes in which, after the prime minister is removed, a new coalition takes power. Fixing the term of service and leaving the line of succession in place encourages continuity of the governing coalition in the event a presidency ends prior to a completed term.

The Second Electoral Reform Amendment specifies that the party leading a successful coalition shall have its preselected slate for president and vice president designated to serve the upcoming four-year term. Party leaders may cede time to other party leaders in the course of negotiations, anticipating that this will help facilitate a coalition they may join even if the coalition isn't one they will lead. The combined rules prevent parties from negotiating a different slate of officeholders than those designated, by whatever means, before the quadrennial House election. The restriction against formulating new slates ensures that voters know who will serve as president and vice president if the party or parties they support when casting district and proportionality ballots prevail. The limitation to predetermined party slates also avoids introducing so many options that party leaders risk failing to form a coalition.[12]

The amendment's goal is to enhance citizen influence and power, not diminish it. The coalition process pulls the presidential nominee, through policy commitments and executive appointments, toward an emerging, if evolving, core that represents the most important interests embraced among coalition partners.

Over the course of their campaign, smaller party leaders will signal which larger parties they're likely willing to join as coalition partners. Voters are empowered to rely on such representations, holding their parties accountable. And for parties that run primaries and caucuses, voters will have substantial input in determining who sits at the top of the party ticket. These processes will improve political engagement and satisfaction.

SENATE CERTIFICATION AND NEGOTIATING TO THE CORE

The Senate will transform into a multiparty chamber over time, although more slowly as compared with the House. Until this transformation takes hold, having the majority and minority leaders certify House party vote tallies in quadrennial elections will enhance the legitimacy of coalition negotiating processes. As these processes become familiar, they will be widely accepted. The Senate will emerge as an increasingly helpful partner in furthering multiparty coalitions, as opposed to pursuing narrower partisan interests within a two-party system.

The amendment provides minimal detail on the terms of negotiating a majority coalition. House party leaders are free to negotiate myriad conditions as the price of joining a coalition. These may include securing favored cabinet positions; judicial appointments, including on the Supreme Court; legislative or other policy commitments; and positions as committee chairs. The amendment specifies that party leaders may cede time to one another as part of this broader negotiation process.

The deliberately fluid nature of coalition bargaining lets leaders position themselves and their constituents across two dimensions: economics/policy and culture/identity. And it lets them signal essential commitments for joining a coalition with the effect of shaping the political core. This broad aspect of negotiation helps explain the greater political satisfaction and accountability associated with multiparty parliamentary systems as compared with the US presidential system or the UK's two-party parliamentary system. This is also evident both in voter survey data and from the considerably higher voter turnout in multiparty parliamentary systems.[13]

Mixed-Member Proportionality
Outranks Ranked Choice

Mixed-member proportionality, or MMP, lets voters place weight on their preferences rather than limiting them to a binary choice to favor or oppose either of two major party candidates. Some notable commentators, including Director of the Edmond and Lily Safra Center for Ethics, Danielle Allen; David Daley, of Fair-Vote; and Andrew Yang, of the Forward Party, support ranked-choice voting, or RCV, also known as instant-runoff voting, or IRV.[14] RCV asks voters to ordinally rank candidates, meaning list candidates in order of priority. In a commonplace version, a voting algorithm sequentially eliminates candidates who rank last in each round. Votes for the dropped candidate are then reallocated each round to the candidates the voters ranked next. The process continues until a single candidate who obtains a majority of votes wins.

RANKED-CHOICE VOTING (ROUND I)

Given the prominence of ranked-choice voting in public conversations over electoral reform, I will be taking it up in two rounds. In this discussion, I'll compare RCV with MMP specifically based on voter accessibility. In Round II (see chapter 10), I'll address several additional concerns that RCV raises and that its advocates have generally overlooked. This includes the problematic claim that RCV empowers voters to weight preferences for candidates without throwing votes for third, fourth, or more parties away.

Despite RCV's intuitive appeal, MMP has important practical and theoretical advantages. This helps explain why among those who study comparative systems, MMP is the most acclaimed.[15] One benefit is that as a practical matter, at the level of retail politics, MMP is far simpler for voters. For each office, RCV considerably raises the information burdens that individual voters face. Rather than identifying a preferred candidate or party, voters are asked to assess how they rank however many candidates are balloted for each office in priority from most to least preferred. When candidates from multiple parties seek a single office, such as the presidency, this is a challenge. It becomes all the more so when we multiply the choices across the many offices to be filled each election cycle: the presidency, the Senate, the House, state governorships, state general assemblies (upper and lower chambers), mayoral and city council elections, elected state judgeships, and more. For voters, this potentially means multiplying the number of offices times the number of approved candidates. Assuming, for example, there are eight offices to fill and five different parties, this calls upon voters to make up to forty ranked choices. There are several possible responses, and each ultimately implies that RCV succeeds best by limiting its scope.

First, we might imagine limiting RCV to the presidency, or perhaps also Congress, with or without multimember congressional districts. Because the president will remain directly elected by voters, whether processed by the Electoral College or through a national popular vote, we will still face two dominating parties. The two major parties that dominate presidential races could either confront party fragmentation in the House, corresponding with notable governance challenges or, through bloc voting strategies, perpetuate a two-party system in Congress as well.

Second, we might imagine RCV infused throughout the federal, state, and local levels and have voters use it selectively for the offices that matter most to them. This risks substantial representational distortions of the very kind multiparty democracy seeks to redress. It also risks having organized voters exert outsized influence strategically. Such voters might designate their preferred third parties at the expense of low information voters, meaning those who are less politically engaged and who are apt to limit themselves to two parties except for select offices such as the presidency and perhaps the Senate or House.

Third, we might imagine reviving party ballots.[16] The voters' preferred party would provide completed ballots ranking candidates for all offices on their behalf. This would potentially help voters sort information. But the scheme will succeed only if each specific voter's preferences precisely match those of the leaders of the preferred party with respect to all rankings.

Ranked-choice voting implicitly assumes that the options voters face neatly align on a spectrum, such as conservative to liberal. For example, we might imagine five candidates with ideologies corresponding to an array of positions: (1) hard right, (2) center right, (3) moderate, (4) center left, (5) hard left. With such a neat alignment, voters preferring the most extreme candidates, (1) hard right or (5) hard left, could easily rank the rest from closest to furthest from their starting point, with the conservative ranking from (1) through (5), and the liberal from (5) through (1), all in succession.

Although this seems intuitive, the premise is doubtful. Our two-party politics suffers because political preferences don't neatly align along a single dimension. Instead, our politics implicates two dimensions: economics/policy and culture/identity. Over those dimensions, choices are confounding. Party ballots, for example, would only avoid the challenge by passing it down one level to the parties themselves. But neither parties nor voters can collapse all choices this way. To borrow a quote attributed to Albert Einstein: "Everything should be made as simple as possible, but not simpler."[17]

Unlike the extreme voters described above, those starting closer to the middle will face more challenging choices as they seek to array options to the right and left. We might imagine voters basing their rankings on some sense of ideological distance (right or left, up or down) from where they position themselves ideologically or what political scientists call their "ideal point." But even for the most knowledgeable voter, that's a truly daunting task. And it gets worse. Various factions sometimes care more about controlling the direction of their party than winning an upcoming general election.

As this book goes to press, the GOP MAGA faction seems poised to fight for party control, even at the cost of failing to nominate a more electable presidential candidate than Donald Trump or Florida Governor Ron DeSantis. That strategy is neither irrational nor limited to the hard right. Consider the "Bernie or Bust" movement on the hard left. Although centrist Democrats, myself included, were frustrated by such voters in 2016, there's nothing inherently illogical (as distinguished from unwise) about taking the view that moderate Democrats like me will learn our lesson and eventually come around to their position. Simply put, however appealing many voters find RCV, ranking choices over candidates is complex, multifactored, and anything but intuitive.

Within the United States, voting turnout has long been notoriously low, especially in non-presidential and state elections. Raising the cost of voting, as RCV does, threatens to make matters worse.

MIXED-MEMBER PROPORTIONALITY

MMP might seem challenging because it's unfamiliar. But there's a significant difference between teaching an unfamiliar system that, once mastered, is easily employed in each election cycle versus embracing a system that initially seems intuitive yet presents confounding choices election upon election. That's the trade-off between MMP and RCV. MMP requires up-front learning but is simple at the level of retail politics. Millions of people all over the world have successfully mastered it, and it is widely regarded as the best available voting system. RCV, which is perhaps more familiar to some American voters, presents a challenge every election, and increasingly so the more widely it's used.

By contrast, we might imagine MMP replicated in state general assemblies, with state voters casting two ballots for the lower chamber instead of voting for the governor. Unlike broadly embracing RCV, which only makes retail politics more complicated, this change would make voting easier at the state level. And even without that change, adopting the scheme proposed here still produces multiple parties, with dominating parties differing across regions and states. Unlike RCV, which operates best when restricted, MMP succeeds by succeeding.

Two Meanings of Political Agency

Under MMP, voters gain power and influence by designating agents rather than dictating outcomes at the polls. The Second Electoral Reform Amendment lets voters express themselves across a two-dimensional space, with party leaders acting as agents on their behalf. Through negotiations with other party leaders, such agents forge coalitions that push or pull—up, down, left, or right— the emerging core of a governing coalition.

In voting, the term "agency" holds two important implications. The first involves designated agents who negotiate on our behalf. The second involves personal agency in choosing parties, advocating for causes, casting ballots, or, more generally, in adopting an ideology. Both meanings of agency are relevant in explaining the benefits of MMP.

Neuroscientists and psychologists have considered the cognitive underpinnings of political ideology.[18] Although the literature offers few definitive conclusions, several strands are helpful. One considers the role personality type plays in forming individual political ideologies. Another emphasizes that the culture/identity dimension of politics tends to dominate the economics/policy dimension in helping form most people's sense of political identity. Although distinct, those are each closely related to the argument advanced here. Voters tend to assume they hold greater personal agency in forming their political identity than they actually do. For most people, political ideology is affected by institutional context and available options more so than abstract philosophical assessments. Introducing more ideological fluidity among options will help blunt extreme ideologies that are often grounded in perceptions of conceptual anchors reflecting the limited choices voters perceive.

Our voting system is so familiar—infused in our culture over a quarter millennium—that the idea of electing agents who negotiate who serves as president will strike many readers as strange.

In many areas of our lives, we routinely entrust agents to press our interests rather than assuming we are best poised to do so on our own. People routinely consult experts in law, finance, medicine, real estate, and even dating. We do so for a simple reason: we believe, or at least hope, that those we hire to help in such pursuits will do better than we can on our own.

Our majoritarian system divides the electorate into two nearly equal and opposing camps.[19] Just as a group close to a majority is needed to win, so too a group close to a majority will inevitably lose. And due to the Electoral College, in two recent elections out of a total of five elections in our history, a minority of the electorate prevailed at the expense of a larger number of voters who preferred the other major party candidate.[20]

Although direct voting seems inherently democratic, we must explore what "democratic" means. The literature on democracy is vast, and writers routinely disagree about lots of questions related to democratic governance.[21] If there is a single point of agreement, it's that there is no settled-upon meaning of that seemingly familiar term. A wide variety of political practices might credibly be called democratic, and yet their antidemocratic features invariably emerge either through experience or when interrogated with probing analysis.

Here are some examples. In a 1912 case, *Pacific States Telephone and Telegraph Company v. Oregon*, the Supreme Court rejected a due process challenge to a referendum procedure that let state voters resolve certain questions of public policy rather than having them resolved in the state legislature.[22] In a notable 1967 exchange with then-Solicitor General Thurgood Marshall during oral argument in the case of *Reitman v. Mulkey*, Justice Hugo Black observed that referendums are more democratic than legislative processes because the former puts policy questions directly to voters.[23] Black's observation is intuitive. And it is mistaken.[24]

Intuitively, balloted measures seem democratic. All voters have the power to weigh in on a policy question and have their vote count equally with all others. The question is what the voters give up in exchange for this power. The price of directly resolving specific public policy questions presented on a ballot is relinquishing the power of our agents in the legislature to negotiate that policy question, along with others, on our behalf. Through such negotiations, legislators are most unlikely to cast a single up or down vote on the question as presented in a plebiscite, whether taking the form of a legislative referendum or citizen ballot initiative. Instead, they will consider lots of competing views and considerations, changing how the issue is framed and resolved. This is apt to include trade-offs, even on seemingly unrelated policy questions.

To be sure, legislative processes are messy. There's more than a kernel of truth to the saying that, as with sausages, it's best not to know how laws are made. In public policy, we routinely make trade-offs, settling upon choices that are all imperfect in some important way. Limiting policymaking to up or down votes on each question is unlikely to make voters happier. There's a reason why despite deep frustrations with legislative processes, no democracy operates by plebiscite across the board. Notwithstanding their inevitable frustrations, legislatures allow input beyond a simple up or down vote on initially conceived questions for which nearly half of participating voters will find themselves destined to lose.

In electoral voting, although we seem empowered by casting our ballots, we are disempowered by the limited choices we face at the polls. The most compelling conception of democracy isn't limited to whether a majority resolves some final choice. Instead, it focuses on the role constituencies, broadly defined, play in determining which options get presented. In our elections, two genuine choices—those with a chance to win—preclude a wider range of options that another forum might reveal. The two-party system not only suffers from the limited range of candidates; it also suffers from the voters' inability to express at the ballot box what they care most deeply about.

The antidemocratic feature of two-party presidential politics is analogous to referendums. The pigs in *Animal Farm* famously observed that "All animals are equal, but some animals are more equal than others."[25] In a two-party system and in plebiscites, those empowered to determine the choices voters face are more equal than the voters themselves. The antidemocratic attribute of the two-party presidential system, as compared with a multiparty parliamentary system, is providing immense power to those who determine the choices we face. Throughout history, voters have lamented choices made by party elites. Today, many voters resent the seemingly disproportionate agenda influence of base voters. In at least this respect, both sets of voters are right. With a better system, voters would not have to face such limiting choices controlled by decision-makers with whom they so sharply disagree.

In the past two election cycles, traditional Republicans faced two choices. First, they could accept Donald Trump, pushing the Republican agenda northward in a two-dimensional space toward nationalism and Anglo-American, or at least European American, cultural identity. Or, second, they could support the Democrats, whose views on economics and public policy they generally disfavored. Missing was the option to support a Democrat in Senate and House district races, hoping to push the party to embrace more conservative views along the dimension of economics/policy. Missing also was an option to vote Republican provided the candidate eschewed Trump's positions on culture/identity and embraced a more moderate view, left or right, along the economics/policy dimension of an emerging core. In the proposed regime, with two ballots, these messages become far easier to convey.

Voters are more equal when empowered by agents who can better press their values and commitments than the voters can do on their own. This includes not only which party's slate of candidates prevails, but also which trade-offs—on policy and appointments—they support as the price of joining a coalition government. Mixed-member proportionality lets voters express preferences outside the over-simplified liberal-to-conservative dimension, one that, like a seesaw, might press up or down, stressing culture and identity.

When people claim to be politically homeless as the Republican Party ascends toward nationalism or the Democratic Party pushes toward democratic socialism, they mean the choices presented to them no longer capture, or allow them to express, their core values. Conservatives who generally distrust government regulation and favor a robust market economy, yet despise Trump's hyper-nationalism, insulting immigrants, and denigrating minorities and women, feel homeless. Progressive Democrats who resist the party's centrist policy pull, with more moderate policies than they prefer on college funding, climate change, racial justice, and more, feel homeless. So too do Democrats who perceive a constant tug toward progressivism beyond a more general commitment to liberal social policies, and who are skeptical that every problem necessarily benefits from a regulatory intervention that risks making matters worse. And yes, those who most enthusiastically embrace Trumpism felt homeless in response to the perceived centrist pull in an earlier era in which their party was controlled by Republican elites.

The immediate point isn't to take sides, at least on this. It's to emphasize that there are more sides than two. Competition among parties lets voters, through their first and second House ballots, go well beyond registering a binary choice between two candidates in a winner-take-all districted race. Voters are empowered to signal, with notable precision, particular policy commitments that matter most deeply to them, and to empower party leaders—their agents—to help form a government by negotiating those commitments on their behalf with other party leaders.

In contrast with our entrenched two-party system, which lets a once-minority segment of the electorate gain control of a party, pushing it up or down as on a seesaw, the proposed regime lets the other side avoid being pushed down or up. Instead, voters can step off and seek a better partner—or agent—willing to join them on a more fruitful ride.

Ending the Zero-Sum Game

Some readers might surmise that it's impossible for public policy to be generally improving, as opposed to improving the plight of some voters at the expense of others in roughly equal measure. They might imagine that politics is inevitably a zero-sum game in which one group's gain invariably corresponds to another group's loss. The prior discussion is intended to dispel this notion. There's a reason why voters are happier in systems that combine proportionality and parliamentary choice as compared with presidentialism or two-party parliamentarianism. Although politics invariably produces winners and losers, the zero-sum nature of our politics is closely tied to the choices in our two-party system. Coalitions that broaden perspectives, accommodate competing views, and moderate the extreme edges of the most strident ideologies improve outcomes for more citizens.

The restricted nature of choice in our politics encourages battles for the souls of the Democratic and Republican parties, with more moderate voices on one side and more ideologically strident ones on the other. As a result of gerrymandering and social media, the primary cycle has encouraged once-moderate politicians to embrace positions that even an election cycle or two earlier were well outside each party's mainstream. When the two parties then compete in the general election, we experience what to a growing number of voters appears as a battle not just for the soul of each party, but of the nation.

If our politics instead allowed a genuine set of choices representing an array of perspectives across the economics/policy and culture/identity dimensions of our politics, moderate voices in the Democratic or Republican parties could let the more extreme members spin off, forming parties of their own. Those parties might succeed or fail, and that's also true for the moderates within the two major parties who remain. More likely, each party will succeed in helping form part of a governing coalition some of the

time, and along the way, party members will grow to accommodate the views of others as needed to succeed.

Returning to agency, many of the views that voters hold arise
from the limited choices our politics present. When our political
fortunes depend upon joining forces within a party with those
whose views we might otherwise discredit, or even disdain, it's
not surprising that over time, we become more tolerant, however
grudgingly, of those views. Within a two-party system, moderates in each party become more open to the strident forces within
their party and more distrustful of the other side. With more
choices among parties, voters could embrace policy views that
more closely align with their core values and not feel compelled
to accept positions that they would otherwise find deeply
troublesome.

Of course, the parties will negotiate in forming a governing
coalition. That, after all, is the point. But with party competition, those positions need not be entrenched. Remember what
the Framers most feared—and on this they were right—was not
factions, but entrenchment, the very result that we are experiencing today.

In a competitive party system, voters can pick and choose.
They can be Democratic, Republican, Progressive, Libertarian,
America First, or something else. And they can signal a desire to
pull the nation's core left, right, up, or down. Yes, there will be
winners and losers. That's inevitable. And there will be frustration. There always is in politics. But compared with the choices
we face today, the vast majority can be better off knowing that
they have a more meaningful voice in a system with party leaders
who share their views and are willing to fight for them.

CHAPTER 9

Reinventing
Presidential Removal

HOW "NO CONFIDENCE" INSTILLS CONFIDENCE

Like the first two Electoral Reform Amendments, the amendment reviewed in this chapter rests on an important counterintuition: abandoning the Framers' conception of separation of powers will restore benign institutional jealousies, thereby benefiting our citizens and society. The Third Electoral Reform Amendment achieves greater institutional safeguards and benign jealousies by holding the president accountable to, and removable by, a majority coalition in the House of Representatives.

The impeachment clause helps illustrate the Framers' misunderstandings as to how separation of powers works in the system they constructed. In nearly a quarter millennium, not a single president has been both impeached and convicted. Conviction removes the president from office, and it allows the Senate to disqualify the president from holding any "Office of honor."[1] The seeming impossibility of a successfully completed impeachment process exacerbates distrust in the presidency and frustration with our two-party system.

In the Trump era, conviction proved impossible despite an amply documented attempted insurrection on January 6, 2021, that, at the very least, President Donald Trump helped incite and failed to call off. After priming his base to decry the illegitimacy of the 2020 election, Trump stoked supporters to march down Pennsylvania Avenue to "Stop the Steal," with the goal of blocking the Electoral College vote certification administered by his own Vice President Mike Pence. The insurrectionists threatened the vice president's life, shouting, "Hang Mike Pence," along with the lives of other officials, including then–Democratic Speaker of the House Nancy Pelosi, as they stormed the Capitol Building and her office. Commentators claimed that if these events, later amply documented in a bipartisan House investigation, didn't warrant impeachment and conviction, nothing ever would.[2]

The Framers assumed that the institutional structures they put in place would avoid entrenched political parties or factions. They failed to appreciate that cross-institutional party loyalties centered on the presidency would overwhelm institutional or geographical jealousies, a problem that became acute in the information age. The Framers' conception of separation of powers depended upon institutional jealousies belied by experience.

Ironically, the only successful impeachment didn't occur. Despite four impeachments—Andrew Johnson, Bill Clinton, and Donald Trump twice—none producing a conviction, the only truly effective deployment of the impeachment clause involved Richard Nixon. Following a Supreme Court decision demanding the release of incriminating evidence, on the advice of his party's congressional leaders, Nixon resigned to avoid the embarrassment of being the first president forcibly removed from office.[3]

The impeachment clause proved feckless again and again because the Framers failed to anticipate that the president isn't merely the head of a governmental branch. Our majoritarian electoral system makes the president the leader of one of only two major parties. And the fortunes of aspiring party members too often depend upon the grace of even their most ungracious leader.

The final counterintuition is that easing presidential removal through a no confidence vote will strengthen separation of powers, restoring institutional confidence. The importance of this insight can't be overstated. Our two-party system largely eviscerates the benign jealousies central to separation of powers and checks and balances. Contrary to the Framers' intuitions, congressional leaders will be more willing to hold a deeply problematic president accountable if their political fortunes no longer depend upon executive grace. Competition among multiple parties lets congressional leaders safeguard their institutional prerogatives by reconceiving the governing coalition without the risk of losing power. Simply put, institutional jealousies are strengthened with separation of powers relaxed.

The Third Electoral Reform Amendment: Reinvigorating Presidential Removal

Before specifying its key terms, it's important to note what the amendment doesn't change. It doesn't affect the meaning of the constitutional provisions related to presidential impeachment or the Twenty-Fifth Amendment. Instead, the Third Electoral Reform Amendment specifies that a motion for no confidence needn't meet impeachment's stringent demands. Rather than resting on "Treason, Bribery, or other high Crimes and Misdemeanors," no confidence allows removal of a president based upon a newly introduced constitutional term: "maladministration." Although the amendment doesn't define that term, it provides qualifying illustrations, letting members of the House of Representatives develop their own understandings based on experience.

The amendment specifies that a no confidence motion needn't allege criminal conduct, although it may. Likewise, not every violation of a criminal code implicates maladministration, and the amendment has no bearing on the decision of law enforcement to press criminal charges against a president or any other government official either during or after an administration.

Behaviors illustrating maladministration include mismanagement of federal resources, including financial or physical resources, offices, or perks for purely personal or partisan advantage; systematic ineffectiveness in working with cabinet members or other officials at the state and federal levels; systematic embarrassment on behalf of the nation in conducting international affairs; a documented pattern of conveying misinformation to the public or in official communications; and other behaviors that produce widening distrust in the president's ability or willingness to govern effectively or to effectuate the office's constitutional responsibilities. As the final and more general category implies, the listed illustrations aren't intended as comprehensive. What the amendment doesn't embrace as a basis for maladministration is mere disagreement with the president's policy objectives, for example, as might result from shifting coalitions following a midterm election.

Following an appropriate investigation as determined by House rules, a no confidence motion shall be voted upon when proffered in either of two ways: first, by the leadership of no fewer than two qualifying parties, defined pursuant to the First Electoral Reform Amendment, with at least one party a member of the original governing coalition that put the president in office; or, second, by petition of rank-and-file members comprising no less than 15 percent of the full House membership, one-third of whom were part of that original coalition.

A no confidence vote is a vote of conscience, as distinguished from a party-line vote. Although the House may set its own quorum requirements for voting no confidence, a successful no confidence vote requires approval by 60 percent of the full House membership, not merely members present when the vote is conducted. Neither the sponsorship of a no confidence motion nor the vote on such a motion may be in secret.

A successful no confidence vote shall immediately remove the president from office. Such a vote does not, of its own force, prevent the president from seeking future office, including the presidency. Whether or not successful, a no confidence vote shall have no effect on the power of the House of Representatives to initiate formal impeachment proceedings against the president or any other individual pursuant to the Constitution.

Following a successful no confidence vote, rules of succession for the Office of President shall be governed by existing constitutional and federal statutory requirements, subject to modification through ordinary processes.

Unpacking the Third Electoral Reform Amendment

This amendment provides a viable means of removing a problematic president. A vote of no confidence doesn't demand the seemingly impossible bar posed by presidential impeachment. In addition, it discourages reliance on no confidence for pure partisanship, as opposed to targeting serious misbehaviors corresponding to a fair understanding of maladministration.

Introducing no confidence as a method of removing a problematic president raises three issues of constitutional policy: identifying conditions qualifying for removal based on maladministration, setting thresholds for a no confidence motion to be voted on and approved, and determining rules of presidential succession. The amendment also implicates subsidiary issues such as the relationship to impeachment, the Twenty-Fifth Amendment, and possible criminal proceedings. Although the amendment addresses each of these concerns, consistent with the more general approach of the combined Electoral Reform Amendments, it does so in a minimalistic way. It resolves essential questions yet leaves the House of Representatives to fill in details informed by experience.

This chapter reviews the essential features of the Third Electoral Reform Amendment and relates them to the larger objective of infusing aspects of parliamentary design into our constitutional system.

THE GENERAL FRAMING

Among the difficulties plaguing presidential impeachment is the inclusion of specific, arcane, and legalistic terms: "Treason, Bribery, or other high Crimes and Misdemeanors." Despite near universal academic consensus that this clause was never intended to require proof of criminality as a precondition to impeaching and removing a president, bribery and treason are criminal offenses.[4] Especially when constitutional text implicates political processes, folk wisdom on public meaning risks superseding even generally accepted academic understandings. The problem is exacerbated by the simple yet troubling fact that there is virtually always an academic willing to embrace a contrarian or populist view.[5]

The greater interpretive challenge involves the more general term, "other high Crimes and Misdemeanors," a phrase unique in American jurisprudence, notwithstanding its historical origins in early English law.[6] Despite a general consensus among academics that the phrasing is intended to capture the broad concern of a president engaged in conduct for personal advantage and against the oath of office, the term has become a political football with the rules of engagement varying depending upon the side of the aisle at which it is thrown.

Treason and bribery provide essential context for understanding this broader term. Within criminal law, bribery isn't obviously or necessarily the most serious offense. In ranking crimes by severity, many would place murder, arson, or rape ahead of it. Specifying a lesser crime, although a serious one, might seem anomalous, that is until the justification is interrogated.

Bribery prevents the public from relying upon the veracity of stated justifications for official conduct. Bribery obfuscates truer motivations as the official on the take explains policies or other decisions on disingenuous grounds. Ironically, the inclusion of bribery, a specific crime, supports the intuition that impeachment isn't about criminality. If it were, the Framers would also have included more serious criminal offenses rather than specifying a lesser offense and leaving an otherwise open-ended term. Instead, they specified bribery to signal their overriding concern that people holding the public trust must be accountable for official conduct.

Treason involves criminal conduct in the form of waging war against the United States or aiding enemies of the United States by giving them comfort or support.[7] We obviously don't want anyone engaged in treasonous acts serving as president, and should that occur, we want that person expeditiously removed from office. "Other high Crimes and Misdemeanors" isn't defined, but in the context of the clause in which it appears, it conveys an intent to have Congress, in its considered judgment, impeach and convict a president engaged in sufficiently egregious behaviors as to no longer be entrusted with the vital responsibilities of that high office.

The impeachment clause demonstrates the difficulty in providing specific terms that must be met as a precondition of conviction and removal. The more precise the proffered terms, the greater the risk that they will run up against a narrow and legalistic defense by the president's most ardent supporters.

The Third Electoral Reform Amendment avoids this risk. It empowers the House of Representatives, for the first time, to unilaterally remove a president based on maladministration. The amendment specifies that maladministration does not imply criminality, although it may include it. It also states that not all criminality warrants removal for maladministration. Maladministration and criminality are orthogonal. Providing a defined list of behaviors constituting maladministration, rather than providing illustrations and leaving the House to interpret the clause, would disregard the importance of humility in constitutional drafting.

The amendment also states that nothing in it changes or affects the meaning of the presidential impeachment clauses or the Twenty-Fifth Amendment. A no confidence motion, whether or not successful, has no bearing on impeachment or possible criminal charges during or after a presidential administration. Introducing a means of removal with a lower bar than impeachment is not intended to raise the impeachment bar. Nor is it intended to eliminate reliance on impeachment when appropriate, especially since impeachment and conviction, unlike no confidence, let the Senate further vote "disqualification to hold and enjoy any Office of honor."[8]

MALADMINISTRATION

While the Third Electoral Reform Amendment illustrates rather than defines maladministration, it also gives the term constitutional status. No confidence based on maladministration provides a viable means of removing a problematic president without having to meet the more stringent proof associated with impeachment or having to implement the difficult processes associated with the Twenty-Fifth Amendment, which include involvement of the president's own subordinates.

No confidence creates its own risk of seeking to dispense with a president based on disagreement by House leadership with either domestic or international policy goals. The amendment takes steps to avoid this result. A pattern of problematic policy objectives supporting an inference that the president is pursuing private rather than national interests is evidence of maladministration. But maladministration demands more than good faith disagreement on policy. The illustrations provided correlate to broader patterns demonstrating the president's inability or unwillingness to effectuate the responsibilities of office in a manner that serves the nation consistent with her or his constitutional authority.

The illustrations fall into four general categories: (1) gross mismanagement of federal resources, (2) a demonstrated inability to work with high-ranking officials, (3) a pattern of embarrassment on the world stage, and (4) a pattern of conveying misinformation to the public or to officials. In addition, a final listing clarifies that these categories are not exhaustive. In general, a single instance of problematic conduct is less likely to demonstrate maladministration than a pattern of misbehavior within or across categories. The illustrations convey that maladministration need not implicate criminality and that not all criminality implicates maladministration. Instead, the focus is on behavior sufficiently contrary to the national interest or incompatible with constitutional obligation as to justify removal from office.

Although mismanagement of resources might not implicate bribery, it may reveal a pattern of conduct consistent with the president using power for personal gain rather than in the interest of the nation or in furtherance of the policy objectives of her or his governing coalition. An inability to work effectively with cabinet members or other high-ranking officials, state or federal, might imply either an unwillingness to work toward the policy agenda defining the governing coalition's core or a general inability or unwillingness to master the requisite information needed to properly pursue such objectives or protect the national interest. There can be no objective measure by which to gauge presidential competence, but a demonstrated lack of commitment to working toward mastering information central to an effective presidency is a legitimate ground for voting no confidence.

A COMMENT ON THE TWENTY-FIFTH AMENDMENT

Failing to work effectively with cabinet members bears some relation to the Twenty-Fifth Amendment. That amendment accomplishes several objectives, including resolving the circumstance that led former President John Quincy Adams to call John Tyler, following the death of William Henry Harrison, "his Accidency."[9] The Twenty-Fifth Amendment clarifies that upon the president's death, the vice president becomes president, not merely acting president. It also lets a president have the vice president temporarily serve as president, as occurred, for example, with Vice President Dan Quayle when George H. W. Bush underwent a medical procedure.[10]

More notably, the Twenty-Fifth Amendment lets the vice president and a majority of cabinet officials notify the president pro tempore of the Senate and Speaker of the House of a president's incapacity to serve, and if a simple majority of both Houses agree, the vice president then assumes the duties of president. This sets in motion a convoluted process that lets the president refute the allegations, leaving Congress to resolve the dispute.

Following the House investigation into the January 6, 2021, insurrection, there was evidence of conversations about invoking the Twenty-Fifth Amendment against Donald Trump, which ultimately didn't occur.[11] More generally, like the presidential impeachment clause, the Twenty-Fifth Amendment has proven ineffective in empowering other actors to remove a sitting president.

Although it doesn't affect the Twenty-Fifth Amendment, the Third Electoral Reform Amendment creates a more direct means of removing a president struggling to work effectively with his own appointed cabinet officials. Rather than relying upon the vice president and cabinet members to initiate removal, this amendment lets the House investigate, including calling upon cabinet members to testify, and then determine if the evidence supports maladministration.

EMBARRASSMENT AND MISINFORMATION

The third illustration is a pattern of embarrassment on behalf of the nation in conducting international affairs. It's not uncommon for presidents to stumble occasionally on the world stage. Isolated missteps don't provide the basis for removal based on maladministration. Rather, a pattern of embarrassment might include failing to work in coordination with recognized allies and elevating the interests of leaders who are generally hostile to the United States. Such behaviors raise questions as to whether the observed conduct is intended to benefit the national interest or instead serves the personal interests of the president. As with the prior illustrations, this one seeks to ensure confidence in the president's capacity to serve as an effective and respected leader both domestically and internationally.

The final illustration involves a documented pattern of conveying misinformation to the public or in official communications. Here it's especially important to distinguish presidential mis-

steps that are commonplace from more serious conduct potentially warranting removal from office. Presidents often make public
statements that political opponents consider tendentious, casting
a favorable spin on a policy or personal conduct that might not
withstand close scrutiny or the test of time.

EXAMPLES: CLINTON, BUSH II, OBAMA, AND TRUMP

Comparing notable examples of presidential misrepresentations
helps to illustrate the point. Consider President Barack Obama's
claim that under the Affordable Care Act, "if you like your doctor, you can keep your doctor," or the later variation changing
"doctor" to "health care plan." Despite his eventual apology and
claim that he mistakenly believed a grandfather clause would suffice to support the claim, PolitiFact declared Obama's misrepre-
sentation its 2013 lie of the year.[12]

Consider also President George W. Bush's May 2003 representations during what proved to be an early stage of the Iraq War,
with the deaths of thousands of US troops to follow. Bush arrived
by jet to a US aircraft carrier that displayed a larger banner boast-
ing "Mission Accomplished."[13] Bush also justified the Iraq invasion
on the ground that Saddam Hussein had stockpiles of weapons
of mass destruction, biological and chemical, claims never cor-
roborated by investigation despite the fact that in the prior six
months, Hussein had gassed Iraqi Kurds. On one account, Hussein himself boasted about the stockpiles as a defensive measure
to ward off aggression by neighboring Iran, leading to a US intelligence failure.[14] Although there's little doubt Bush emphasized
favorable data, downplaying the rest, what's less clear is whether
Bush genuinely believed the overall weight of the evidence supported his claims. More difficult still was Bush's attempt to link
Saddam Hussein to the terrorist group Al-Qaeda, and thus the
deadly 9/11 attacks on US soil.[15]

Compare these claims with President Bill Clinton's public
statement concerning White House intern Monica Lewinsky
when he said, "I did not have sexual relations with that woman."

A later investigation revealed that Lewinsky had performed oral sex but that the two had not engaged in sexual intercourse. Clinton clearly intended to mislead, and for a time, he did. The president was later impeached, in part, for a related statement to cabinet officials: "There's nothing going on between us."[16] He defended the statement before a grand jury, famously asserting it "depends on what the meaning of 'is' is."[17] Of course, Clinton's audience was focused on whether Clinton, while serving as president, had ever engaged in a sexual relationship with a White House intern. And clearly he had.

Some Clinton supporters defended him by claiming that he was wrongly impeached for having engaged in a sexual act or that by comparison, "Bush lied, People died."[18] This too is disingenuous, especially when considering the hard left's embrace of allegations in the infamous Steele dossier, a product of former British spy Christopher Steele claiming that Russia held tapes of Russian prostitutes engaging Donald Trump in golden showers, the so-called "pee tapes." The concern in such matters, as the right claimed respecting Clinton and the left claimed respecting Trump, isn't the alleged sexual impropriety. Instead, it's the vulnerability to which the cover-up exposes high-level officials, especially the president. And everyone, regardless of which side of the aisle they occupy, knows this.

My point isn't to litigate specific misinformation conveyed by Clinton, Bush, and Obama. Nor is it to compare them to the amply documented history of Trump's persistent pattern of public misstatements, which the *Washington Post* tabulated in excess of 30,000 in four years as president, averaging twenty per day.[19] I will, however, offer a few observations.

First, it's mistaken to imagine a correlation between political ideology and truthfulness. The benign end of politics is service, but the means of accomplishing it is by gaining power. For those who seek it, power can be the ultimate aphrodisiac. And it's no secret that men especially have been known to lie for power and sex.

Second, determining whether public or official misinformation rises to a level that justifies removing a president from office based on maladministration is ultimately a political rather than legal determination. Those evaluating claimed misstatements must assess their substantive importance, frequency, and context, and there is no formula by which to weigh these mixed considerations.

As a general matter, I'm personally more inclined to cut some slack to a president who puts spin on a preferred policy, especially when it is apt to get considerable scrutiny by news media and the public. The greater concern arises from lies involving unverifiable claims where few have access to potential disconfirming evidence.

Although at points I've expressed considerable disagreement with the Framers, it's worth mentioning an important consideration they got right. In a democracy, it's vital to have mechanisms that hold leaders in our highest offices to account. That's why, of all possible criminal offenses, the Framers singled out bribery. It's also why the Third Electoral Reform Amendment disallows no confidence motions to be advanced or voted in secret. The Framers erred in how they imagined some mechanisms they created would improve accountability, but that criticism focuses on means, not ends.

Finally, it's important to bear in mind that, as with any institutional reform, presidential behavior will be affected by the very changes the Electoral Reform Amendments introduce. In a coalition government subject to a no confidence vote, the president will be more strongly motivated to embrace inclusive views, not only those narrowly tied to the base of one party. Success in a coalition regime helps break down the binary of us versus them, and it avoids casting all disputes as left or right. That's all for the good. After all, the goal is not to remove presidents; it is to hold them accountable. If the threat of removal encourages greater accountability—requiring at most its rare invocation—that implies the scheme is working effectively.

VOTING AND REMOVAL THRESHOLDS

The essential players in building a coalition are party leaders, who will exert greater discipline over rank-and-file party members than in our two-party system. The Third Electoral Reform Amendment specifies that no confidence motions are votes of conscience, not party-line votes. The Second Electoral Reform Amendment recognizes that parties, as nongovernmental bodies, have association rights and their own internal rules of discipline.[20] By making no confidence voting a matter of conscience, this amendment carves out a narrow but important exception. No confidence motions may not be sponsored or voted in secret; the electorate is entitled to full knowledge of the voting record on no confidence by all House members, whether elected by a district or party-list ballot.

The amendment specifies thresholds for moving and voting a no confidence motion. The thresholds strike a balance, discouraging such motions from being leveled frivolously and encouraging those advancing them to seek broad support.

Any such motion, meritorious or not, will impose considerable burdens on the president given the near limitless competing responsibilities of that office. In the Supreme Court decision *Clinton v. Jones*, Justice John Paul Stevens notably miscalculated.[21] The case let former Arkansas state employee, Paula Corbin Jones, sue then-President Clinton for sexual harassment based on alleged "abhorrent sexual advances," rather than suspending the suit for the duration of Clinton's presidency. In allowing the suit to proceed, Stevens asserted that any burdens this or some other suit, even a frivolous one, imposed ought not to put an excessive demand on the president's time. The Jones suit ultimately led to independent counsel Ken Starr's discovery of the Monica Lewinsky affair, and Clinton's attempted denial then led to the impeachment proceeding.

My point certainly isn't to defend Clinton's misbehavior. Nor is it to assess whether his lies about his relationship with Lewinsky justified impeachment or would have justified a vote of no confidence. Rather it is to take seriously the concerns of time burdens of any investigation implicating a sitting president.

This problem can be likened to a classic example of type one versus type two error, or false positives versus false negatives. Setting the bar for raising a claim too low risks inviting too many claims, thereby unduly interfering with the president's obligations (false positives). Conversely, setting the bar too high risks too many instances of problematic presidential conduct going uninvestigated and undeterred (false negatives). A pervasive issue in constitutional design, and regulatory design more broadly, is recognizing the inevitability of this trade-off. There's no way to avoid it, so the best we can do is devise a balanced solution that reasonably accounts for the risks associated with each error type. The Third Electoral Reform Amendment strikes an appropriate balance.

The Third Electoral Reform Amendment offers two methods of bringing a no confidence motion. The first approach requires support by the leaders of two qualifying parties, at least one of which joined the original governing coalition appointing the president. Both leaders could be part of that original governing coalition, or one could be in, and the other outside, the original coalition. The second approach is by petition of at least 15 percent of rank-and-file House members, at least one-third of whom were part of the original coalition. Requiring support by leaders of two parties, one in the original governing coalition, or of a substantial minority of rank-and-file members in that coalition, provides credible evidence of plausible merit to the no confidence motion.

The amendment doesn't fix the percentage of rank-and-file members that leaders of qualifying parties must represent. Instead, it relies upon either the default 5 percent threshold or the threshold revised by the Senate, which might be lowered, or might be raised, provided doing so doesn't exceed 10 percent or reduce the number of qualifying parties below eight. With the higher 10 percent threshold, two parties would carry, at least presumptively, no less than 20 percent of the rank and file; with the lower threshold, that percentage would correspondingly decrease. The representation is presumptive because the ultimate vote is one of conscience.

The Third Electoral Reform Amendment rests on the intuition that in Parliamentary America, the Senate will emerge a genuine partner to the now proportional House. That means the Senate won't be motivated to produce hyper-fractional parties in the House, as opposed to a number within the optimal range between five and eight. The lower the number of parties, the higher the percentage of the membership two qualifying leaders presumptively represent. The threshold rule generally discourages frivolous motions. Allowing just one party to move for no confidence risks having a party outside the governing coalition use the process for partisan gain rather than to safeguard against a problematic president.

The flip side of setting the bar too low, risking frivolous motions, is setting it too high, risking unraised meritorious motions. The harder question is whether a two-party motion arising entirely from outside the original governing coalition should suffice. Here we must consider the two separate Congresses coinciding with a single four-year presidential term. In the first two years, except in the unlikely event of a minority-led government following five failed coalition attempts, the governing coalition will constitute a majority. In the second two years, it's possible that the respective size of the governing coalition and opposition might shift, making the coalition that put the president in power a minority and elevating the opposition leader to Speaker of the House. Requiring support of at least one party that formed part of the president's original coalition government reduces the likelihood of a no confidence motion motivated strictly by partisan gain. Instead, such a motion is intended to remove a problematic president engaged in maladministration, not to change the party in power following a midterm election.

Although this means the president might serve with minority House support, that's also true now. But unlike in our two-party presidential system, the greater fluidity of a multiparty House will allow restructuring the governing coalition following a midterm election. Forming part of the governing coalition might be a helpful strategy in planning for an upcoming quadrennial presidential election by demonstrating a capacity to deliver something of value to party constituents. Courting other party leaders will also prove an effective strategy for a president seeking reelection or in positioning a chosen successor for the presidency.

If the governing coalition becomes a minority following a midterm election, disallowing two opposition parties to move for no confidence avoids yet another risk. It makes it less likely that the new majority coalition will advance two successive motions, the first unseating the president and the second unseating the newly elevated former vice president. Such a scheme would let the new coalition then install its leader, serving as Speaker of the House, to the Oval Office based on the Presidential Succession Act.[22]

There's another possible defense against this strategy. Under the Twenty-Fifth Amendment, an elevated vice president serving as president may nominate a vice presidential successor, although doing so requires the approval of both houses of Congress. It's impossible to know how such a scenario might play out, but the threshold rules of the Third Electoral Reform Amendment inhibit such gaming. The requirement that one party leader hail from the original governing coalition promotes stability while allowing a meaningful mechanism—lower than the impeachment bar—for removing a problematic president.

The final threshold rule involves removal itself. The 60 percent removal threshold, four times the rank-and-file threshold for a motion not sponsored by party leaders, is steep enough to prevent the out-coalition from removing a president with just a few defectors from the original governing coalition. On the other hand, 60 percent is less steep than two-thirds, the nearly impossible-to-reach threshold for Senate removal following impeachment. And the entire process takes place within the single House chamber. This departure from the more general majoritarian removal threshold in parliamentary systems emphasizes the uniquely American attributes of these amendments.

If we assume a minimal governing coalition, at 51 percent, the 60 percent threshold for removal requires that just over one-fifth, 20 percent of the coalition, join with the opposition for the motion to succeed. This significant level of support from within the original governing coalition is sufficient to inhibit attempts to pluck just a handful of members with promises of greater perks, thereby inhibiting non-meritorious motions from passing. The scheme appropriately balances concerns of presidential stability and accountability.

SUCCESSION

The final feature of the Third Electoral Reform Amendment involves succession rules. The amendment takes a minimalist approach, leaving the existing rules in place, dictated by the Twenty-Fifth Amendment for the vice president and the Presidential Succession Act for the remaining line of succession, subject to change in the usual course.

This feature produces a distinctly American parliamentary system. The scheme embraces a different approach to succession than is observed more generally in parliamentary regimes, including some we have seen in the world tour. As one example, Germany requires that the Bundestag first settle upon a successor to the chancellor as a precondition to a no confidence vote.[23] This ensures stability, but the bar is extremely high.

Israel takes an opposite approach that's generally more consistent with pure parliamentary governance.[24] A vote of no confidence removes the prime minister with no assurance as to a successor. Instead, a new coalition must form to appoint one, and if that fails, the president may call a new election of the Knesset with the hope that a subsequent coalition will form. This hasn't always succeeded, sometimes producing multiple successive elections until a governing coalition forms.[25]

Parliamentary systems more generally closely align the head of government with the legislature. But absent a clear line of succession, instability in the governing coalition also risks producing instability for the head of government. By contrast, this amendment balances flexibility with stability. And because the line of succession, other than the vice president, is statutory, Congress may change succession rules based on experience.

This completes the survey of the three Electoral Reform Amendments. Together these amendments infuse essential parliamentary features into the US constitutional system, and they do so in a manner that remains uniquely American. For the final part of our journey, part IV, we'll consider the politics of passing these amendments, making them part of our constitutional design, and compare them with alternatives. We'll then consider the optimistic vision that Parliamentary America promises for us and for future generations.

The Politics of Ratification and Envisioning Parliamentary America

CHAPTER 10

Achieving Coalition Governance

THE POLITICS OF PASSING THESE AMENDMENTS

We've now surveyed the history of the third constitutional crisis, the foundations of the third-party dilemma, and three Electoral Reform Amendments that promise to radically repair our broken democracy. Even now you might remain skeptical about the plausibility of the amendments being adopted. The amendments will not only fix the crisis we are in—they also can pass.

This chapter presents two central arguments supporting this claim. First, the amendments significantly enhance the prestige and power of vital institutions. The amendments create novel pathways to power, both at the federal level and for state and local officials. Second, the amendments are far more attractive than alternative proposals. They avert the considerable political risks to key institutional actors that other commonly discussed, yet less effective, reforms pose.

Although arguments concerning political attractiveness versus merit are distinct, both matter when assessing proposed reforms. The first two constitutional crises, and other crises that democracies around the world have faced, demonstrate that such challenges don't arise in a singular moment or in a necessarily dramatic fashion. Crises can fester for years, even decades, along with the processes of ending them. What's essential is ensuring that those called upon to make decisions—political leaders and our electorate—are well informed before charting a course based upon the menu of available options.

Before explaining why the proposed amendments are both viable and superior to alternatives, it's appropriate to offer a personal reflection. I'm an unlikely advocate for the radical reforms proposed in this book. I've devoted over thirty years to studying and teaching constitutional law. I spent the first part of my academic career, now less than half, at the conservative/libertarian George Mason University School of Law, later aptly named for the iconic conservative Justice Antonin Scalia. And I've now spent the longer part of my career at the progressive/liberal University of Maryland Francis King Carey School of Law, proudly associated with the revered liberal Justice Thurgood Marshall, for whom its library is named, even as Marshall himself was disallowed to enroll at Maryland due to racial segregation.[1] I've always been a center-left Democrat, often finding myself to the left of colleagues at George Mason and to the right of those at Maryland.

For the most part my scholarship, integrating tools of economic analysis with constitutional law, has been what legal scholars describe as "positive." That means helping to explain the world as it is, as opposed to "normative," which means explaining how one thinks the world should be. Over the years, I've been asked if my focus was intended to avoid conflicts with more ideological colleagues—right then left—especially as I thankfully progressed through the various academic benchmarks typically used to assess an academic career. It wasn't. I've always been fascinated by institutions, viewing their most anomalous features as puzzles to be solved, not problems to be fixed. At least initially.

And yet here I am, over three decades later, claiming that the Framers fundamentally misconceived how our electoral system and system of executive accountability would affect our politics and culture, and advocating my own admittedly radical set of reforms. I didn't arrive here easily. I did so because over these many years, I've developed an expertise and perspective rare among reform advocates. Our democracy is in crisis, and I agree on the need for reform. I disagree that most reforms gaining attention will extricate us from the crisis we're in or that they can be adopted. We can and must do better.

Like each chapter in part III, this one rests on a counter intuition: The most promising means of getting past our constitutional crisis is to avoid reforms whose primary benefit is their widespread appeal. The features of the Electoral Reform Amendments that might seem most troublesome—leaving the Senate intact, leaving House members incumbents, and not limiting congressional terms—make them politically viable. In considering how to repair our democracy, appealing to key political actors is at least as important as appealing to the electorate even though the electorate, not political actors, are the ultimate beneficiaries of reform. The greatest challenge of reform is that to be effective, its solutions, especially when compared with alternatives, must appeal to the very institutions—both Houses of Congress and to the political parties themselves—it seeks to rectify.

Although intended fundamentally to change a vital national conversation, this book isn't a mere thought experiment. It contains serious and practical proposals for reforming our constitutional democracy that leverage concerns of powerful political actors and vital institutions in a manner that benefits the citizenry. The amendments I propose create a robust pathway to Parliamentary America. They will let our children and grandchildren work toward further reforms guided by their inevitably wiser lights. This isn't pie in the sky. It's deeply personal and existential. My goal is for the United States to emerge from this crisis a beacon to other nations and finally, after a quarter of a millennium, a genuine, thriving democracy.

The Amending Bar

In Article V, the Constitution sets out two ways to amend. By a two-thirds vote in each House, Congress may propose amendments, or two-thirds of the states may call a convention to propose amendments. In either case, at Congress's election, amendments are ratified when approved by three-quarters of state legislatures or state ratifying conventions. The bar is extraordinarily high.

The Constitution has been amended only twenty-seven times. If we exclude the first ten—the Bill of Rights—and the Twenty-Seventh Amendment, which took over two hundred years to ratify, that leaves sixteen. That averages one amendment every fourteen years.

Enacting federal legislation is more like running hurdles than a marathon or a sprint. To add another sports metaphor, it's easier to block than pass. That's even truer of amending. In amending, there are many points at which supporters can be tripped up or blocked. That might suggest the proposed amendments are futile. They're not. But it means proposals that fail to consider the blocking power of those who benefit from the current system cannot succeed.

Let's start with the affirmative case.

The Affirmative Case for the Electoral Reform Amendments: More Pathways to Influence and Power

To many pundits, our political polarization seems insurmountable. Our system has let the GOP seize disproportionate power relative to its demographics. Rural midwestern and southern states, the Republican base, hold outsized power in the Senate and the Electoral College. Liberal California, with nearly forty million people, has the same number of senators as conservative Wyoming, with under 600,000 people, an astonishing ratio of sixty-seven voters to one. The smallest twenty-one states together have forty-two of one hundred senators, yet their combined populations equal that of California. The power imbalance has repeatedly let the GOP control the White House and Senate despite its shrinking base. Why would Republicans consent to constitutional reforms that dilute this advantage?

Constitutional reform demands careful attention to how groups make decisions and how individuals respond to incentives. Consider the incentives that will incline leaders of both major parties, and other political actors, to support these Electoral Reform Amendments:

- House party leaders will gain the tremendous power to choose and remove the president through coalition building and a no confidence vote. House leaders in both parties thrive on power, and these amendments give them considerably more.
- Senators will gain prestige as members of an even more exclusive club as compared with the enlarged House—100 versus 870—retaining special powers, including advice and consent over cabinet appointees, judicial nominees, and treaties. And they will gain the important new power to set qualifying party thresholds for the House.
- Politicians committed to narrow constituencies or policy positions will be better able to focus their advocacy. Less prominent members of Congress will gain the opportunity to lead smaller parties focused on ideological positions embraced not only within a geographical district, but also appealing to like-minded voters statewide. Supporters of gun rights, religious freedom, or the right to life, on the right, and of racial justice, climate action, gun control, gender equality, or reproductive rights, on the left, will gain greater influence and access to power, donations, and media.
- Today's rank-and-file House members have only two parties through which to gain access to power. With more

parties, they gain more channels. They will no longer be compelled to cater to leaders holding strongly divergent, sometimes deeply troubling, policy views or commitments on ideology and culture.

- State legislative leaders will play an instrumental role in devising lists for party-based House elections, and many will become list candidates themselves. Mixed-member proportionality (MMP) provides a highly desirable fast track from the statehouse to Capitol Hill, with many state office holders then finding their way into the national spotlight.

- Politicians who lead third, fourth, or more parties, will play a fundamental role in forming the government and working policy toward their preferred location within a richer space that captures both the economics/policy and culture/identity axes of our politics. They and their constituents will no longer be locked into a simplistic right-left divide.

- The party-list track doesn't require grueling biannual campaigns focused intensely on fundraising. Instead, it embraces politicians with varied skills, including collaborating, problem-solving, and forging coalitions, and for whom compromise isn't a dirty word.

At all levels of government, these amendments empower aspiring leaders who regard the unerring insistence upon the strident demands of an ideological base as a threat to our democracy. Together, the amendments provide an inspiring path forward, with more parties and more choices.

In addition to appealing to politicians, the proposed amendments will bring new optimism to voters. Across the spectrum, citizens are frustrated by Washington's endless, worsening gridlock and the systemic difficulties in tackling the nation's dire challenges. These amendments offer voters more meaningful options and a way out of endless hyper-partisanship.

The Defensive Case for the Amendments: Preserving Power and Prestige

The Electoral Reform Amendments are a compelling defensive measure against reform proposals that, although gaining broad public attention, threaten the power and prestige of those whose support is needed to approve them, and that will not produce a robust multiparty democracy. Such alternatives include reapportioning the Senate; redistricting and enlarging the House with multimember districts; employing ranked-choice voting; limiting House and Senate terms; and replacing the Electoral College with the national popular vote (including by interstate pact). The Electoral Reform Amendments by no means exhaust the possibilities for worthwhile reform. But unlike these and other proposals, the Electoral Reform Amendments will solve the constitutional crisis we face and create a robust democracy that opens pathways to further reforms.

The goal of reform shouldn't be a long list of ideas that makes everyone happy. Instead, it is to identify and resolve the underlying problem from which others derive. Although the three Electoral Reform Amendments are radical, they're also narrowly targeted. They focus on what's required to solve the pending crisis and leave tackling other problems to the future, including problems we might wrongly anticipate or fail to foresee. The first two constitutional crises counsel against hubris. Both revealed that we are better at resolving a clearly identified problem than at anticipating future challenges that might arise.

The defensive case for supporting these Electoral Reform Amendments begins with the possibility of a national constitutional convention. Tracking the precise number of states calling for a convention is challenging. Some states have rescinded earlier calls, and several have coupled calls with limited mandates, making it difficult to determine when calls can be properly combined. As of this writing, approximately twenty states of the required thirty-four have pending resolutions of some sort.[2] In two earlier periods the calls came extremely close to passing the threshold. In the late 1980s, we missed it by only two states, and in the 1960s, we missed it by just one.[3] Although these calls generally involved specified mandates, such as calls for a balanced budget amendment, it's impossible to know whether such limitations would stick.

The only example we have of a convention was when, governed by the Articles of Confederation, the Framers ditched their mandate and started from scratch. In an important respect, the Framers were right. Rejecting the Articles let the Framers change the premise concerning the ultimate source of federal sovereign authority from the states to "We the People." Even so, that historical event offers little guidance as to what might happen in a convention pursuant to the Constitution itself.

In evaluating the Electoral Reform Amendments, it's helpful to consider two perspectives on a convention.

The first perspective focuses on the threat a convention poses for key institutional actors: elected members of the House and Senate. As the threat of a convention looms larger, the Electoral Reform Amendments can serve as a pressure release valve, offering an increasingly attractive alternative to those in office. Although the amendments will end the benefits to small states of disproportionate voting weight in the Electoral College, those states retain outsized power in the Senate, something a convention might take away. As the need for reform becomes imminent, this trade-off becomes all the more compelling. Beyond early primaries or caucuses, presidential candidates rarely focus campaigns on small states, which virtually never control outcomes.

The second considers the public, which will become increasingly focused on reform as calls for a convention approach thirty-four states or when Congress entertains such reform proposals on its own. Public pressures will focus on two conditions: first, the likelihood of proposals being enacted, and, second, assurances that whichever proposals are advanced are able to end our constitutional crisis. These combined pressures strongly favor the Electoral Reform Amendments. As defensive measures, the amendments can gain the support of both houses of Congress. And in combination, they provide a genuine solution.

To see why, let's compare the menu of alternatives.

The Reform Menu

REAPPORTIONING THE SENATE

The Senate is among the most antidemocratic elective bodies in the world.[4] No credible democratic theory can justify the twenty-one smallest states, whose combined population equals California's, holding 42 percent representation in the Senate, while California holds 2 percent, or California, with near forty million people, and Wyoming, with 600,000, a ratio of sixty-seven to one, having the same size delegation. The historical defense is wanting: States were once independent sovereigns that ceded attributes of sovereignty in exchange for accepting the Constitution. Equal apportionment in the Senate was essential to that compromise.[5]

There are several responses.

First, the unequal voting power of citizens is contrary to a long line of Supreme Court equal protection cases that insist upon avoiding even the smallest representational disparities in virtually all other contexts: state legislatures, including upper chambers; the US House of Representatives; and local governmental bodies.[6] The Senate entirely thwarts these values, which are otherwise infused throughout our system.

Second, the state sovereignty compromise has long had problematic racial implications. Although historically such states as Rhode Island and Delaware favored equal Senate apportionment as a counterweight to large Southern states that had negotiated the three-fifths clause, over time, as population trends favored the North, the resulting power imbalance let the Senate obstruct efforts to work toward overcoming our tragic racial history. Recall, for example, Senator Strom Thurmond's filibuster to thwart civil rights legislation.[7]

Third, the notion that historical conceptions of state sovereignty justify Senate apportionment is itself dubious. Although the original states were nominally sovereign, the Supreme Court has recognized the limited nature of that sovereignty. The Court has clarified that the states were never sovereign in the international sphere. International sovereignty passed directly from the Crown to the United States in its corporate capacity.[8] And this occurred when the United States became independent, not when it ditched the Articles of Confederation for the Constitution. With respect to domestic powers, the Court has emphasized that states couldn't reserve powers they never held, including those that came into being with the Constitution itself.[9]

Given these limitations, it's important to ask what sovereignty in this context actually means. States hold power to enact legal policies within their domain, which are referred to as police powers. Unlike the federal government, state powers are presumed, meaning they needn't rest on delegated authority from an external source such as the Constitution. But that doesn't mean that each state, as a matter of sovereign right and without regard to population, holds an inherent moral claim, in perpetuity, to egregiously disproportionate Senate representation.

Although thirteen states were party to the original pact, the remaining thirty-seven were not. Another thirteen states are so small that despite each having two senators, they have only one or two members in the House of Representatives. Here are the states with one House member from smallest to largest: Wyoming, Vermont, Alaska, South Dakota, North Dakota, and Delaware. And now the two-member states: Montana, Rhode Island, New Hampshire, Maine, Hawaii, West Virginia, and Idaho. Of this combined group, only three states, Delaware, Rhode Island, and New Hampshire, were part of the original pact. Equal Senate apportionment, favoring other regions of the country, hardly serves the interest of these three blue states.

Yes, there's textual support for equal state suffrage in the Senate. But that's all there is.

The textual limit on Senate apportionment appears in the Constitution's amending clause: "no state, without its consent, shall be deprived of its equal suffrage in the Senate."[10] This might be read to require unanimous consent among states to reapportion the Senate. A better reading is that the Constitution imposes a double barrier to Senate reapportionment, demanding two amendments. First, we'd have to amend the amending clause to allow an amendment reapportioning the Senate. Then we'd amend to reapportion. Despite the moral case for doing so, this is obviously more easily said than done. Small red and purple states especially will inevitably resist ceding power.[11] And although the present apportionment scheme is unjust, it's not irrational for states to protect whatever power they hold.

Despite the political impracticality of Senate reapportionment, it's important that citizens appreciate the moral case for doing so. For one thing, broadening public support for remedying this egregious imbalance puts pressure on other reforms, especially those proposed here. But even if Senate reapportionment were plausible, doing so will not extricate us from the current crisis. A fairly apportioned Senate won't end the two-party system or hyper-partisanship. That's why despite supporting Senate reapportionment, I haven't included it as part of the Electoral Reform Amendments. Along with other worthwhile reforms, a precondition to Senate reapportionment is a genuine, robust democracy, which the proposed amendments will produce.

With those amendments in place, the Senate will, in time, emerge as a multiparty chamber. Each Senate contest will continue to be dominated by two parties, but in the multiparty democracy these amendments will create, the dominant parties won't be the same throughout the country. A multiparty Senate will incline toward coalition politics, which will become essential to enacting legislation and to performing other institutional functions. One possibility is that the Senate will itself ameliorate some of its antidemocratic features, such as the filibuster, and that a growing coalition of senators will come to appreciate the call for modest reapportionment, even if the end result isn't strictly population-based. But for now, it's best to turn to other proposed reforms.

RETHINKING THE HOUSE

Reform advocates have proposed three sets of proposals for the House—enlargement, multimember districts, and term limits—with term limits also proposed for the Senate. The proposals gaining the most attention don't change how the president and vice president are elected, meaning they retain presidentialism. This is a vital feature to bear in mind when evaluating these proposals. Let's take each proposal in turn.

ENLARGING THE HOUSE: THE CUBE ROOT RULE

Proposals to enlarge the House of Representatives begin with a famous 1972 study by Estonian physicist and political scientist Rein Taagepera.[12] Taagepera observed that looking across democratic nations, lower legislative chambers demonstrated a notable mathematical correlation. Graphing a nation's population on one axis and the number of legislators on the other revealed a relationship now called the cube root rule.[13] Simply put, if you begin with the numerical size of the lower chamber and multiply it by itself, and then multiply the product once more by the same figure, the grand total roughly corresponds to the population.

In 2020, a group of political scientists in the United States produced a study in which they argued for reforming the House of Representatives based upon the cube root rule and considered several proposals to bring the larger 700-member House to fruition.[14] Seven hundred cubed is 343 million, which is close to the 2022 population of 332 million, although the study figures were based on 2015. The authors considered bringing this about incrementally or in a single shot, ultimately settling upon a system they call primary allocation. This entails a two-step voting process, with an initial statewide vote by party and a second vote, based

ACHIEVING COALITION GOVERNANCE   251

on proportional results, that allocates to each party the number of state "districts" corresponding to its seat allocation.

The same study explained the cube root correlation in a manner that bears notable parallels to the calculus of consent.[15] Recall that Buchanan and Tullock posited that legislative bodies should minimize the sum of decision costs, which increase with the number of lawmakers, and external costs, which decrease with the number of lawmakers. Supporters of the cube root rule advance two parallel considerations. First, as the legislative body grows, each member represents a relatively smaller constituency, thereby improving constituent communications and service. More closely tying legislators to their constituents reduces external costs. Conversely, as the legislative body grows, legislative deliberations become more difficult, raising decision costs.

The cube root rule suffers the same limitations as the calculus of consent. If we set aside India's lower chamber, Lok Sabha, with 543 members representing over 1.4 billion people (2.6 million citizens per representative),[16] the US House of Representatives is a notable outlier as compared with other democracies around the globe. Each member today represents approximately three-quarters of a million people. Even at seven hundred members, each House member would represent 474,000, still an outlier.

The 2020 study, mentioned above, included the United States but not India among thirty-seven nations based on 2015 population data. The study generally included only the membership of the lower legislative body when bicameral, although it combined both chambers of the United States Congress. Excluding the Senate makes the numbers for the United States more of an outlier. Based on the reported numbers, Congress has one member per 597,998 constituents with the Senate included, and one member per 735,468 constituents counting only the House. Even the lower figure is more than double the next highest of the other countries included: Colombia (290,536), Japan (269,421), then Mexico (251,782).[17] Here's a comparison to our world-tour nations included in the study: France (111,710), Germany (129,695), the United Kingdom (110,611), and Israel (67,208). Raising the House to 700 members would still leave Congress as a significant outlier at one member per 399,911 constituents, with the Senate included, and one member per 457,055 constituents counting only the House. Finally, if we double the House, as proposed in the First Electoral Reform Amendment, the result is closer to others at the high end of the study, at one member per 329,823 constituents with the Senate included, or per 367,734 including just the House.

The cube root rule can't explain how constituent communications and service are sufficiently improved with such a high representational ratio. Although a House with 870 members is at the high end for a single chamber, so too is our population. Concerns about size and meaningful deliberation confront the same limits of the Buchanan and Tullock analysis of decision costs.[18] Identifying key decision-makers and assessing the role of party discipline is more important to decision costs than strictly focusing on legislative size.

RESTORING MULTIMEMBER HOUSE DISTRICTS

Political scientist Lee Drutman seeks to break what he aptly describes as the doom loop of our two-party system. His proposals include expanding the House to 700 members based on the cube root rule; abandoning single-member geographical districts in favor of five-member districts, which can be achieved by statute; and abolishing congressional primaries. In his book, *Breaking the Two-Party Doom Loop*, Drutman advocated giving voters the choice either of ranked-choice voting (RCV) or voting by party, and extending RCV to the Senate and presidency, with the latter still chosen by voters. Drutman has separately suggested a system called open list proportional representation, or OLPR, discussed later in the chapter, might be preferable to RCV.[19] Drutman's combined proposals retain presidentialism but change how elected federal offices are chosen.

Drutman's thoughtful scheme presents several challenges. Here I focus on two: first, generating opposition among political actors whose support is likely necessary to bring it about, and second, failing to solve the constitutional crisis and third-party dilemma.

The political challenge is that the scheme transforms each sitting House member from incumbent in an existing geographical district or state into a functional incumbent in newly drawn, competitive multimember districts. I said competitive, not *more* competitive, because of hyper-partisan gerrymandering. As previously explained (see chapter 3), this process, which the Supreme Court has greenlighted, renders the overwhelming majority of House districts noncompetitive. Or it makes them competitive only in primary contests, thereby sharpening our ideological divides, rendering each state a deeper shade of red or blue.

The one thing Republican and Democratic members of Congress are apt to agree upon is the desire to retain their safe, noncompetitive districts. At the end of the day, we must always remember that whatever benign objectives politicians wish to advance, politics is about power. Some members of the House might fare well in newly drawn districts or in a multimember at-large races, but others won't, and we can count on legislators protecting their turf.

There is yet another concern with these proposals revealed through the lens of history. As we've seen, in the United States, combining multimember districts with at-large voting hasn't produced the benefits advocates envision. Among House districts in the nineteenth century, even following the 1842 Apportionment Act, and in city council voting in southern jurisdictions as late as the 1980s,[20] at-large voting instead entrenched a singular majority rather than inviting greater competition. In our two-party system, at-large voting can allow even a slim majority party to capture all seats, and with racialized politics, the same system can systematically empower whites.

INTEGRATION WITH OTHER PROPOSALS

Some advocates claim that combining multimember districts with other measures, such as RCV, encourages more parties by lowering the threshold for electoral success.[21] While possible, that benign outcome isn't guaranteed. Another possibility is that each state's controlling party will engage in strategies to ensure its full slate of candidates wins all seats in as many multimember districts as possible through bloc voting. Multimember districts might contribute to such strategies by easing the process of hyper-partisan gerrymandering as compared with the more complex mapping of multiple single-member districts. This would entail having closer dominant-party majorities across as many multimember districts as the numbers will allow while packing the opposition into as few multimember districts as possible.[22]

Separately, if the combined scheme does add more parties to the House, it nonetheless fails to tie the success of smaller parties, through the process of parliamentary coalition building, to that of the president, who is elected independently. Alternatively, if we lowered the bar for running for president, as done in the first of two electoral stages in France, while still maintaining separate presidential and congressional elections, the combination risks presidential alignment with a small congressional coalition giving rise to other governance challenges.

Overall, multimember districting schemes risk perpetuating existing governance challenges and adding new ones. These challenges persist in virtually all presidential and semi-presidential systems, or hybrids, precisely because those systems fail to tie the success of legislative parties to that of the government itself.

ENACTMENT CHALLENGES

Beyond these challenges lie the practical ones in getting the previously discussed proposals passed. Repealing single-member districts removes every member of the House from the district that elected her or him. Under that system, representatives must campaign in a new district, in at-large multimember districts, or statewide based on a party list. Some will succeed; others will fail. But for House members, now elected from largely noncompetitive blue or red geographical districts, the overall trade is risky, at their expense, and with no obvious payoff. If the scheme succeeds, a good many sitting House members will be displaced. Indeed, that's the point.

Members of Congress are unlikely to endorse a plan—and are likely to fight one—that's designed to intensify competition for the very seats they hold. By contrast, the Electoral Reform Amendments leave every single member of Congress an incumbent in the district or state in which he or she was elected. Beyond that, the amendments give them significant additional powers. To be sure, with the exception of single district states, MMP adds a new cohort of party-based House members in what we can characterize as statewide multimember districts. But the two-vote MMP process, with the party vote controlling state level proportionality, avoids the sort of at-large gaming that lets a narrow majority block out significant minorities within the state.

LIMITING CONGRESSIONAL TERMS: HOUSE AND SENATE

Constitutional reformers also advocate limiting congressional terms. This reform originated decades ago from within the GOP, forming part of Newt Gingrich's 1994 Contract with America, although his Republican-led House ultimately abandoned it.[23] It might not be surprising that after gaining power, Republican leaders no longer prioritized congressional turnover.

Twenty-three states attempted to impose term limits on their congressional delegations—typically twelve years each in the House and Senate—only to be thwarted in the Supreme Court.[24] The Court held that the Constitution's list of electoral qualifications—age (twenty-five for the House; thirty for the Senate), years of citizenship (seven for the House; nine for the Senate), and in-state residency—were exhaustive. The Latin phrase for the argument is *expressio unius est exclusio alterius*, meaning that the expression of one thing is the exclusion of others. Law professors routinely point out the weakness of this argument and the selectivity with which the Court deploys it.[25] To paraphrase Justice Robert Jackson, the Supreme Court doesn't get the last word because it's right; it's right because it has the last word.[26]

Beyond the constitutional question, it's not at all clear that limiting congressional terms will have the moderating effect its advocates claim. Members of Congress interact with one another again and again without knowing when such repeat interactions are likely to end. Game theorists refer to this dynamic as an iterative game.[27] The problem is that knowing when the game will end changes player incentives. Without future interactions, any benefits of interparty cooperation, or even cooperation among differing factions within a party, decline.[28] Instead, members of Congress are apt to focus intensely on what comes next. Committing firmly to positions that might benefit them as lobbyists or consultants may take priority. Academic studies on the relationship between term limits and party moderation are mixed, but more recent ones, focusing on state-level data, dispel claims that term limits reduce partisanship. Indeed, they tend to demonstrate an opposite effect.[29]

The political lessons on term limits are more important than constitutionality since limiting congressional terms would require amending. Even beyond enhancing the risk of polarization, the history of term limits emphasizes another general lesson of congressional reform. State term limits were invariably enacted with statewide initiatives that bypassed state general assemblies.[30] This isn't surprising. Once again, we can count on legislators protecting their turf.

The Efficacy of Reforms Not Targeting Congress

Members of Congress might more willingly entertain amendments targeting other institutions than their own. Two commonly discussed proposals are replacing the Electoral College with the national popular vote and employing ranked-choice voting (RCV), including a common version known as instant-runoff voting (IRV), for the presidency. As previously noted, RCV could also affect Congress, and even state general assemblies, if filtered more deeply into federal and state elections. That too creates challenges (see chapter 8), but the deeper problem, explained below, is that neither reform will extricate us from the crisis we face.

THE NATIONAL POPULAR VOTE

In addition to the Senate, it's near impossible to defend the Electoral College with a credible democratic theory. Providing a number of Electoral College votes equal to each state's congressional delegation, regardless of population, extends the inequities of Senate apportionment, albeit in less extreme form, given the influence of population-based House delegations. The scheme continues to provide small states with outsized voting power even as it centers the presidential election on the handful of large states whose Electoral College delegations almost always turn outcomes Democratic or Republican under winner-take-all rules.

The most famous, or infamous, illustration is the 2000 election between Al Gore and George W. Bush, a deeply confusing, exceedingly close contest that sent two cases to the Supreme Court.[31] In perhaps the most iconic coverage of that election, with Tom Brokaw and Tim Russert explaining the possibility of an upside-down outcome to viewers, Russert finally held up a small whiteboard, bearing three words in black marker: "Florida Florida Florida." Russert went on to tell Brokaw that if they just stuck with those simple boards instead of "highfalutin computers," it would all be easier to understand.[32]

In the 2000 election, the presidential outcome turned on 537 voters in Florida, despite a majority of voters nationwide coming out the other way. Even so, Russert's whiteboard revealed a curious benefit to the Electoral College. Florida wasn't the only state in which the outcomes were disputed in that election.[33] But it was the only one that mattered.

In criminal law there's a concept called harmless error. Not every mistake that occurs in a trial warrants reversal. Sometimes you'd have gotten the same result even if the mistake hadn't been made. The Electoral College creates a harmless error rule for presidential elections.[34] Not all state outcomes matter in the sense of changing who ultimately wins even if the mistakes are corrected. Eliminating the Electoral College and replacing it with a national popular vote would produce a benefit but not without a cost. I agree the benefit is larger, but the cost isn't trivial, especially considering the history of the 2020 election, with the Donald Trump team, despite lacking any evidence, decrying the illegitimacy of outcomes across several states to the point of fomenting an attempted insurrection to block the official tally.

The principal benefit of replacing the Electoral College with the national popular vote is eliminating upside-down elections. The two most recent examples were the 2000 election, with George W. Bush defeating Al Gore, and the 2016 election, with Donald Trump defeating Hillary Clinton, both times despite a contrary national popular vote. That's a big deal. And it's certainly more democratic to have every single vote in the country counted equally. But if we embrace the national popular vote, electoral harmless error disappears. In close elections—as we've experienced again and again—we can expect election disputes in precinct upon precinct across the United States. With contests suddenly relevant wherever they are raised, we can expect more of them and a correspondingly greater distrust of electoral outcomes. After January 6, 2021, it's not hyperbolic to imagine opposition turning, once more, into political violence.

A final and very real concern is that the national popular vote won't eliminate the two-party system. And the scheme won't stop the two parties from growing ever distrustful and ideologically distant.

THE STATE VOTING PACT

There is one more layer to the national popular vote. Various organizations have advocated for the National Popular Vote Interstate Compact (NPVIC). Multiple states enter the compact to "guarantee the Presidency to the candidate who receives the most popular votes across all 50 states and the District of Columbia."[35] In May 2023, Minnesota became the sixteenth state to join the pact. Those states, plus the District of Columbia, which also joined, represent 205 of the required 270 votes (just 65 votes short) for a majority of the total 538 Electoral College Votes.[36] Although Congress has 535 members (435 in the House and 100 in the Senate), per the Twenty-Third Amendment, the Electoral College also includes three votes for the District of Columbia, the same delegation as the smallest states.[37]

The NPVIC states that once the majority threshold is met, participating states will commit to selecting as their slate of electors those matching the national popular vote, not their individual state outcomes, and they will do so winner-take-all. The plan makes the Electoral College more democratic in the sense that the nationwide vote count would control who's chosen as president, rather than the problematic Electoral College algorithm.

The democratic objective is compelling. It also has costs. The effect on voter incentives is unclear. Although there are exceptions, our elections are notoriously subject to low turnout, even accounting for an uptick in highly contentious presidential elections.[38] From the perspective of individual voters, the effects of the NPVIC are ambiguous. Some voters, knowing their presidential ballots won't affect the state delegation, which instead will be controlled by the national popular vote, might be less motivated to vote at all. Voters might also experience frustration when their state's majority vote outcome, assuming they supported it, was for the candidate who lost the national popular vote. Others, knowing their votes will influence every pact states' Electoral College delegation, might feel more strongly motivated to vote. If the pact is approved, voters must be educated so that they appreciate the trade-offs.

Because the scheme leaves direct election of the president in place, along with districted House elections and statewide Senate elections, it likewise leaves in place the two-party system.

Overall, the case for ending the Electoral College, like Senate reapportionment, is compelling, but it won't solve our constitutional crisis. The Second Electoral Reform Amendment also ends the Electoral College, but it does so by creating a genuine multiparty system with improved incentives to turn out and vote.

RANKED CHOICE VOTING (ROUND II)

Several organizations, including FairVote, the Forward Party, and Our Common Purpose, have proposed various plans involving RCV. RCV is often combined with other reforms.[39]

Under RCV, voters are presented a menu of candidates for whichever office it applies to, for example, president, senator, representative (including possibly in multimember districts), governor, and state general assemblies. But instead of simply choosing the candidate the voter prefers, next to each candidate's name appears a place to rank based on the number of candidates for the office. With five candidates, for example, voters rank each candidate on a scale from one to five, although they needn't complete the entire process. Most commonly, the candidate that receives the lowest number of votes in the initial round is dropped, and those who ranked that candidate first have their second-choice rankings allocated as votes for those candidates in the next round. Absent a majority winner in round two, the candidate who gets the fewest votes is then dropped, and the process is repeated (sometimes going into voters' third, fourth, or further rankings) until the candidate with a majority of votes wins.

This version of RCV is also known as instant-runoff voting (IRV). This conveys the idea that the voting scheme immediately recaptures voter preferences, avoiding the need for a second (or more) staged election. In theory, it can be handled near instantaneously, all in one go. Indeed, a claimed benefit of RCV is the possibility of collapsing the traditional two-stage election process into one.

Studies suggest that candidates in such voting systems tend to engage in less hostile campaigns.[40] A successful strategy requires persuading voters that even if you, as a candidate, are not their first choice, you respect their preferences and hope to gain their support as their second or third choice. The goal is to produce a dominant middle position, meaning a candidate who would defeat the others in direct comparisons in a field of several candidates, none of whom has majority support in the first round (also called a Condorcet winner). Advocates of RCV tout the system's democratic-enhancing, or majoritarian, objectives and that it lets voters support third parties without falling prey to the spoiler effect.

RCV doesn't live up to its hype. Candidates can still be spoilers or randomizers with voters supporting them harming their interests. More generally, under the very conditions that characterize our politics and that have given rise to our constitutional crisis, outcomes can thwart majoritarian preferences.

AN ALASKA CASE STUDY ILLUSTRATING
THE PROBLEMS WITH RCV

RCV's anomalies are helpfully illustrated by a special House of Representatives election in Alaska conducted in August 2022. The outcome of that election was reaffirmed in the regular midterm election three months later.[41]

The special election took place in two stages, an open primary followed by RCV over the top three candidates. The most well-known candidate was former Republican vice presidential candidate Sarah Palin, who emerged first in the primary with 27 percent of the vote. The other runoff candidates were Nick Begich, also Republican, who received 19.1 percent support, and Mary Peltola, a Democrat, who emerged fourth, with just 10.1 percent.[42] Peltola made the runoff because third-place finisher Al Gross, an Independent, with 12.6 percent support, dropped out.[43] In the RCV election, Palin emerged second and Begich third. With Begich knocked out, Peltola, who came in first in the three-way contest, also defeated Palin.

Several studies have shown that the Alaska election thwarted a majoritarian, or Condorcet-winning, outcome.[44] Once more, a

262 THE POLITICS OF RATIFICATION

Condorcet winner is an option, when there's no first-choice majority winner, that defeats all others in direct comparisons. These studies show that that RCV undermined the interests of two-thirds of Palin backers who would have done better simply by staying home. Had they done so, Palin would not have knocked out Begich. In a direct contest, Begich would have defeated both Peltola and Palin, making him the Condorcet winner. Mathematics professors David McCune and Adam Graham-Squire rightly observe that even without RCV, the Alaska primary and general election system would have produced the same outcome.[45] But we shouldn't embrace a reform that fails to improve upon the system in place and that risks making matters worse.

A study by the Center for Election Science demonstrated that the special Alaska House election refutes each of three central arguments pressed by RCV advocates: (1) ensuring voters can vote sincerely for their first choice without generating a disfavored outcome; (2) helping second (or lower) voter preferences win as higher-ranked preferences drop out in successive rounds; and (3) ensuring majoritarian outcomes. Instead, the Alaska election exposed the risk that RCV thwarts each claimed benefit: (1) Palin supporters harmed their interests just by showing up; (2) two-thirds of her supporters undermined the prospects of their second choice prevailing; and (3) the Peltola victory thwarted majoritarianism.

The Alaska election was widely criticized. One commentator claimed RCV mistakenly elevated a candidate receiving an initial 10 percent support at the expense of the plurality winner.[46] But that's not the problem. A majoritarian, or Condorcet, winner can sometimes receive low initial first-choice support. RCV can't ensure a Condorcet winner prevails even when one is available, and the problem is generalizable. With a bimodal electorate, RCV risks removing a candidate with low initial support who occupies a median position. Aaron Hamlin, for the Center for Election Science, dubbed this the "center-squeeze effect."[47] This means candidates to either side of a Condorcet candidate who get more votes can prevail by knocking out the centrist candidate in an early elimination round.

RCV produces a majority vote for a winning candidate in the final round. But that can't justify RCV. For purposes of promoting democratic values, what matters most isn't who wins the final round. Instead it's how the voting system determines which candidates advance to that round.

Whatever the merits of the Alaska election outcome, as a general matter, when RCV confronts a bimodal distribution, outcomes risk favoring extreme candidates. That, of course, is the very problem we have now. After all, the danger of our politics, especially in national elections, is increasing bimodalism. However well-intended, advocates touting RCV's tendency toward moderation and democracy-enhancing values are simply mistaken.

FURTHER REFLECTIONS ON RCV

FairVote, which supports RCV, rests on data from a variety of electoral settings, domestic and international.[48] Translating these data more broadly to the United States context is challenging. If RCV were widely embraced within the US, as needed to forge a multiparty system, voters would face confounding choices over multiple offices in each election. Ranking choices is complex even assuming the candidates align on a single right-left spectrum (see chapter 8). The challenges become greater once we recognize that our politics implicates two dimensions: economics/policy and culture/identity. It's hard to expect all but the rarest of voters to manage the challenge of assessing candidates based on intuitions concerning how distant the candidates appear to be from the voter's ideal point.[49] Voters might have a sense as to how to rank two candidates, even three, but beyond that rankings risk becoming arbitrary, even guesswork.

The RCV data aren't helpful in answering how voters would meet such challenges. Voter satisfaction scores aren't straightforward. Survey data generally favor single-voting regimes, whereas the experience-based data with the systems in place show more favorable RCV satisfaction scores.[50] These data are less helpful in considering the experience of US voters in multiple complex electoral contests or in national elections where electoral distributions are more likely bimodal than in local elections. Limiting RCV to particular offices might simplify matters, but doing so implies that RCV succeeds best if it doesn't succeed too much.

To pull us out of our constitutional crisis, we must infuse greater fluidity among candidates and parties. In two dimensions, political entrepreneurs can reconceive coalitions that thwart neat ordinal rankings assessed along the two-party right-left divide. The goal of electoral reform is to stop having either party control the seesaw, taking voters on an increasingly troubling ride. Instead, we must let voters step off and take a ride that's more fulfilling. RCV can't achieve that, but Parliamentary America can.

EMPOWERING OR DISEMPOWERING PARTIES: FINAL FIVE OPEN PRIMARY VOTING, OPEN LIST PROPORTIONAL REPRESENTATION, AND APPROVAL VOTING

RCV isn't the only innovative voting protocol gaining attention. Other notable proposals include final five open primary voting; open list proportional representation, or OLPR; and approval voting. Although each system has variations, describing their common attributes helps contrast the different approaches they generally offer as compared with the Electoral Reform Amendments. Along with RCV, these voting systems tend to disempower parties with the goal of achieving centrism. By contrast, Parliamentary America empowers voters through genuine party competition.

Institute for Political Innovation Founder Katherine Gehl advocates final five open primary voting. Unlike closed primaries, which limit voting to registered party members, this scheme lists all primary candidates for office, such as the House of Representatives, regardless of party, and lets all voters choose among all listed candidates.[51] Voters then use ranked-choice voting over candidates who advance to the final round. The system encourages moderate candidates because non-party members counterbalance the stronger ideological commitments of elites and base members of other parties.

Open list proportional representation has conflicting effects on party control of candidates and platforms. It lets parties police access to candidate lists, and it has voters across parties select one candidate from a menu of party lists, typically in a multimember district, often resolving the election in a single combined round.[52] OLPR encourages moderate outcomes to the extent voters select candidates from the lists from other parties because crossover voters tend to counter the stronger ideological commitments of base party members. The Center for American Progress nicely captures this intuition: "In an OLPR system in the United States, there could be no real red or blue states, as every vote cast would help determine how red or blue."[53] Although OLPR potentially limits the power of parties to ensure their favored candidates succeed, there is a countervailing consideration: by controlling which candidates are balloted initially, party elites can deny access to most extreme candidates.

The Center for Election Science advocates approval voting.[54] This system lets voters choose from a menu of candidates representing multiple parties. But unlike other voting systems, approval voting places no limit on the number of candidates an individual voter may approve. Unlike RCV, the scheme doesn't differentiate based on relative voter preferences over candidates. Instead, voters make a simple binary choice—approve or not—for each listed candidate. Approval voting encourages centrist candidates because voters approving lists of candidates from multiple parties are likely to favor more moderate candidates than each party's own members in a closed system.

Although every electoral system introduces its own nuances, for our purposes it's helpful to consider the common features that distinguish these voting protocols from the Electoral Reform Amendments. First, these protocols don't empower House party coalitions to choose the president, and therefore they won't forge a system that genuinely empowers third parties. Second, with the caveat that OLPR lets party elites exclude extreme candidates from their own party lists, these proposals let voters outside a party limit the offerings of candidates and platforms parties provide rather than empowering the parties themselves to make such determinations.

At a superficial level the second attribute—weakening parties—might seem appealing given the genuine frustration US voters routinely experience with the limited and increasingly divergent choices the Democratic and Republican parties offer. Disempowering parties might intuitively imply empowering voters. But a central theme of this book has been to demonstrate why that premise is flawed. Just as it is unwise to control media by regulating its content (see chapter 4), so too it is unwise to control elections by limiting the ability of parties to offer distinct choices to voters. The wiser pathway to reform is to motivate private actors—media and parties—to offer our citizenry better options. The problem with our electoral system isn't that parties hold power. Instead it's that with only two major parties, voters lack the choices meaningful party competition will bring.

As political scientist Jack Santucci has rightly observed, "The choice between two and no parties is false. The real choice is between two and more parties."[55] Parties are inevitable in a democracy. Ending the third constitutional crisis requires that we avoid the central mistake the Framers made of imagining they could supersede party competition with a different game (see chapter 1). A fundamental insight from the world tour (see part III) is that in a democracy, no matter the game, parties quickly learn how to play it. That includes working to defeat proposals designed to disempower them. The better approach is to ensure that our electoral system encourages parties to adopt playbooks that benefit them and the electorate.

The goal of electoral reform is to produce an appropriate number of parties—not too many, not too few—giving voters more and better choices. Mixed-member proportionality, or MMP, empowers voters and parties. With genuine party competition, parties will offer meaningful choices, with multiple visions captured across the economics/policy and culture/identity ideological landscape. And voters will choose among leaders motivated to produce governing coalitions within a continuously evolving core.

Parliamentary America will solve our crisis and is politically viable. And it offers a vision of America that we'll be proud to leave as our legacy to future generations.

CHAPTER 11

Parliamentary America

TOWARD BETTER POLITICS,
FURTHER REFORMS, AND A CIVIL SOCIETY

As we near the end of our journey, it's appropriate to take stock. We've traveled the world, met notable thinkers, and evaluated the theoretical and practical challenges of our electoral system. We've enriched childhood games with social science insights. We've placed information-age technologies—computer-based hyper-partisan gerrymandering and algorithmic social media news feeds—that wreaked havoc with our constitutional system and culture in a broad, historical context. And we've evaluated three constitutional amendments that will end the third constitutional crisis and third-party dilemma, compared them with alternatives, and probed the politics of getting them passed.

This chapter takes the final step. Imagine we succeed. Our children and grandchildren become the beneficiaries of Parliamentary America, and the United States emerges as a beacon to aspiring democracies across the globe. That's not because our new system is final or perfect. When it comes to democracy, there's no such thing. What will make Parliamentary America a beacon aren't the specific reforms, even as they proved critical to ending our nation's immediate crisis. Instead, Parliamentary America will inspire other nations for having confronted the imminent threat of governmental collapse or autocracy and for taking careful steps to right our nation's path. That task demands a clear-eyed recognition of how the foundational premises of our constitutional system have undermined collective efforts to meet our nation's existential challenges. This will emerge as the central lesson of all three constitutional crises. Just as we've learned from the rich experiences of other democracies, so too other nations, including those struggling to become or to remain democratic, will be inspired by Parliamentary America.

The last step is considering three transformations that Parliamentary America will help bring about: changing the dynamics of ordinary lawmaking, inviting future structural reforms, and improving our cultural and political discourse. The Electoral Reform Amendments aren't a cure-all for our politics and culture. Our divides have festered for decades or longer and are deeply rooted, even as the past several years have pushed them ever closer to the breaking point. Structural reforms immediately following the first two constitutional crises marked the beginning of protracted mending processes, inviting later changes that, as the Framers aptly phrased it, made us "a more perfect union." More perfect implies always striving to improve. Healing may take decades or longer, and some wounds never truly heal. But part of the healing process in a healthy democracy is creating pathways for future generations to tackle their own challenges, including ones we can't foresee. Our vantage point is limited, yet we can envision possibilities, once foreclosed by our two-party system, made possible in Parliamentary America.

Politics in the Core: From Endless Division
to Sober Compromise

Imagining the future benefits from a brief recap of the past. Prior to Parliamentary America, the United States was characterized by unbridgeable divides with respect to nearly every aspect of public policy and culture. Notable examples included race, gender and reproductive rights, climate change, the COVID-19 pandemic, and guns.[1] Party leaders split sharply on these and other topics with intensifying disagreements echoed across social media and beyond. Among the greatest challenges was a pervasive unwillingness to credit those on the other side of nearly any issue as having engaged in a fair assessment of underlying data yet discerning contrary implications.

Identifying the causes of our growing political and societal dysfunction proved easier than devising a cure. During the decades defining the information age, both the traditional processes of acquiring news and news-like information, and of electing officials to represent us, broke down.[2] For much of our history, educated elites served as a check against the potential harms of threatening populist impulses. Elites played an important vetting role both within news media and for aspiring politicians.

Modern technology confounded the media. In the information age, fewer people subscribed to and read traditional print media sources or watched televised news broadcasts featuring trusted anchors. Information fractured. Algorithmic social media news feeds, especially on Facebook and Twitter, inverted the relationship between news sources and readers, with sources emerging as consumers and all of us as the product. Studies repeatedly confirmed the powerlessness of disconfirming data to change minds.[3] Presented with reliable evidence challenging the factual predicates of core beliefs, people tended to double down, rarely changing their views, and instead shifting discourse to arguments that were easier to defend. Core political identity—

sometimes called tribalism—proved more powerful than the elusive quest for truth.

The information age also changed our electoral system as aspiring politicians bypassed party elites. Hyper-partisan gerrymandering carried out with laser-like precision let state and congressional maps provide a shrinking Republican Party disproportionate power and influence. Just as the media chose readers, not the other way around, elected officials chose voters, not the other way around. As congressional districts became less competitive, each party pushed further toward its respective base. The only real challenges came in primaries, which rarely favored the center. National policy increasingly turned on the fate of the few remaining competitive districts in a system that, once set into motion, even its creators struggled to control.[4]

Minuscule voting differences had profound lasting impacts. This was most evident in the 2000 and 2016 elections where the Electoral College outcomes thwarted the popular vote. Fewer than six hundred votes mistakenly cast for Pat Buchanan in Palm Beach County, Florida, due to the peculiar, if well-intended, butterfly ballot, would have flipped the 2000 presidential election from George W. Bush to Al Gore.[5] In 2016, had just three border counties been mapped into neighboring states—with Lucas County, Ohio, and Lake County, Illinois, included as part of Michigan, and with Mercer County, New Jersey, included as part of Pennsylvania—Hillary Clinton would have defeated Donald Trump, all without changing a single vote.[6]

In the two-party winner-take-all system, Republican leaders understood politics first and foremost as a battle for power—gaining it, holding it, and exercising it. Because Republicans are a minority party, control of the ballot box emerged as a primary battleground.

The 2000 and 2016 elections didn't just empower electoral minorities; they also entrenched a conservative Supreme Court. George W. Bush appointed Chief Justice John Roberts (replacing

Chief Justice William Rehnquist) and Associate Justice Samuel Alito (replacing Sandra Day O'Connor). Donald Trump, in a single four-year term, appointed Associate Justices Neil Gorsuch (replacing Antonin Scalia), Brett Kavanaugh (replacing Anthony Kennedy), and Amy Coney Barrett (replacing Ruth Bader Ginsburg). Three of these five appointments played a pivotal role in profoundly transforming longstanding doctrine. Replacing two moderate conservatives, Justices O'Connor and Kennedy, and one liberal, Justice Ginsburg, with three core conservatives, Justices Alito, Kavanaugh, and Barrett, paved the way for greenlighting partisan gerrymandering, ending a woman's right to choose, eroding separation of church and state, and further entrenching Second Amendment rights.[7] As this book went to press, the Supreme Court also ended race-based affirmative action, albeit with a possibly notable caveat.

The seismic shift in power following each election cycle, with the battle for the Supreme Court carrying decades-long implications, heightened the tensions of our two-party politics. The stress of electoral outcomes simplistically cast in terms of right or left masked weighty divisions implicating both the economics/policy and culture/identity dimensions of our political landscape. The political strain foisted upon voters the difficult choice either to subordinate core ideological commitments, supporting the less problematic of two major party candidates, or to vote consistently with their sincere policy preferences while contributing to an outcome so troubling as to be viewed an existential threat.

A dynamic feedback loop—siloed news sourcing feeding polarized tribal camps supporting increasingly ideological politicians rewarding ever-divisive news feeds—transformed nearly every political decision into a moral battle for America's soul. This included who controlled access to the ballot box, who drew districting boundaries, and who controlled judicial appointments, especially on the Supreme Court.

In the information age, the two-party system might be likened to complex braiding—separate intricate ponytails each comprising interwoven strands, reflecting suppositions of fact, ideological commitments, and layered personal identities. The media-to-voter-to-politician-to-media ecosystem rendered the task of untangling daunting or impossible. Factual or historical challenges were routinely met with endlessly creative shifts in discourse, producing antics variously resembling high school debates or a high-stakes parlor game, too often premised on "alternative facts."[8] Parliamentary America lets us comb through the knots, allowing newer, looser strands to form and reform, all by changing the rules of the game.

On the world tour, we saw isolated examples of unusual political marriages—Ireland's Greencons, England's odd couple, Israel's Arab-party/right-wing alliance. These anomalies are more plausible in a system less prone to the permanent and widening entrenchment of winner-take-all politics. Unusual alignments can shake up politics—like reshuffling a deck of cards or loosening tightly interwoven strands—even if those alliances are generally temporary and their goals targeted. More generally, unlike the two-party system, which fed ever-widening political and cultural divides, competition among several parties—Democrats, Progressives, Republicans, Libertarians, America First, and others—encourages seeking common ground in the quest for a developing core and a successful governing coalition.

In Parliamentary America, Democratic and Republican leaders, extricated from the extreme demands of their base, have become freer to negotiate with one another and with other party leaders. Effective leaders realize that building a coalition inevitably invites trade-offs and that moral courage in politics isn't an ideologically driven suicide mission. Compromise isn't weakness.

Voters have also come to appreciate these lessons. Libertarians who insisted upon staying home or voting for Trump, despite the threat, and progressives who went Bernie or Bust, no longer face the third-party dilemma. Instead, they, and party leaders they favor, confront the choice to make accommodations as a means of gaining power and influence or instead to insist rigidly on an uncompromising ideology. More and more voters now realize that coalition building lets them prioritize core values, but that doing so demands joining with others who don't necessarily share their overriding ideological commitments.

We can't know how specific policy questions will be resolved in the rough-and-tumble world of Parliamentary America. But we can sketch some examples of the sorts of approaches that hold far greater promise than in Presidential America's earlier intractable two-party world.

RACIAL PREFERENCES

Consider race-based affirmative action. The Supreme Court's 2023 decision, *Students for Fair Admissions, Inc. v. Presidents and Fellows of Harvard College*, banned racial preferences in public and private university admissions subject to a caveat. Chief Justice Roberts's majority opinion let student essays express "how race affected [the applicant's] life, be it through discrimination, inspiration, or otherwise."[9] The practical implications are uncertain, including whether Congress could authorize broader reliance on race. A grand coalition of now smaller Democratic and Republican parties may agree on two points: first, as an aspirational matter, permanently entrenched racial preferences are problematic, and second, the long-dominant framing of racial preferences, dating to the 1978 Supreme Court decision *Regents of the University of California v. Bakke*, served the nation, and minorities, less well than intended.[10]

The controlling *Bakke* opinion limited consideration of race in admissions to furthering diversity and disallowed racial quotas. Two majority Supreme Court opinions in 2003 involving the University of Michigan reaffirmed *Bakke*. The Court upheld the law school's consideration of race as a soft variable in admissions yet struck down the undergraduate policy, which attached specified points based on race.[11] The distinction overlooked evidence that law school outcomes closely correlated to the undergraduate program's formulaic approach and that the point system saved considerable resources given the undergraduate program's larger scale.

Party leaders might agree that the nation would be better served with a candid acknowledgment that a more sincere basis for racial preferences is remedying the longstanding effects of past racial discrimination. Discriminatory practices were too often fashioned in complex ways by the interplay between countless private decisions and tacit approval, even encouragement, by governmental policies. Ample research has demonstrated the long history of such practices as redlining, steering, lending discrimination, disparate public school resource allocations, teaching personnel decisions, higher education access, and zoning laws.[12] These practices effected enormous differences in wealth accumulation, educational opportunities, access to quality housing and food, and more, at overwhelming cost to African American communities. And with some irony, given partisan alliances, such practices also often disadvantaged poor white communities.

It's not possible to predict the precise set of policies that might emerge from these discussions. But opening the door to conversations that get beyond such superficial claims as Chief Justice John Roberts's earlier assertion that "the way to stop discrimination based on race is to stop discriminating on the basis of race,"[13] or conversely presuming a racial animus accounts for all disparate outcomes, creates helpful space for new ideas and policies to flourish. The direction those conversations take will be affected by the influence of other parties that might join as coalition partners, and that's as it should be. Whether the menu on offer includes funding commitments to historically Black colleges and universities, greater resource allocations to inner-city schools, pipeline programs that let lower-income college students more quickly enter professional schools, and other aspects of remediation in housing, urban development, and more, the possibility of constructive compromise is far better outside the divisive world of two-party politics.

THE POLITICS OF REPRODUCTIVE RIGHTS

Immediately following the controversial 2022 Supreme Court decision in *Dobbs v. Jackson Women's Health Organization*,[14] several states enacted highly restrictive abortion regulations. Republican Senator Lindsey Graham went so far as to propose a national fifteen-week abortion ban, raising the ire of fellow Republicans who feared, and then witnessed, a 2022 midterm election backlash.[15] Opposing views on reproductive rights reached a fever pitch.

Abortion rights have long been a divisive issue. In *Planned Parenthood of Southeastern Pennsylvania v. Casey*,[16] the joint authors of the controlling opinion claimed to reach a middle ground. They retained *Roe v. Wade* while providing states with greater regulatory latitude under a newly minted, and laxer, "undue burden" test. The opinion claimed to "resolve the . . . intensely divisive controversy reflected in *Roe*" in a manner that "call[ed] the contending sides . . . to end their national division by accepting a common mandate rooted in the Constitution."[17] It didn't turn out that way.

Our partisan divisions intensified despite an emerging electoral consensus favoring a woman's right to choose. When *Dobbs* was issued, 62 percent of Americans believed abortion "should be legal in all or most cases," and 57 percent of the American public opposed the specific case result.[18] Pew Research Center and Monmouth University studies demonstrated even stronger opposition to a previously enacted Texas abortion law. That statute banned abortions as early as six weeks, even in cases of rape or incest, imposed criminal penalties on physicians or other abortion providers, and let private individuals directly sue those helping a woman seeking to have an abortion.[19] The Monmouth study showed that as many as 70 percent of those polled disapproved of allowing private lawsuits to prevent women from seeking an abortion, and 81 percent opposed the Texas statute's specific financial compensation scheme for successful suits.

Consider once more how an evolving grand coalition might frame the issue, unencumbered by a once-minority faction foisting its restrictive views, out of keeping with those of the American public, onto the rest of the Republican Party. We must start by acknowledging that many individuals hold a sincere religious belief that personhood begins at conception. Even so, party leaders might agree on several points: First, any individual capable of pregnancy has an absolute right to terminate the pregnancy within a reasonable period of time when it was the product of rape or incest or when the person seeking to do so is too young to have lawfully consented to sexual activity. Second, anyone experiencing a pregnancy that threatens her life or health has an absolute right to terminate the pregnancy at whatever point is required to ensure personal safety. Third, contrary to the suggestion of Justice Amy Coney Barrett, the ability to give up an infant without penalty, or to choose adoption, doesn't overcome the unique burdens on a woman forced to carry a fetus to term against her will.[20]

The harder questions involve when a woman may terminate an unwanted pregnancy in the more general course, meaning when it was not the product of such limiting circumstances as rape, incest, or age below lawful consent, or when the pregnancy doesn't pose any of the previously identified special risks. A right that's strictly limited to the first trimester disregards that not all women's reproductive cycles operate with clocklike precision and that not all fetal abnormalities are discovered, or discoverable, early in pregnancy. Party leaders might agree that, in general, the right to early abortion must be absolute, and work out more detailed policies concerning rights later in pregnancy, tied to specific circumstances. They may determine that some of these choices can be left to states to resolve, provided the basic right to terminate an unwanted pregnancy is protected, and that those seeking to terminate a pregnancy, and those helping them do so, are not penalized for exercising their rights, including traveling across state lines.[21]

Once more, the point isn't to predict precisely what an evolving core reflects on these divisive issues. Rather, it is to demonstrate that once the Republican Party is no longer captive to one faction holding views widely out of keeping with a substantial majority of American voters, and once the Democratic Party has more policy latitude without fear of alienating those who find no basis, ever, for restricting the choice to terminate a pregnancy, the possibilities of more granular inquiries and meaningful compromise greatly improve.

GUNS

Parliamentary America also invites the possibility of meaningful compromise on the daunting issue of access to guns. Prior to the Electoral Reform Amendments, Pew Research data showed cross-cutting agreement on modest gun reforms, including preventing those with mental illness from purchasing guns (87 percent), creating a federal database of gun sales (66 percent), requiring background checks for private sales and sales at gun shows (81 percent), and banning high-capacity magazines and assault-style weapons (64 percent and 63 percent, respectively).[22]

What is sometimes referred to as the gun-show loophole is a misnomer. Dating to the Brady Act, private-to-private sales, in contrast with Federal Firearms License–registered sales, were exempt from the requirement of background checks but subject to the general requirement of disallowing sales to prohibited persons, such as felons or others known to pose a risk of harm to self or others.[23] Gun shows became associated with such private sales, giving rise to the loophole characterization.

For decades, the National Rifle Association (NRA) effectively held Republican politicians hostage based on a ratings system for proposed gun laws that tolerated virtually no dissension from its extreme anti-regulatory stance on Second Amendment rights.[24] Following the tragic Uvalde, Texas, school shooting, Congress enacted the Bipartisan Safer Communities Act.[25] Although this was the first gun safety regulation in decades, the reforms were exceedingly modest. Key provisions included clarifying who must obtain a federal license to engage in a firearms transaction and ending what was known as the boyfriend loophole, thereby preventing persons convicted of misdemeanor domestic violence from buying or possessing firearms for five years. Other provisions included funding for various state programs designed to help reduce the incidence of violent crime.

The bill didn't tackle the pervasive rise of dangerous weapons, including military-grade AR-15 rifles often used in school shootings, or prevent private-to-private sales exemptions from required background checks.[26] Although some cross-national comparisons are dubious, such as simply comparing gun crime rates in the United States to those in nations with far smaller populations, two overriding facts remain: first, the US stands alone on the world stage in having a fundamental right to acquire and own weapons, including especially dangerous ones; and second, the US is an outlier with an astounding 20 percent more firearms than people.[27] Contrary to claims of "more guns, less crime,"[28] we have more gun crimes for the simple reason that the United States has far more privately owned guns, in the aggregate and per person, than any other nation in the world.

Tackling this issue will be far more plausible in Parliamentary America. With the Republican Party split among Republican, America First, and Libertarian parties, the NRA will lose its iron grip on the GOP, allowing that party to become a meaningful partner in addressing the increasingly existential drumbeat of gun crime and school shootings.

We might once more imagine a grand coalition, Democrats and Republicans, perhaps joined by Progressives or Libertarians, agreeing on several principles. First, the Supreme Court's 2008 decision, *District of Columbia v. Heller*, which found an individual right to keep and bear arms, rested on a tendentious reading of the Second Amendment.[29] The Second Amendment states in full: "A well regulated Militia, being necessary to the security of a free State, the right of the people to keep and bear Arms, shall not be infringed."[30] Most notably, the *Heller* Court effectively read out the amendment's prefatory clause. And even then, the *Heller* decision provided greater regulatory latitude to prohibit access to unusual weapons, which may well include AR-15 rifles, than the pre-Parliamentary America Republican Party and conservative Supreme Court majority has since been willing to allow.[31] Second, the ultimate problem with guns is their pervasiveness—more guns than people—and durability. Guns are the ultimate durable good, capable of deathly harm as long as ammunition is available. Third, no matter how responsible an original owner of any weapon might be, there is no guarantee that someone dangerous will never come into its possession. Reducing gun crime demands reducing guns. And no, this does not mean through confiscation. There are better, more creative, ways to achieve fewer guns *and* less gun crime.

A grand coalition with a developing core might prospectively ban large-capacity rapid-fire rifles or firearms other than as a form of entertainment in highly controlled and licensed venues, completely ban private-to-private sales of such weapons, and require those in possession of such weapons to enter them in a central registry. This would allow the government to ensure that upon the death of a present owner of an unusually dangerous weapon there is a record of who might come into its possession, and to gain an opportunity to buy that weapon and remove it from circulation. The coalition might agree more generally to a government-funded weapons-purchasing program, including high-capacity weapons and others as well.[32] It might consider tax incentives that motivate voluntarily relinquishing guns to law enforcement authorities. The plan might include special incentives, no questions asked, with attractive bounties well in excess of market value, for guns most commonly used in urban street crimes. Just consider the potential return on investment for such a combined program in reducing the most damaging instances of urban crime and in confronting the numbingly frequent, tragic recurrence of mass shootings, including in schools. Truly pennies on the dollar.

Second Amendment enthusiasts are sure to push back on these suggested reforms, and even to suggest they mark the danger of Parliamentary America. But that's disingenuous. Our Constitution once protected the right to own other human beings, and although far too late, we rightly ended that over a century and a half ago, at the price of the Civil War and over 600,000 troop casualties. The Second Amendment doesn't declare a private *individual* right to own high-capacity rifles or to acquire weapons without background checks. Until the *Heller* decision, so from 1789 through 2008, few scholars or jurists claimed otherwise. Rightness or wrongness doesn't matter in a world that only rewards power, but it does matter in a world, like Parliamentary America, that changes the rules of the game to demand more—a coalition with a shared purpose to improve the lives of all Americans by shaping, then governing in, the political core.

SOME GENERAL OBSERVATIONS

Not everyone reading this book will agree with what I've described as core areas of agreement. In each instance, there's almost certainly something for everyone to dislike. That's usually the sign of productive debate and compromise. Even if what I've proposed emerges only as a possible starting point for future deliberations, that's helpful. Politics is messy, and details matter. In Parliamentary America, parties can always count on future elections and future coalitions that will seek to move the core ever closer to where their most effective, high-valence leaders wish to take it.

Readers will undoubtedly observe that my starting point was a possible grand coalition that included the now-smaller Republican and Democratic parties. That was not to make building a coalition easier; it is because doing so made finding a core more difficult. The process began by identifying granular areas of consensus and cabining, without necessarily resolving, more contentious questions. It would be far easier to achieve outcomes favored by those on the left, which, based on voting in the 2016 and 2020 presidential elections, make up a majority of the electorate, thereby excluding newer parties whose members previously formed the GOP. But that would be counterproductive. In a mixed-member proportionality system, the Democratic or Republican parties are apt to lead coalition negotiations, at least initially. We can expect power to sometimes volley back and forth between those parties, with smaller parties helping form a coalition, and other times the Democrats and Republicans joining to form a grand coalition.

I have not surmised possible odd coalitions that principally marry parties that are naturally opposed, such as Progressives and Libertarians, or even America First. It's impossible to predict the sort of events captured by the saying "Politics makes strange bed-fellows."[33] Such alliances might occur when a highly unsuccessful president's failings garner cross-cutting support for removal. One reason why no-confidence motions are based on conscience, not party discipline, is to learn from history, and thus to avoid the expectation that such combinations will necessarily endure beyond the temporary mutual benefits they typically provide.

We could devise comparable stories in policy domains beyond those discussed here. It's certainly mistaken to imagine parties suddenly joining in harmony over issues that previously divided Democrats and Republicans in the earlier two-party presidential system. Intense policy disputes will inevitably arise. But Parliamentary America lets parties tackle these policy areas in two important stages: first, in negotiating governing coalitions, and second, in ironing out the details of proposed legislation. Not all legislative negotiations will succeed, of course, but the more fluid coalition process helps lay the groundwork for greater and more meaningful compromise than in the earlier two-party winner-take-all world.

Further Structural Reforms

The goal of the Electoral Reform Amendments was to produce a robust multi-party democracy. The amendments were the beginning of reform, not the end. In Parliamentary America, leaders of several parties will be better situated to continue the process of making the United States an ever more perfect union. Let's consider some notable further reforms.

THE SUPREME COURT

In the two-party era, the Supreme Court emerged the ultimate political battleground. The Republicans perfected a blocking strategy so powerful that Donald Trump, who served a single four-year term, replaced Justices Antonin Scalia (Neil Gorsuch), Anthony Kennedy (Brett Kavanaugh), and Ruth Bader Ginsburg (Amy Coney Barrett), even though Justices Scalia and Ginsburg died four years and seven months apart. Reformers pressed for two possible changes: expanding the Supreme Court, thereby making the conservative majority a minority on a larger, more liberal Court, and imposing term limits, typically eighteen years, with staggered retirements to facilitate appointments on a predictable two-year schedule.[34]

Expansion proposals, which were never popular to begin with, are apt to lose whatever steam they may have had once the two-party system ends. Supreme Court expansion could lead to further and further increases in size, making it unsustainable. Term limits also present challenges, including reduced collegiality. The Court might experience further erosion of respect for precedent, including opinions of sitting jurists, when faced with a preset retirement schedule. Even so, let's imagine the eighteen-year-term proposal gets approved.

The predictability of appointments might itself partly ameliorate the problem of diminished cooperation both among senators and among justices. The two largest parties—Democrats and Republicans—will predictably lead early governing coalitions. Because seats on the Supreme Court are apt to emerge as one of the most powerful bargaining chips, smaller parties can negotiate appointments to the highest court as the price of joining a governing coalition, and over time, party leaders will anticipate justices being appointed from multiple parties through such bargaining. Although political bargains won't be judicially enforced, failing to honor them politically could invite a credible risk of a no confidence vote, or at the very least a threat to exit the coalition. Among the justices, predictable turnover may reward cooperation as they come to realize that new appointees bring perspectives reflecting a range of jurisprudential ideologies, thus diminishing emphasis on individual views of jurists who previously sat on the Court for decades on end.

With a staggered eighteen-year limit, each four-year presidential term produces two scheduled Supreme Court appointments. While Supreme Court appointments would remain powerful, the new system will reduce incentives for high-stakes gaming. Senate leaders are more likely to use the power of advice and consent as the Framers intended: to ensure those appointed have outstanding qualifications and a proper judicial temperament as needed to perform the important duties on the nation's highest court. Otherwise, they can predict—with scheduled accuracy—that when coalition parties change, others might game the system every two years, just as they had.

Making Supreme Court appointments more predictable and routine would provide another benefit. Although inevitably there will be some strongly ideological appointments, overall, the predictable turnover should have a moderating effect. Justices will increasingly appreciate that their opinions will have a more lasting influence when they are well grounded in sound constitutional commitments and policy rather than in an absolutist ideology.

THE SENATE

In Parliamentary America, debates will almost certainly continue concerning this most undemocratic institution. Although the Electoral Reform Amendments don't resolve the issue, they will have the salutary effect of making the Senate a multiparty institution. Smaller states are apt to find themselves allied on some issues, but not on all or even most. State size is rarely as unifying as geographical proximity to neighboring states and the general ideological views in the relevant region. Delaware and Rhode Island have more in common with larger northeastern and mid-Atlantic states than with Wyoming or Montana, which have stronger ties to other western states. Once the two-party system ends, it might become increasingly difficult for the Senate to bear the weight of individual members blocking bills with enormous public backing and on which the fate of the coalition-based presidency depends.

In the new regime, we might envision two major reform proposals affecting the Senate: reapportionment and legislative bypass. As we've seen, reapportioning the Senate would require first amending the amending clause, and then amending the Article I requirement of equal apportionment among states.[35] Reapportionment would make the Senate more like the House, albeit with smaller numbers and a still more elite status.

Political scientist Lee Drutman offers an appealing proposal that avoids reapportionment but that would require amending. Drutman proposes providing the House with a greater and more direct policymaking role, leaving the Senate to fulfill its traditional obligations of advice and consent over appointments, treaties, and some areas of legislative policy.[36] The idea, which has much to commend it, finds precedent in some of the nations we've toured, such as England and Germany. In those nations, the upper chambers generally play a lesser role in formulating public policy as compared with the lower chambers, which form the governing coalition that selects the head of government.

There is a sound logic to the arrangement. First, upper chambers tend to have an aristocratic, and thus antidemocratic, heritage. Consider, for example, the difference between England's House of Lords and House of Commons. Our Senate is analogous to the House of Lords, and indeed, state legislatures originally held the power to choose senatorial delegations without election. The House of Representatives was known as "the People's House." The Seventeenth Amendment changed this, mandating Senate elections. Even so, the whiff of upper-chamber aristocracy remains. It's embodied, for example, in the power of individual members to filibuster, thus blocking legislation often with broad national support, or at least holding it subject to a supermajority requirement of 60 percent.[37]

Although the filibuster has been chipped away at over the decades, Parliamentary America may motivate abandoning it altogether. This simple change to an internal rule might be a prudent exercise in institutional self-defense, more so than a product of democratic enlightenment. With the fate of the presidency closely tied to a majority House coalition, it makes little sense to continue empowering individual senators, especially from small states, to block key proposals forming part of a coalition platform. Over time, senators might relinquish this power to avoid the risk of still more radical reforms.

Building upon Lee Drutman's suggestion, I propose an amendment that, once more, leaves the Senate intact, yet improves the democratic attributes of our lawmaking process. The amendment would retain ordinary lawmaking processes, which includes bicameralism and presentment, but add a Senate bypass for bills with supermajority, two-thirds, House support. In this regime, the House may send a bill directly to the president either by initially approving it with a two-thirds vote, or, if following simple majority House approval, the Senate opposes the bill, by overriding the Senate vote with a two-thirds vote.

In Parliamentary America, the president hails from the majority House coalition, so the override would rarely occur without presidential support. Should the president veto the bill, the usual two-thirds vote by each chamber would be required. By requiring such a high level of House consensus, the proposal would ensure broad national support prior to enacting any bill bypassing the Senate into law.

Providing the lower of our two houses with a more powerful role in legislating enhances the democratic values of our system of government. I personally favor reapportioning the Senate. These two Senate reform proposals aren't mutually exclusive. They accomplish many of the same objectives of enhancing the

democratic aspects of lawmaking, thereby improving the legitimacy of resulting policy. And there's an additional benefit: the
scheme encourages a supermajority House coalition at least on
major issues, motivating politics in the core.

The bypass approach leaves a relic, an upper chamber that
smacks of aristocracy and nods to a sovereignty the states never
truly held. But the Senate would no longer retain the pretense of
holding the same force in creating public policy as the House. Reapportionment is a more direct means of achieving this goal. I
would support either, or both in combination, but I suspect the bypass might be more tractable politically. Although appearances
matter, constitutional reform should be driven first and foremost by
the need to solve problems. Giving the Senate a secondary policymaking role while retaining its other unique powers might prove a
helpful defense against threatened reapportionment.

REALIGNING THE PRESIDENTIAL, SENATE, AND HOUSE
TERMS AND ELECTION CYCLES

In the European world tour (see chapter 5), we saw that in 2000,
France aligned its previously mismatched presidential and parliamentary terms of office. A final reform that also would require
amending entails aligning our own presidential and congressional terms, this time by adopting Brazil's term alignment for its
two legislative chambers and presidency.[38] The United States now
has terms of two, four, and six years respectively for the House,
presidency, and Senate. This scheme produces potential misalignments following midterm elections between the presidency and
House, and more general misalignments with the Senate. Like
Brazil, we could instead set the presidential and House terms at
four years each and Senate terms at eight. This would better align
the House and presidency politically, avoiding the problem of
midterms altogether. Senate elections would then stagger, with
half the membership elected each quadrennial cycle.

This scheme would operate best if conditioned on the separate
proposals of Senate bypass and a diminished Senate lawmaking

role. If the Senate retained its present equal lawmaking status with the House, the new calendar would risk misaligning every other presidential term with a Senate whose political core potentially differs from that of a newly formed House coalition and presidency. But even without changing the calendar, Parliamentary America promises to render the Senate a multiparty institution and thus to encourage greater cooperation.

I didn't include this reform among the three Electoral Reform Amendments because the realignment isn't necessary to extricate us from the constitutional crisis we are facing and because it raises fundamental questions concerning the Senate's lawmaking role. This term-alignment proposal introduces yet another trade-off for senators who would gain the prestige of an enhanced term, now carried over two full presidential terms, albeit at the possible price of a diminished lawmaking role and with a greater emphasis on advice and consent. For any reform, we must consider trade-offs facing institutional actors who hold blocking power.

Improving Our Culture and Discourse

Our politics and cultural discourse have fallen prey to a problematic feedback loop. Parliamentary America will help to break that loop, thereby improving cultural cohesion. I'm not Pollyannaish. There's no magic bullet that will end, at least anytime soon, the strident discourse in which too many regard those with whom they disagree not merely as misled or uninformed, but far too often as stupid or evil. This deeply problematic dynamic undermines any capacity to come together toward a common mission as a nation.

As we've seen, the history of news media substantially evolved through different periods (see chapter 4). Each press period is significant in assessing the cultural breakdown we're experiencing today. For many readers, the benchmark for media may resemble a perhaps idyllic conception of the period of press professionalization. That period tended to correspond to elite control not only of news gathering and dissemination, but also of vetted political candidates. The histories of media and of political parties are parallel, and as with politics, it's easy to imagine elite media control as more virtuous than it was in the rough-and-tumble coverage at the time. But an era needn't be perfect to mark a substantial improvement in comparison with where we are now.

We must acknowledge genuine benefits associated with other periods that weren't marked by elite control, including the party press, penny press, and modern social media age. The party press helped sharpen competing conceptions of the public good. The penny press democratized news access, sometimes introducing salacious coverage (especially by standards of the time); interspersed entertainment, including personal ads; and occasionally manipulated distribution to lure in advertisers with exaggerated circulation claims. Social media has likewise democratized access and not always, or entirely, in deleterious ways, even if the overall results for our democracy have been deeply problematic. One benefit has been broadening access to readers by those producing news and news-like content.

The tight controls over news media in the era of press professionalization undoubtedly left far too many individuals, especially marginalized groups, such as African Americans, immigrant groups, and others, without adequate venues to challenge mainstream, widely accepted institutional norms and channels to power. Although such groups often had their own print media, tight editorial controls of dominant media forced an insularity that discounted voices of dissension. A candid assessment of media mustn't excessively or entirely condemn social media, failing to appreciate the benign role it has played in encouraging us to listen more attentively to once marginalized voices.

As with electoral systems, no system of news dissemination is perfect. In the United States, having the government determine how news is gathered, processed, and distributed would not only be unseemly; it would be unconstitutional. The press is the only entirely private institution expressly protected in the Constitution's text.[39] Once ratified, the First Electoral Reform Amendment would give political parties special status. Throughout history, political parties and the press have had a synergistic relationship. The best means of ensuring that our press satisfies the interests of our electorate is not to dictate its structures, and certainly not its content. The better approach is to improve the incentives of private institutions that do.

The combined Electoral Reform Amendments have this effect, not only on political parties, but also on news media. They do so by favorably affecting incentives of social media, which has increasingly been the source through which readers access news and news-like content. The amendments will encourage algorithms informing individual customized news feeds that no longer cater to their most divisive, tribal features. In Parliamentary America, social media profitability will more readily correlate with appealing to a range of subscribers with varying political and ideological perspectives. In growing numbers, content generators and subscribers will be less motivated to demean or insult others whose goodwill might prove essential in joining together to pursue common objectives. In this new landscape, voters will often disagree on which of several parties are most appealing yet realize that for whichever party they prefer, gaining power and influence demands working effectively with others holding differing views.

The Parliamentary America news media certainly won't end sharp divisions. But it will reduce incentives to castigate those outside one's tribe. In Presidential America, each of the two major parties tended to be more accommodating of their own more strident voices for fear of alienating base members and to avoid the risk of losing power. By contrast, in Parliamentary America each party and its constituents will come to realize that accommodating views of other parties is essential to effective governance and a productive society.

The feedback loop of media-to-voters-to-politicians-to-media today encourages a sharpening divergence on all fronts, fundamentally undermining any sense of cultural cohesion. Although breaking the loop is essential to fulfilling a promise that future generations might live in a thriving democracy, it needn't entail dictating the processes through which parties form or media thrive. Instead, it demands producing benign incentives that encourage political parties and media to improve themselves. The Electoral Reform Amendments accomplish this goal.

Yogi Berra, baseball's favorite philosopher, is credited with saying, "It's difficult to make predictions, especially about the future."[40] Author William Faulkner famously stated, "The past is never dead. It's not even past."[41]

Despite Berra's characteristically wise admonition, sometimes we have no choice but to make predictions. The best we can do is cover our bases in making them. That requires ensuring our predictions are well grounded, as Faulkner observes, in present experiences too often ascribed to the past.

Many thoughtful commentators have described the crisis we face as a nation, and others have offered up prescriptions concerning how best to improve our constitutional democracy. This book seeks to bridge these contributions with a set of radical reforms, each grounded in past—and present—learning from the experiences of millions of persons across the globe whose nations confronted their own existential challenges and who forged a better, more productive path than the one we are now on.

The future of our constitutional democracy is truly in our hands. We are the Framers.

From "We the People" to "We the Framers"

O say does that star-spangled banner yet wave
O'er the land of the free and the home of the brave?
—Francis Scott Key, "Star Spangled Banner"

I wanna see you be brave.
—Sara Bareilles, "Brave"

As we come to a close, it's appropriate to return to where this book began, perhaps earlier. For several years I've started my course in constitutional law with two questions: Are we in a constitutional crisis? And how would we know?

The pedagogical goal for my first-year law students is the same as it is for you. It's important that our citizenry appreciate that although there are many troubling aspects to our nation's history, culture, and constitutional system, not all of them produce a constitutional crisis. Systems founded upon even deeply problematic moral foundations sometimes function effectively, if egregiously unfairly. Similarly, although there are many improvements we might hope for in our constitutional system, several of which are explored in this book, not all of them will resolve the crisis our nation faces. Solving the crisis demands a careful analysis of its root causes.

The reverence with which many people hold the Framers is often based on a set of understandings filtered through the media or biased histories that bear only a faint resemblance to, or understanding of, the problems they faced or the solutions they devised. No constitution is ever complete. Although the Framers prefaced the Constitution with "We the People," they didn't intend to imply that only those who lived hundreds of years ago had the stature or wisdom to meet the task.

The Framers that are often most relevant didn't meet in Philadelphia in 1787; instead, they fought against Southern secession and added a series of amendments designed to combat racial injustices going back hundreds of years, starting long before the United States emerged as a nation. Those Framers rejected the premises of the Constitution's original Framers, understanding that states must further relinquish sovereignty to ensure that we remain a union and that the national government must play a vital role in protecting our most vulnerable citizens from harms variously imposed or condoned by states. When we extol the genius of the Framers meeting in Philadelphia in the late 1780s, we miss the larger call of our constitutional history.

Over the past several years, many thoughtful people have asked whether I truly believe the ambitious proposals advanced here might be approved. Would members of the House give up whatever powers they hold in a chamber half the size of what the First Electoral Reform Amendment proposes to gain the power to choose the president as set out in the Second Electoral Reform Amendment, even if doing so will end our constitutional crisis? Would citizens give up directly voting for the president and vice president in exchange for empowering leaders of parties more closely matching their personal ideologies to bargain in forging a governing coalition on their behalf?

Consider this thought experiment: As you'll recall, Germany voted in March of 2023 to modify its MMP voting system in response to particular challenges posed by its changing size Bundestag and various voting anomalies. In reforming its system, Germany didn't embrace presidentialism or semi-presidentialism. Imagine you had the power to offer Germany the chance to do just that. You meet with a fair cross section constituting half the Bundestag, and with an equally fair, but smaller, cross section of Germany's electorate. You offer both groups the following deal: For the Bundestag members, you offer to cut the soon-fixed body—630 members—by half, to 315, thereby doubling each member's voting strength, in exchange for the body relinquishing its power to choose the chancellor. To the citizens, you offer to give them the power to vote directly for chancellor, but at the price of giving up the Bundestag's power, based on party proportionality, to choose the chancellor on their behalf through negotiated governing coalitions.

None of us will ever be able to offer those in Germany such a deal. But if we did, I'm confident we'd find few takers. Germany's new electoral system seeks to avoid specific challenges the Bundestag faced, but not to abandon proportionality, coalition governance, and parliamentary design. Parliamentary America doesn't diminish the power and influence of House members. Nor does it diminish the power and influence of American voters. It does the opposite.

The Electoral Reform Amendments don't transform the House of Representatives into the older Bundestag or the one soon to take effect. The proposals advanced here are uniquely American, leaving the presidency in a fixed four-year term, leaving the line of succession intact, and keeping members of the House as incumbents. The proposed regime avoids the central problem Germany faced. The House remains constant in size. Congress may adjust that size with ordinary legislation provided it retains half districted and half party-based seats, and state-level party proportionality. Parliamentary America accepts the inevitable imperfections of a vastly improved—yet far more proportional—system of democratic accountability.

Consider one more thought experiment: Imagine we have Parliamentary America. Would members of the House give that up to restore the present House at half the seats, relinquishing the power to form a governing coalition that chooses the president? Would American voters seek to revert to the Electoral College or perhaps a national popular vote? Again, I'm confident both answers are a resounding no.

Ironically, assuming I'm right might support or challenge the case for Parliamentary America. If the stopping point for saving our democracy is inertia, one might imagine that whether the starting point is where we are or where we should be, it's impossible to enact even the most vital change. I don't believe this, and I hope you don't either. Inertia's a powerful force. But we can overcome it as we have in the past. We can, indeed must, be more hopeful when the future of our democracy is at stake.

Especially in periods of constitutional crisis, "We the People" must become "We the Framers." That was the lesson of the first constitutional crisis when we rejected the premise of the Articles of Confederation that states were the ultimate source of sovereign power. And it was the lesson of the second constitutional crisis when we came to appreciate that ensuring the protections of the most vulnerable of our citizens, newly freed African Americans, could no longer be entrusted to the very states that condoned their servitude, with some continuing to do so even after emancipation.[1]

The transformation from We the People to We the Framers will not end with us. The three Electoral Reform Amendments—transforming the House of Representatives, changing the process for selecting the president, and introducing a viable means of removing a failing president—are necessary to extricate ourselves from the constitutional crisis that we face and to ensure future generations a robust democracy. We must abandon the notion that our constitution's quarter-millennium duration counsels against change.

Returning once more to our world tour, I had the opportunity to visit one of Israel's many ancient ruins, Apollonia National Park, located near Herzliya. The picturesque site, along the Mediterranean shoreline north of Tel Aviv and south of Haifa, conveys the layered history of five separate civilizations, all come and gone—Illyrians, Greeks, Romans, Mamelukes, and Crusaders. While walking the ruins, I tried to imagine the intricate lives of those who called that beautiful seashore site their home over thousands of years. As I did so, I could not stop one recurring thought. I was certain that all of them believed that they, and their descendants, would remain there forever. We humans struggle to appreciate just how fleeting it all is.

If this book conveys a single lesson, please let it be this: Our generation is not inferior to any others, including the original Framers or the Framers of the Reconstruction Amendments. The Greatest Generation was great, and we can be too. Every generation gets some things right and other things profoundly wrong. Rigid insistence on the rightness of the past is no wiser than hubristic confidence that we alone have insights into the future. The greatest check against hubris is testing our insights against the genuine experience of millions upon millions of people, past and present, throughout the world.

The true test of a system's soundness and wisdom isn't its longevity. A system adapted to the needs of diverse nations and peoples is a far stronger signal of wisdom and efficacy than an outlier nation struggling to remain democratic and for which its remarkable longevity is owing to other considerations intertwined, or tightly braided, as William Faulkner recognized,[2] with its always present past.

Change is scary. It demands wisdom and confidence. And yes, it takes bravery.

ACKNOWLEDGMENTS

I owe a tremendous debt of gratitude to those who supported me throughout this project. This book differs from anything I've previously written. While writing it, I have stood on the shoulders of brilliant theorists, incisive political leaders, and poignant writers, all grappling in their own way with the challenges of democracy and how to achieve its highest ideals. Despite a long career as a teacher and scholar, I realized that for this project to succeed, I had to learn to write all over again. I needed to convey the most insightful learning on a wide range of topics and draw upon a variety of disciplines in a manner that would let citizens not only understand sometimes intricate concepts, but also appreciate their importance in the fight to reclaim our democracy. If I've succeeded, it's owing to the support, wisdom, guidance, and encouragement of everyone mentioned here, and, undoubtedly, so many others who in casual conversation, over social media, or through various informal interactions planted the seeds of ideas the origins of which I've forgotten but that have nonetheless germinated in this book.

My colleagues at the University of Maryland Francis King Carey School of Law provided the time and resources to undertake a project that has required four years to bring to fruition. From the initial proposal, to hiring various consultants, to the time required to produce the final manuscript, my deans and colleagues and have provided unerring encouragement and support. Special thanks to Dean Donald Tobin and Dean Renée Hutchins and to Peter Danchin, Deb Eisenberg, Barbara Gontrum, and

Mike Pappas, associate deans, for recognizing the importance of this book and for their willingness to provide me the time and resources to write it.

In addition to those listed above, I am especially indebted to the following colleagues: Richard Boldt, Bob Condlin, Larry Gibson, Leigh Goodmark, Mark Graber, Leslie Henry, Russell McClain, Michael Van Alstine, and Liza Vertinsky. Thanks also to my students both in Constitutional Law and in Law and Economics. Although it's a cliché to say professors learn more from their students than their students from them, that doesn't make it less true. My students have vigorously probed and questioned, making me a better teacher, writer, and thinker. I have benefited from comments at the Maryland Carey Law Legal Theory Workshop and from the Maryland Carey Law Virtual Constitutional Law and Economics Workshop.

Special thanks to Michael Abramowicz, Danielle Allen, Jack Balkin, Brian Bix, E. Elliot Bulmer, Jim Chen, David S. Cohen, Michael Gilbert, Tom Ginsburg, Alon Harel, Melinda Henneberger, Peter Huang, Guha Krishnamurthi, Kathryn Lamp, Mark Lemley, Orly Lobel, Scott Mainwaring, Alexander Morell, Vanessa Otero, Richard Painter, Mike Pappas, Bob Pushaw, Dan Rodriguez, Paul Root Wolpe, Djavad Salehi-Isfahani, Tiago Santos, Jack Santucci, Matthew Shugart, Ilya Somin, Nicolaus Tideman, Robert Tsai, Nina Varsava, Elaine Weiss, and David Wolpe. The members of this group possess a rich assortment of academic backgrounds, disciplinary expertise, and extensive knowledge of democracy in the United States and abroad. Their comments on the proposal, specific chapters, and sometimes complete drafts have helped me immeasurably.

I benefited from insightful comments from faculty and students when presenting this project as part of the University of Nebraska Lane Lecture Series. I also benefited from comments during a virtual presentation to the Baltimore Bar Association.

I am indebted to a wide group of thoughtful readers, old friends and new, who generously helped me improve this book, including by asking for greater clarity and more accessible presentations. Their feedback always furthered the goal of rendering the book suitable to its broad ambition of improving upon public conversations concerning what we must do to ensure our nation successfully emerges from the crisis we face as a thriving democracy: Bruce Brod, Lorre Cuzze, Brandon Draper, Mary Draper, Nancy Herring, Michael Krampner, Roger Machlis, Kenn Moss, Mark Paris, Art Robinson, and Abra Walter.

Securing a literary agent is no small task. Will Weisser brilliantly steered me through the process, helping me translate an inchoate vision into an effective proposal. Matt Carlini at Javelin is a wonderful agent who became a trusted friend. From the start, Laura Davulis and Kait Howard of Johns Hopkins University Press appreciated that this book's ambition is to reach out broadly to our concerned citizenry even as it also aspires to provide something of value to scholars across a variety of disciplines: politics, media studies, sociology, law, history, social psychology, and more. Ezra Rodriguez painstakingly ensured the success of the manuscript and graphics, including the various images. Inksplash, the copyeditor, helped improve expositional clarity; and Juliana McCarthy and Robert Brown, from JHU Press, together helped guide the book through the entire production process.

I benefited greatly from the remarkable assistance of several outstanding research assistants: Ghina Ammar, Katie Aumiller, Hannah Cybart, Meredith Johnston, Anna Manogue, Rachael Morrissey, Jennifer Nigro, Marica Sharashenidze, Elizabeth Stamas, and Catherine Wilkins.

My law school provides truly exceptional library support. Sue McCarty has always gone above and beyond, providing brilliant guidance no matter the project. Jennifer Chapman is beyond dedicated, and her remarkable assistance throughout this specific book project was simply unparalleled. I can truly say that without her constant guidance, this book would not have been possible, and certainly not as well-written. Nathan Robertson has been a source of wisdom and guidance throughout this project. I am grateful to my amazing assistant, Frank Lancaster, not only for his patience and insights, but also for his talent in producing the book's line graphics. A thank-you also to Natalie Anne Jones, who was so helpful in the final stages of this book's production.

Special thanks to my wonderful publicist, Jessica Krakoski, for her ongoing guidance on conveying the book's central ideas across a wide variety of platforms.

Finally, I owe the greatest debt to my family. Without them, I wouldn't have been able to write this book, which in so many ways is about *their* United States of America, one I truly hope they'll continue to love and enjoy. My parents, Herb and Audrey Stearns, passed away prior to the events that motivated me to write this book. My love of the United States and what it aspires to be began with them, and it extends to my own family. Thank you for everything to my wife, Vered, and my wonderful children, Shira, Keren, and Eric. And also to my sister, Wendy Bornstein. The boundless love and support you have all provided me means more than you will ever know.

APPENDIX

The First Electoral Reform Amendment: An Enlarged House of Representatives

Section 1: The membership of the House of Representatives shall be doubled, with half the membership elected in single-member geographical districts and half elected by party, and the full membership shall be based on proportional representation assessed by state.

Section 2: Eligible voters may cast two ballots for their state's House of Representative delegation: the first for a candidate representing their district and the second for a qualifying party representing the state. Unless the Senate alters the qualification threshold pursuant to Section 3, qualifying parties must meet a 5 percent national threshold for seating. Qualified district election winners shall be seated and, to the extent practically feasible, each state's House delegation shall be adjusted to ensure proportionality when the outcomes of both sets of ballots are combined. Congress may alter the total size of the House of Representatives by statute, which shall take effect following an intervening election, provided the House retains equal numbers of district and party seats for each state.

Section 3: The Senate may lower the initial 5 percent party-qualification threshold by simple majority vote provided the new threshold is set in advance of the biennial election prior to the election in which it applies. If eight or more parties meet the party-qualification threshold in an election cycle, the Senate may raise the threshold to a maximum of 10 percent provided that based on the two prior election cycles, doing so would not reduce the number of qualifying parties to fewer than eight.

Section 4: Congress shall have the power to enforce the first two sections of this amendment.

The Second Electoral Reform Amendment: A Parliamentary Presidency

Section 1: Within forty-eight hours of a quadrennial presidential election or subject to a calendaring change pursuant to this amendment, the Senate majority and minority leaders, as determined by Senate rules, shall certify seat totals of all qualifying parties in the House of Representatives. The relative number of seats shall determine the ordering of party negotiations in forming a governing coalition to select from the predetermined party slates for president and vice president. If either Senate leader declines timely certification, or if the Senate leaders certify different results, coalition negotiations may commence when a majority of qualifying House party leaders approve certification by a single leader.

Section 2: A qualifying party holding a majority of House of Representative seats shall have its preselected slate for president and vice president fill those offices. In the absence of a majority party in the House, the leader of the party with a plurality of seats shall commence negotiations with other qualifying party leaders. Such leaders shall be authorized to commit their party delegations in these negotiations. If the plurality party leader fails to negotiate a majority coalition, then the leader of the party holding the next highest number of seats shall be given the opportunity to negotiate a majority coalition, and this process shall continue until a majority coalition forms or until up to five qualifying party leaders, in descending order of party seats, fail do so.

Section 3: The party leading a successful coalition negotiation shall have its preselected slate of candidates serve as president and vice president. If no party leader forms a majority coalition, the plurality party's preselected slate shall serve as president and vice president. The president and vice president shall each serve a four-year term, unless the term is otherwise ended.

Section 4: Congress may change the dates of election, of swearing in House members, and of swearing in the president and vice president; and the House of Representatives may change the date for swearing in members to facilitate coalition negotiations. Other than for the first presidential election governed by this amendment, calendar changes shall take effect following one biennial election cycle after approval and shall remain in effect until changed pursuant to this amendment.

Section 5: The House may adjust the timing of negotiations, subject to the following conditions: Each qualifying party leader must be offered equal time, but no less than one week, to negotiate a majority coalition until a majority coalition forms, and party leaders may cede time to other leaders during negotiations. In the absence of a House resolution altering this schedule, up to five party leaders shall be granted two weeks in succession to engage in coalition negotiations, with the process ending when leaders of all parties forming a majority coalition certify that result to the sitting vice president. Coalition negotiations shall be self-executing.

Section 6: Rules of presidential succession shall remain, subject to statutory revision for all but the vice president. Other than empowering qualifying party leaders to commit their delegations in coalition negotiations, this amendment does not affect internal rules of party discipline. Parties possess rights of association and may choose how they produce slates for the offices of president and vice president, candidates for the Senate and

House districts, party lists for selection based on each state's proportionality vote, and party leaders for facilitating House coalition negotiations.

Section 7: The terms of this amendment shall be self-executing.

The Third Electoral Reform Amendment: No-Confidence Motions for Presidential Removal

Section 1: A vote of conscience of 60 percent of the full membership of the House of Representatives based on a finding of maladministration shall remove the president from office.

Section 2: Maladministration may include mismanagement of federal resources, such as financial or physical resources, offices, or perks, for purely personal or partisan advantage; systematic ineffectiveness in working with cabinet members or other officials, state and federal; systematic embarrassment on behalf of the nation in conducting international affairs; a documented pattern of conveying misinformation to the public or in official communications; and other behaviors that produce widening distrust in the president's ability or willingness to govern effectively or to effectuate the office's constitutional responsibilities. This listing is not intended to be exhaustive.

A no-confidence motion need not allege criminal conduct, and violations of a federal or state criminal law do not necessarily demonstrate maladministration. This amendment shall have no bearing on the authority of law enforcement to pursue criminal charges against a president or other government official during or after an administration, or on other lawful methods of presidential removal.

Section 3: Following an investigation subject to governing rules in the House of Representatives, a no-confidence motion shall be voted upon when proffered by the leadership of no fewer than two qualifying parties as defined in the First Electoral Reform Amendment, with at least one party a member of the original

governing coalition that selected the sitting president, or by petition of rank-and-file members composed or no less than
15 percent of the full House membership and with at least
5 percent of the full House membership as part of the original
governing coalition that selected the sitting president. Neither
the sponsors of a no-confidence motion nor the vote on such a
motion may be in secret.

Section 4: A successful no-confidence vote shall immediately remove the president from office, and a vote of no confidence shall
not prevent the president from seeking future elective office, including the presidency.

Section 5: The provisions of this amendment shall be self-
executing.

NOTES

Introduction

1 "You Can't Handle the Truth!—*A Few Good Men* (7/8) Movie CLIP (1992) HD," Movieclips, October 21, 2012, video, 0:15, https://www.youtube.com /watch?v=9FnO3igOkOk.

Chapter 1. The Third Constitutional Crisis

1 Ezra Klein, *Why We're Polarized* (London: Profile Books, 2020); Anne Applebaum, *Twilight of Democracy: The Seductive Lure of Authoritarianism* (New York: Doubleday, 2020); Steven Levitsky and Daniel Ziblatt, *How Democracies Die* (New York: Crown, 2018); Mark A. Graber, Sanford Levinson, and Mark Tushnet, eds., *Constitutional Democracy in Crisis?* (Oxford: Oxford University Press, 2018).

2 Maxwell L. Stearns, Todd J. Zywicki, and Thomas J. Miceli, *Law and Economics: Private and Public* (St. Paul, MN: West Academic, 2018), 499–574.

3 *The Federalist Papers*, no. 10, ed. Lawrence Goldman (Oxford: Oxford University Press, 2008): 48–55 (James Madison); *Federalist*, no. 54, 269–73 (Alexander Hamilton or James Madison); *Federalist*, no. 55, 273–78 (Alexander Hamilton or James Madison); Bond v. United States, 564 U.S. 211, 221–22 (2011); United States v. Lopez, 514 U.S. 549, 576–77 (1995).

4 Edward G. Carmines and Matthew Fowler, "The Temptation of Executive Authority: How Increased Polarization and the Decline in Legislative Capacity Have Contributed to the Expansion of Presidential Power," *Indiana Journal of Global Legal Studies* 24, no. 2 (2017): 369–98; Exec. Order No. 14076, 87 Fed. Reg. 42,053 (July 13, 2022) (Protecting Access to Reproductive Healthcare Services); Exec. Order No. 14079, 87 Fed. Reg.

49,505 (Aug. 3, 2022) (Securing Access to Reproductive and Other Health-care Services).

5 Klein, *Why We're Polarized*; Applebaum, *Twilight of Democracy*; Levitsky and Ziblatt, *How Democracies Die*; Graber, Levinson, and Tushnet, *Constitutional Democracy in Crisis?*

6 Threatened to be doesn't mean proved to be. "The Ross Perot Myth," FiveThirtyEight, accessed September 12, 2022, https://fivethirtyeight.com /videos/the-ross-perot-myth/.

7 "Toward a More Responsible Two-Party System: A Report of the Committee on Political Parties," *American Political Science Review* 44, no. 3 (Supplement) (1950): 1–99; Chester J. Pach, Jr., "Dwight D. Eisenhower: Campaigns and Elections," *University of Virginia Miller Center*, accessed October 19, 2021, https://millercenter.org/president/eisenhower/campaigns-and -elections.

8 David Daley, *Ratf**cked: Why Your Vote Doesn't Count* (New York: Liveright Publishing Corporation, 2017).

9 Mason Walker and Katerina Eva Matsa, *News Consumption Across Social Media in 2021*, Pew Research Center, September 20, 2021, https://www .pewresearch.org/journalism/2021/09/20/news-consumption-across-social -media-in-2021/.

10 Kyle Langvardt, "Regulating Online Content Moderation," *Georgia Law Journal* 106 (2018), 1373 (describing social media platforms of "news media conduits").

11 Steve Rathje, Jay J. Van Bavel, and Sander van der Linden, "Out-Group Animosity Drives Engagement on Social Media," *Proceedings of the National Academy of Sciences* 118, no. 26 (June 29, 2021): e2024292118, https://doi.org /10.1073/pnas.2024292118; Elizabeth Dwoskin, "Misinformation on Facebook Got Six Times More Clicks than Factual News during the 2020 Election, Study Says," *Washington Post*, September 4, 2021, https://www .washingtonpost.com/technology/2021/09/03/facebook-misinformation-nyu -study/.

12 *Federalist*, no. 10, 48–55 (James Madison).

13 Max Farrand, ed., *The Records of the Federal Convention of 1787* (New Haven: Yale University Press, 1911), 428.

14 Elvin T. Lim, *The Lovers' Quarrel: The Two Foundings and American Political Development* (New York: Oxford University Press, 2014), 1–59.

15 Philip A. Klinkner and Rogers M Smith, *The Unsteady March* (Chicago: University of Chicago Press, 1999), 83–105; Michael Klarman, *From Jim Crow to Civil Rights* (Oxford: Oxford University Press, 2004), 40–41, 72–75, 344–442.

16 "Voting Laws Roundup: October 2021," Brennan Center for Justice, October 4, 2021, https://www.brennancenter.org/our-work/research-reports /voting-laws-roundup-october-2021.

17 "The Constitution Drafting Project," National Constitution Center, accessed October 20, 2021, https://constitutioncenter.org/debate/special -projects/constitution-drafting-project; Sanford Levinson, *Our Undemocratic Constitution: Where the Constitution Goes Wrong (and How We the People Can Correct It)* (New York: Oxford University Press, 2006); Lee Drutman, *Breaking the Two-Party Doom Loop: The Case for Multiparty Democracy in America* (New York: Oxford University Press, 2020); Jedediah Britton-Purdy, "The Constitutional Flaw That's Killing American Democracy," *The Atlantic*, August 28, 2022, https://www.theatlantic.com/ideas/archive/2022 /08/framers-constitution-democracy/671155/; "Our Reforms," FairVote, accessed September 13, 2022, https://fairvote.org/our-reforms/.

18 Stearns, Zywicki, and Miceli, *Law and Economics* 499–655.

19 "To James Madison from Thomas Jefferson, 6 September 1789," *Founders Online*, National Archives, https://founders.archives.gov/documents /Madison/01-12-02-0248 ("Every constitution then, & every law, naturally expires at the end of 19 years."); Stephen Holmes, *Passions and Constraint: On the Theory of Liberal Democracy* (Chicago: University of Chicago Press, 1995), 152–58.

20 Zachary Elkins, Tom Ginsburg, and James Melton, *The Endurance of National Constitutions* (New York: Cambridge University Press, 2009), 129–31.

21 Pew Research Center, *The Partisan Divide on Political Values Grows Even Wider*, October 5, 2017, https://www.pewresearch.org/politics/2017/10/05 /the-partisan-divide-on-political-values-grows-even-wider/; Klein, *Why We're Polarized*.

22 Daley, *Ratf**cked*.

23 "The Battle of Wits," *The Princess Bride*, directed by Rob Reiner (1987; Los Angeles, CA: 20th Century Fox), film, 16:24.

24 Levitsky and Ziblatt, *How Democracies Die*.

25 Stearns, Zywicki, and Miceli, *Law and Economics*, 516; Harold Demsetz, "Information and Efficiency," *Journal of Law and Economics* 12, no. 1 (1969): 1–22.

26 Arend Lijphart, *Patterns of Democracy: Government Forms and Performance in Thirty-Six Countries*, 2nd ed. (New Haven: Yale University Press, 2012); Christopher J. Anderson and Christine A. Guillory, "Political Institutions and Satisfaction with Democracy: A Cross-National Analysis of Consensus and Majoritarian Systems," *American Political Science Review* 91, no. 1 (1997): 66–81.

27 Russell J. Dalton, *Political Realignment: Economics, Culture, and Electoral Change* (Oxford: Oxford University Press, 2018).

28 Norman Schofield and Itai Sened, *Multiparty Democracy: Elections and Legislative Politics* (New York: Cambridge University Press, 2006).

Chapter 2. The Third-Party Dilemma

1 "What Is the Electoral College?," *National Archives*, December 23, 2019, https://www.archives.gov/electoral-college/about.

2 "Distribution of Electoral Votes," *National Archives*, March 6, 2020, https:// www.archives.gov/electoral-college/allocation; J. Miles Coleman, "The Electoral College: Maine and Nebraska's Crucial Battleground Votes," *University of Virginia Center for Politics*, January 9, 2020, https://centerforpolitics .org/crystalball/articles/the-electoral-college-maine-and-nebraskas-crucial -battleground-votes/.

3 "2000 Electoral College Results," *National Archives*, November 27, 2019, https://www.archives.gov/electoral-college/2000.

4 Maurice Duverger, *Political Parties: Their Organization and Activity in the Modern State*, trans. Barbara North and Robert North (London: Methuen, 1964), 217.

5 Matthew S. Shugart and Rein Taagepera, *Votes from Seats: Logical Models of Electoral Systems* (Cambridge: Cambridge University Press, 2017), 99–124 (explaining that reliance on Duverger's Law is often misplaced and the greater predictive force of the seat-product model, which correlates the effective number of parties in elections and legislatures to a formula based upon the number of districts and seats per district).

6 David Freedlander, "One Year in Washington," *New York Magazine*, January 6, 2020, https://nymag.com/intelligencer/2020/01/aoc-first-year-in -washington.html.

7 Steven Greenhouse, "The 2000 Campaign: The Green Party; Nader, in Harlem, Attacks Gore and Bush with Gusto," *New York Times*, November 7, 2000, https://www.nytimes.com/2000/11/07/us/2000-campaign-green -party-nader-harlem-attacks-gore-bush-with-gusto.html.

8 Bush v. Gore, 531 U.S. 98 (2000).

9 Real Time with Bill Maher, "Real Time with Bill Maher—Nader Moment," YouTube Video, 0:51, March 6, 2012, https://www.youtube.com/watch?v =EI1Y_rRPy40. The interview took place on July 30, 2004.

10 Richard L. Smith, "A Statistical Assessment of Buchanan's Vote in Palm Beach County," *Statistical Science* 17, no. 4 (2002): 441–57.

11 CNN, "NAFTA 20th ANNIV—Perot Giant Sucking Sound," YouTube Video, 0:34, July 21, 2016, https://www.youtube.com/watch?v=W3LvZAZ -HV4.

12 "The Ross Perot Myth," FiveThirtyEight, accessed September 15, 2022, https://fivethirtyeight.com/videos/the-ross-perot-myth/.

13 PBS NewsHour, "Ronald Reagan on 'There You Go Again,' Other Notable Debate Moments," YouTube Video, 9:46, February 3, 2011, https://www .youtube.com/watch?v=T43EzCUtSwQ.

14 PBS NewsHour, "Carter vs. Reagan: The Second 1980 Presidential Debate," YouTube Video, 1:33:46, September 26, 2020, https://www.youtube.com /watch?v=3HB2sz4bAbU.

15 "Reagan Buries Carter in a Landslide," in *CQ Almanac 1980*, 36th ed. (Washington, DC: Congressional Quarterly, 1981), 3-B–5-B, https://library .cqpress.com/cqalmanac/document.php?id=cqal80-860-25879-1173496.

16 Paul R. Abramson, John H. Aldrich, Phil Paolino, and David W. Rohde, "Third-Party and Independent Candidates in American Politics: Wallace, Anderson, and Perot," *Political Science Quarterly* 100, no. 3 (1995): 349–67; Neal Allen and Brian J. Brox, "The Roots of Third Party Voting: The 2000 Nader Campaign in Historical Perspective," *Party Politics* 11, no. 5 (2005): 623–37.

17 Barbara Sprunt, "GOP Ousts Cheney from Leadership over Her Criticism of Trump," *NPR*, May 12, 2021, https://www.npr.org/2021/05/12 /995072539/gop-poised-to-oust-cheney-from-leadership-over-her-criticism -of-trump.

18 Bob Woodward and Robert Costa, *Peril* (New York: Simon & Schuster, 2021).

19 "About," *Select Committee to Investigate the January 6th Attack on the United States Capitol*, accessed September 21, 2022, https://january6th.house.gov /about; Stephen P. Mulligan, Jennifer K. Elsea, Peter G. Berris, and Michael A. Foster, "The Mar-a-Lago Search Warrant: A Legal Introduc- tion," *Congressional Research Services: Legal Sidebar* (August 29, 2022), https://crsreports.congress.gov/product/pdf/LSB/LSB10810.

20 "Factbox: The Legal Troubles of Former US President Donald Trump," Reuters, August 24, 2023, https://www.reuters.com/legal/government /legal-troubles-former-us-president-donald-trump-2023-08-24/; Jonah E. Bromwich, Ben Protess, William K. Rashbaum, and Michael Gold, "The Case Against Donald Trump: What Comes Next?," *New York Times*, April 5, 2023, https://www.nytimes.com/article/trump-indictment-criminal-charges .html.

21 Benjamin Weiser, Lola Fadula, and Kate Christobek, "Donald Trump Sexually Abused and Defamed E. Jean Carroll, Jury Finds," *New York Times*, May 9, 2023, https://www.nytimes.com/2023/05/09/nyregion/trump-carroll-trial-sexual-abuse-defamation.html.

22 David Jolly, Christine Todd Whitman, and Andrew Yang, "Opinion: Most Third Parties Have Failed. Here's Why Ours Won't," *Washington Post*, July 27, 2022, https://www.washingtonpost.com/opinions/2022/07/27/forward-party-new-centrist-third/; "Why Forward?," *Forward Party*, accessed September 22, 2022, https://www.forwardparty.com/whyforward; Ariel Edwards-Levy, "CNN Poll: Most Voters Say Neither Republican nor Democratic Congressional Candidates Have the Right Priorities," *CNN*, July 19, 2022, https://www.cnn.com/2022/07/19/politics/cnn-poll-midterms/index.html.

23 Federal Election Commission, *Federal Elections 2016: Election Results for the U.S. President, the U.S. Senate and the U.S. House of Representatives*, December 2017, https://www.fec.gov/resources/cms-content/documents/federalelections2016.pdf.

24 Davis Wasserman, Sophie Andrews, Leo Saenger, Lev Cohen, Ally Finn, and Griff Tatarsky, "2020 National Popular Vote Tracker," *Cook Political Report*, accessed May 24, 2021, https://cookpolitical.com/2020-national-popular-vote-tracker; "2020 Electoral College Results," U.S. National Archives and Records Administration, last reviewed April 16, 2021, https://www.archives.gov/electoral-college/2020.

25 Matthew Yglesias, "Progressives Don't Love Joe Biden, But They're Learning to Love His Agenda," *Vox*, July 18, 2020, https://www.vox.com/21322478/joe-biden-overton-window-bidenism.

26 Both the Trump and Biden administrations' notable legislative successes resulted from party-line votes. For Trump, the largest legislative victory was the Tax Cuts and Jobs Act. Tax Cuts and Jobs Act of 2017, Pub. L. No. 115-97, 131 Stat. 2054 (codified in scattered sections of 26 U.S.C.). For Biden, notable legislative actions include the American Rescue Plan and the Inflation Reduction Act. American Rescue Plan, Pub. L. No. 117-2, 135 Stat. 4 (codified in scattered sections of 15 U.S.C., 26 U.S.C. & 42 U.S.C.); Inflation Reduction Act, Pub. L. No. 117-169 (2022). When legislation proved impossible, the Trump and Biden administrations often resorted to executive orders, more frequently than their predecessors. The averages per year in office for President Biden and his three predecessors are George W. Bush (36); Barack Obama (35); Donald Trump (55); Joe Biden (51, as of March 6, 2023). "Executive Orders," *American Presidency Project*, accessed March 6, 2022, https://www.presidency.ucsb.edu/statistics/data/executive-orders.

27 Dave Roos, "5 Presidents Who Lost the Popular Vote but Won the Election," *History*, November 2, 2020, https://www.history.com/news/presidents -electoral-college-popular-vote. The five presidents are John Quincy Adams (1824); Rutherford B. Hayes (1876); Benjamin Harrison (1888); George W. Bush (2000); and Donald Trump (2016).

28 Justin Wm. Moyer, "#HillarySoQualified: Pro-Clinton Hashtag Goes Wrong Fast," *Washington Post*, April 7, 2016, https://www.washingtonpost .com/news/morning-mix/wp/2016/04/07/hillarysoqualified-pro-clinton -hashtag-goes-wrong-fast/; Susan Milligan, "Poll: Millennials Would Settle for Clinton," *U.S. News and World Report*, April 25, 2016, https://www .usnews.com/news/articles/2016-04-25/millennials-would-settle-for-hillary -clinton-harvard-poll-shows.

29 Anthony Downs, *An Economic Theory of Democracy* (New York: Harper and Brothers, 1957).

30 Chester J. Pach, Jr., "Dwight D. Eisenhower: Campaigns and Elections," *University of Virginia Miller Center*, accessed May 24, 2021, https:// millercenter.org/president/eisenhower/campaigns-and-elections.

31 Frank Bruni, "The 2000 Campaign: The Gun Issue; Gore and Bush Clash Further on Firearms," *New York Times*, May 6, 2000, A8; James Flanigan, "Gore, Bush: Two Different Futures for the Economy," *Los Angeles Times*, October 8, 2000, https://www.latimes.com/archives/la-xpm-2000-oct-08-fi -33242-story.html; "Comparing Al Gore and George W. Bush's Military Agendas," *Frontline*, accessed September 22, 2022, https://www.pbs.org /wgbh/pages/frontline/shows/future/agenda/.

32 Pew Research Center, *The Partisan Divide on Political Values Grows Even Wider*, October 5, 2017, https://www.pewresearch.org/politics/2017/10/05 /the-partisan-divide-on-political-values-grows-even-wider/.

33 Lee Drutman, "Political Divisions in 2016 and Beyond: Tensions Between and Within the Two Parties," *Democracy Fund Voter Study Group*, June 2017, https://www.voterstudygroup.org/publication/political-divisions-in-2016 -and-beyond; Shawn Treier and D. Sunshine Hillygus, "The Nature of Political Ideology in the Contemporary Electorate," *Public Opinion Quarterly* 73, no. 4 (2009): 679–703; Gary Miller and Norman Schofield, "The Transformation of the Republican and Democratic Party Coalitions in the U.S.," *Perspectives on Politics* 6, no. 3 (2008): 433–50.

34 Thomas M. Holbrook and Scott D. McClurg, "The Mobilization of Core Supporters: Campaigns, Turnout, and Electoral Composition in the United States Presidential Elections," *American Journal of Political Science* 49, no. 4 (2005): 689–703; Matthew Yglesias, "The Debate Over Swing Voters Versus Mobilizing the Base, Explained," *Vox*, September 11, 2019, https://www.vox

.com/2019/9/11/20856802/swing-voters-base-democrats-trump-2020
-election.

35 Stuart Anderson, "A Review of Trump Immigration Policy," *Forbes*,
    August 26, 2020, https://www.forbes.com/sites/stuartanderson/2020/08/26
    /fact-check-and-review-of-trump-immigration-policy/?sh=4f69115556c0;
    Jim Key, "Three Years into his Presidency, What's the Impact of Trump's
    Anti-Muslim Actions?," *USC Dornsife Magazine*, January 15, 2020,
    https://dornsife.usc.edu/news/stories/3147/three-years-into-his-presidency
    -whats-the-impact-of-trumps-anti/; Katie Rogers, Lara Jakes, and Ana
    Swanson, "Trump Defends Using 'Chinese Virus' Label, Ignoring Growing
    Criticism," *New York Times*, March 18, 2020, https://www.nytimes.com
    /2020/03/18/us/politics/china-virus.html; Jason Lange, "Trump Wins
    Backing of Largest U.S. Police Union as he Touts 'Law and Order'," *Reuters*,
    September 3, 2020, https://www.reuters.com/article/us-usa-election-law
    -enforcement/trump-wins-backing-of-largest-u-s-police-union-as-he-touts
    -law-and-order-idUSKBN25V22V; Michael D. Shear, "Jewish Trump Staff
    Silent on His Defense of Rally with Anti-Semitic Marchers," *New York
    Times*, August 16, 2017, https://www.nytimes.com/2017/08/16/us/politics
    /trump-jewish-neo-nazi-jared-kushner-ivanka.html.

36 Eliza Collins, "Trump: I Consult Myself on Foreign Policy," *Politico*, March 16,
    2016, https://www.politico.com/blogs/2016-gop-primary-live-updates-and
    -results/2016/03/trump-foreign-policy-adviser-220853; Yoni Appelbaum,
    "'I Alone Can Fix It,'" *Atlantic*, July 21, 2016, https://www.theatlantic.com
    /politics/archive/2016/07/trump-rnc-speech-alone-fix-it/492557/.

Chapter 3. Constitutional Gridlock

1 John Quincy Adams Diary 9, 22 August 1784, in *The Diaries of John Quincy
   Adams: A Digital Collection*, (Boston, Mass.: Massachusetts Historical
   Society, 2004), page 38 [electronic edition], https://www.masshist.org
   /jqadiaries/php/doc?id=jqad09_38.

2 *The Adams-Jefferson Letters: The Complete Correspondence between Thomas
   Jefferson and Abigail and John Adams*, ed. Lester J. Cappon (Chapel Hill, NC:
   University of North Carolina Press, 1959).

3 Sidney M. Milkis, *Political Parties and Constitutional Government* (Baltimore: Johns Hopkins University Press, 1999); Bruce Ackerman, *The Failure
   of the Founding Fathers* (Cambridge, MA: Harvard University Press, 2005).
   The United States has the oldest continuing national constitution. Massachusetts has the oldest continuing state constitution. "John Adams & the
   Massachusetts Constitution," Massachusetts Court System, accessed

October 5, 2022, https://www.mass.gov/guides/john-adams-the
-massachusetts-constitution.

4   The complete list: John Quincy Adams, 1824; Rutherford B. Hayes, 1876;
Benjamin Harrison, 1888, George W. Bush, 2000; and Donald Trump,
2016. Dave Roos, "5 Presidents Who Lost the Popular Vote but Won the
Election," *History*, July 23, 2020, https://www.history.com/news/presidents
-electoral-college-popular-vote.

5   Sidney M. Milkis and Michael Nelson, *The American Presidency: Origins and
Development, 1776–2018*, 7th ed. (Thousand Oaks, CA: CQ Press, 2016),
72–75. In the 1792 election, Governor George Clinton ran unsuccessfully
against John Adams for vice president.

6   From Alexander Hamilton to James A. Bayard, 16 January 1801, Hamilton
Papers, Founders Online, National Archives, Washington, DC, https://
founders.archives.gov/documents/Hamilton/01-25-02-0169.

7   "Alexander Hamilton," featuring Leslie Odom Jr., MP3 audio, track 1 on
Lin-Manuel Miranda, *Hamilton: An American Musical (Original Broadway
Cast Recording)*, Atlantic, 2015.

8   U.S. Const., amend. 12, sec. 4 (presidential impeachment clause).

9   The election of 1864, with Abraham Lincoln and Andrew Johnson succeed-
ing under the National Union Party name, is the exception proving the rule.
Eric Foner, *The Fiery Trial: Abraham Lincoln and American Slavery* (New
York: W. W. Norton, 2010), 298–302.

10 Andrew Johnson was impeached in 1868 but not convicted; Richard Nixon
resigned before he could be impeached in 1974; Bill Clinton was impeached
in 1998 but not convicted; and Donald Trump was impeached twice, once in
2019 and again in 2021, and not convicted either time. Milkis and Nelson,
The American Presidency, 195–97, 380, 449–50; Nicholas Fandos and
Michael D. Shear, "Trump Impeached for Abuse of Power and Obstruction
of Congress," *New York Times*, December 18, 2019, https://www.nytimes
.com/2019/12/18/us/politics/trump-impeached.html; Weiyi Cai, "A
Step-by-Step Guide to the Second Impeachment of Donald J. Trump," *New
York Times*, February 13, 2021, https://www.nytimes.com/interactive/2021
/02/08/us/politics/trump-second-impeachment-timeline.html.

11 Donald Ratcliffe, *The One-Party Presidential Contest: Adams, Jackson, and
1824's Five-Horse Race* (Lawrence, KS: University Press of Kansas, 2021).

12 Peter H. Argersinger, "'A Place on the Ballot': Fusion Politics and Antifu-
sion Laws," *American Historical Review* 85, no. 2 (1980): 287–306.

13 Timmons v. Twin Cities Area New Party, 520 U.S. 351, 369–70 (1997).

14 *Timmons*, 520 U.S. at 370 (Stevens, J., dissenting); *id.* at 382 (Souter, J.,
dissenting).

15 Milkis and Nelson, *The American Presidency*, 132, 137; Donald A. Cole, *Martin Van Buren and the American Political System* (Princeton, NJ: Princeton University Press, 1984), 147–48; Maurice G. Baxter, *Henry Clay and the American System* (Lexington, KY: University Press of Kentucky, 1995), 134–43.

16 Lynn Hudson Parsons, *The Birth of Modern Politics: Andrew Jackson, John Quincy Adams, and the Election of 1828* (New York: Oxford University Press, 2009), xii, 142–45, 151, 164–65.

17 Michael F. Holt, *The Rise and Fall of the American Whig Party: Jacksonian Politics and the Onset of the Civil War* (Oxford: Oxford University Press, 1999), 142.

18 Wood v. Broom, 287 U.S. 1, 8 (1932).

19 2 U.S.C. § 2c.

20 Hugh T. Lovin, "The Fall of Farmer-Labor Parties, 1936-1938," *Pacific Northwest Quarterly* 62, no. 1 (January 1971): 16–26.

21 Lee Drutman, *Breaking the Two-Party Doom Loop* (New York: Oxford University Press, 2020), 184–85 (proposing five-member congressional districts, a variation on at-large voting) and 240–43 (discussing 1842 election).

22 John H. Aldrich, *Why Parties? The Origin and Transformation of Political Parties in America* (Chicago: University of Chicago Press, 1995), 283; John H. Aldrich, *Why Parties? A Second Look* (Chicago: University of Chicago Press, 2021), 276.

23 Holt, *Rise and Fall of the American Whig Party*, 1–32.

24 Lincoln emerged the Condorcet winner, meaning an option that absent a majority winner, defeats all others in pairwise comparisons. Maxwell L. Stearns, Todd J. Zywicki, and Thomas J. Miceli, *Law and Economics: Private and Public* (St. Paul, MN: West Academic, 2009), 508.

25 Dred Scott v. Sandford, 60 U.S. 393 (1857).

26 White House, "Remarks by President Biden at Signing of Juneteenth National Independence Day Act," June 17, 2021, https://www.whitehouse .gov/briefing-room/speeches-remarks/2021/06/17/remarks-by-president -biden-at-signing-of-the-juneteenth-national-independence-day-act/.

27 Charles W. Calhoun, *The Presidency of Ulysses S. Grant* (Lawrence, KS: University Press of Kansas, 2017); Ron Chernow, *Grant* (New York: Penguin Books, 2017), 613–860.

28 See, e.g., Constitution of the Republic of South Africa, 1996, ch. 2, §§ 26, 27. ("Everyone has the right to access to adequate housing . . . Everyone has the right to have access to . . . sufficient food and water"); Daniel Schneider, "The Constitutional Right to Housing in South Africa: The Government of

the Republic of South Africa v. Irene Grootboom," *International Journal of Civil Society Law* 2, no. 2 (April 2004): 45–62.

29 Eric Foner, *Forever Free: The Story of Emancipation and Reconstruction* (New York: Vintage Books, 2005), 148.

30 Shelby Cnty. v. Holder, 570 U.S. 529, 560 (2013) (Ginsburg, J., dissenting).

31 Rogers v. Lodge. 458 U.S. 613, 616–22 (1982).

32 City of Mobile v. Bolden, 446 U.S. 55, 65–66 (1980), *rev'd* by 1982 Amendments to the Voting Rights Act, Pub. L. 97-205, 96 Stat. 131 (1982) (codified at 52 U.S.C. § 10301).

33 Roy A. McKenzie and Ronald A. Krauss, "Section 2 of the Voting Rights Act: An Analysis of the 1982 Amendment," *Harvard Civil Rights–Civil Liberties Law Review* 19, no. 1 (Winter 1984): 155–92; William E. Schmidt, "South Abandoning At-Large Voting," *New York Times*, May 30, 1984, https://www.nytimes.com/1984/05/30/us/south-abandoning-at-large-voting .html.

34 Mary McGrory, "Voting Rights Make Strange Bedfellows," *Washington Post*, May 9, 1982, D1.

35 Ismail K. White and Chryl N. Laird, *Steadfast Democrats: How Social Forces Shape Black Political Behavior* (Princeton, NJ: Princeton University Press, 2020).

36 David Daley, *Ratf**ked: Why Your Vote Doesn't Count* (New York: Liveright Publishing Corp., 2017).

37 Aldrich, *Why Parties?*; Aldrich, *Why Parties? A Second Look.*

38 Nick Gass, "Jeb Bush: Trump 'Trying to Insult His Way to the Presidency,'" *Politico*, September 3, 2015, https://www.politico.com/story/2015/09/jeb -bush-donald-trump-2016-fight-insults-213300; David Smith, "Republicans Fear Trump's Parade of Insults Might Help Him Cost the Election," *Guardian*, November 1, 2016, https://www.theguardian.com/us-news/2016 /nov/01/donald-trump-insults-us-election-result-republicans-gop.

39 Bob Phillips, *Phillips' Treasury of Humorous Quotations* (Carol Stream, IL: Tyndale House, 2004), 67.

40 John H. Aldrich, "Political Parties in a Critical Era," *American Politics Quarterly* 27, no. 1 (Jan. 1999): 21, 30; Aldrich, *Why Parties? A Second Look.*

41 For example, see Balsam v. Sec'y of N.J., 607 F. App'x 177, 183 (3d Cir. 2015), *cert denied* in Balsam v. Guadagno, 577 U.S. 870 (2015) (holding that New Jersey's closed primary system for nominating political party candidates did not violate the First and Fourteenth Amendments); Clingman v. Beaver, 544 U.S 581 (2005) (rejecting a challenge by the Libertarian Party of Oklahoma to Oklahoma's semi-closed primary system). For an unusual case rejecting a state Republican Party's First Amendment association claim, see *Washington State Grange v. Washington State Republican Party*, 552 U.S. 442 (2007) (sustaining

against facial challenge a Washington State primary voting method allowing candidates to self-identify party affiliation, without party endorsement, culminating in a runoff between the top two candidates regardless of party). That case, with Justice Thomas joined in his majority opinion by liberal Justices Stevens, Souter, Ginsburg, and Breyer, none of whom remain on the Court, played a central role in the Alaska Supreme Court decision, *Kohlhaas v. State of Alaska*, 518 P.3d 1095 (Alaska 2022), which sustained that state's open primary and ranked-choice voting scheme. Chapter 10 discusses a special Alaska election pursuant to that scheme. See pp. 261–63.

42 Azi Paybarah, "Here's Where Trump's Endorsement Record Stands So Far," *New York Times*, May 24, 2022, https://www.nytimes.com/2022/05/24/us /politics/trump-endorsements-primary-elections.html.

43 "The Birth of the Gerrymander," *Massachusetts Historical Society*, September 2008, https://www.masshist.org/object-of-the-month/objects/the-birth -of-the-gerrymander-2008-09-01.

44 Today, the breakdown is as follows: twenty-eight by state legislature; seven by advisory body (subject to approval by the legislature); four by independent commission; and five by political appointee or politician commission (generally by the controlling party). Alaska, Wyoming, North Dakota, South Dakota, Vermont, and Delaware do not have House redistricting procedures because each state comprises a single congressional district. Michael Li, Gabriella Limón, and Julia Kirschenbaum, "Who Draws the Maps?," *Brennan Center for Justice*, September 16, 2021, https://www .brennancenter.org/our-work/research-reports/who-draws-maps-0.

45 Shaw v. Reno, 509 U.S. 630, 635 (1993).

46 Bush v. Vera, 517 U.S. 952, 1003 (1996) (Stevens, J., dissenting) ("The great irony, of course, is that by requiring the State to place the majority-minority district in a particular place and with a particular shape, the district may stand out as a stark, placid island in a sea of oddly shaped majority-white neighbors.").

47 Baker v. Carr, 369 U.S. 186 (1962); Reynolds v. Sims, 377 U.S. 533 (1964).

48 Davis v. Bandemer, 478 U.S. 109 (1986).

49 Vieth v. Jubelirer, 541 U.S. 267, 315–17 (2004) (Kennedy, J., concurring in the judgment); Gill v. Whitford, 138 S. Ct. 1916 (2018).

50 Rucho v. Common Cause, 139 S. Ct. 2484 (2019).

51 Daley, *Ratf**ked*.

52 "'Gerrymandering on Steroids': How Republicans Stacked the Nation's Statehouses," WBUR, July 19, 2016, https://www.wbur.org/hereandnow /2016/07/19/gerrymandering-republicans-redmap.

Chapter 4. The End of Trust

1 Claudia Deane, Kim Parker, and John Gramlich, "A Year of U.S. Public Opinion on the Coronavirus Pandemic," Pew Research Center, March 5, 2021, https://www.pewresearch.org/2021/03/05/a-year-of-u-s-public -opinion-on-the-coronavirus-pandemic/; Ashley Parker, Josh Dawsey, Matt Viser, and Michael Scherer, "Trump's Erratic Behavior and Failure on Coronavirus Doomed His Reelection," *Washington Post*, November 7, 2020, https://www.washingtonpost.com/elections/interactive/2020/trump -pandemic-coronavirus-election/.

2 Meridith McGraw, "Trump's Election Fraud Claims Were False. Here Are His Advisers Who Said So," *Politico*, June 13, 2022, https://www.politico .com/news/2022/06/13/trumps-election-fraud-claims-were-false-here-are -his-advisers-who-said-so-00039346; Aaron Blake, "A Conservative Group Debunks Trump's Voter-Fraud Claims (Yet Again)," *Washington Post*, December 9, 2021, https://www.washingtonpost.com/politics/2021/12/09 /trumps-voter-fraud-myth-dies-another-death-conservative-group-debunks -it-again/.

3 Glenn Kessler, "What the Steele Dossier Said vs. What the Mueller Report Said," *Washington Post*, April 24, 2019, https://www.washingtonpost.com /politics/2019/04/24/what-steele-dossier-said-vs-what-mueller-report-said/; Burton Speakman, "A Knight's in Sheep's Clothing: Media Framing of the Alt-Right Can Alter the Image of Racist Groups," *Journal of Creative Communications*, 16, no. 1 (2021): 81–96; Anna Dubenko, "Right and Left on the Violence in Charlottesville," *New York Times*, August 19, 2017, https://www.nytimes.com/2017/08/14/us/politics/trump-charlottesville-left -right-react.html.

4 Keith Coffman, "CNN Settles Defamation Lawsuit with Kentucky Teen in Lincoln Memorial Case," *Reuters*, January 7, 2020, https://www.reuters.com /article/us-usa-media-cnn/cnn-settles-defamation-lawsuit-with-kentucky -teen-in-lincoln-memorial-case-idUSKBN1Z70CL; Bill Chappell, "BYU Says It Has No Proof That the Fan Banned over Racist Slurs Said Them," *NPR*, September 2, 2022, https://www.npr.org/2022/09/02/1120558306 /byu-volleyball-racist-slurs-fan.

5 Kristen Weir, "Why We Believe Alternative Facts," *American Psychological Association* 48, no. 5 (May 2017), https://www.apa.org/monitor/2017/05 /alternative-facts; Silvia Knobloch-Westerwick et al., "Confirmation Bias, Ingroup Bias, and Negativity Bias in Selective Exposure to Political Information," *Communication Research* 47, no. 1 (2020): 104–24.

6 See Figures 2.5 and 2.6 in chapter 2. Mark Jurkowitz, Amy Mitchell, Elisa Shearer, and Mason Walker, *U.S. Media Polarization and the 2020 Election: A Nation Divided* (Washington, DC: Pew Research Center, 2020).

7 See chapter 2.

8 James Boswell, *Life of Samuel Johnson* (Chicago: Scott, Foresman and Company, 1923), 272.

9 William J. Baumol and Hilda Baumol, "On the Economics of Musical Composition in Mozart's Vienna," *Journal of Cultural Economics* 18 (1994): 171–98.

10 Carol Sue Humphrey, *The American Revolution and the Press: The Promise of Independence* (Evanston, IL: Northwestern University Press, 2013), 23–58.

11 Kyle Scott, *The Federalist Papers: A Reader's Guide* (New York: Bloomsbury, 2013), 40–43; "Federalist Papers: Primary Documents in American History," Library of Congress Research Guides, accessed December 12, 2022, https://guides.loc.gov/federalist-papers/full-text.

12 Patrick Henry et al., *The Anti-Federalist Papers*, ed. Jim Miller (Mineola, NY: Dover Publications, Inc., 2020), xi, 90, 103, 160.

13 Jeffrey A. Smith, *Printers and Press Freedom: The Ideology of Early American Journalism* (New York: Oxford University Press, 1988), 142–61; Humphrey, *The American Revolution and the Press*.

14 See chapter 3.

15 Douglas Bradburn, "A Clamor in the Public Mind: Opposition to the Alien and Sedition Acts," *William and Mary Quarterly* 65, no. 3 (July 2008): 565–600.

16 Donald K. Brazeal, "Precursor to Modern Media Hype: The 1830s Penny Press," *Journal of American Culture* 28, no. 4 (2005): 405–14.

17 Mark Wahlgren Summers, *The Press Gang: Newspapers and Politics, 1865–1878* (Chapel Hill, NC: University of North Carolina Press, 1994), 59–75; Hy B. Turner, *When Giants Ruled: the Story of Park Row, New York's Great Newspaper Street* (New York: Fordham University Press, 1999).

18 Ralph O. Nafziger, "International News Coverage and Foreign News Information," *Annals of the American Academy of Political and Social Science*: 219 (Jan. 1942): 136–37; Susan R. Brooker Gross, "News Wire Services in Nineteenth-Century United States," *Journal of Historical Geography* 7, no. 2 (1981): 167–70, 175.

19 Randy Bobbitt, *Us against Them: The Political Culture of Talk Radio* (New York: Rowman & Littlefield Publishers, Inc., 2010), 3–5.

20 "Editorial: Mourn Rush Limbaugh's Death, Then Bury His Shock-Jock Approach to Politics," *Baltimore Sun*, February 18, 2021, https://www.baltimoresun.com/opinion/editorial/bs-ed-0219-rush-limbaugh-20210218

-lvbpkznruvbnpgcsrtd5gdam3m-story.html; Michael Carlson, "Rush
Limbaugh Obituary: Rightwing Broadcaster Known for a Brand of
Attacking 'Shock Job' Radio That Set Tone for the Internet Age of Politics,"
Guardian, February 17, 2021, https://www.theguardian.com/media/2021/feb
/17/rush-limbaugh-obituary.

21 Jeffrey M. Berry and Sarah Sobieraj, "Understanding the Rise of Talk
Radio," *PS: Political Science and Politics* 44, no. 4 (2011): 762–67.

22 Yochai Benkler, Robert Faris, and Hal Roberts, *Network Propaganda:
Manipulation, Disinformation, and Radicalization in American Politics* (New
York: Oxford University Press, 2018), 3–99; William G. Mayer, "Why Talk
Radio Is Conservative," *Public Interest* 156 (Summer 2004): 86–103.

23 Benkler, Faris, and Roberts, *Network Propaganda*, 145–221.

24 Jury Trial Demand, Dominion's Combined Opposition to Fox News Network,
LLC's and Fox Corporation's Rule 56 Motions for Summary Judgment at
131-80, U.S. Dominion, Inc. v. Fox News Network, No. N21C-03-257 EMD
(Del. Sup. Ct. Feb. 27, 2023); Dani Anguiano, "Rupert Murdoch Testified
That Fox News Hosts 'Endorsed' Stolen Election Narrative," *Guardian*,
February 27, 2023, https://www.theguardian.com/media/2023/feb/27/rupert
-murdoch-deposition-dominion-lawsuit-fox-news; Matt Taylor, "Fox News
Reaches $787.5 Million Settlement in Dominion's Defamation Lawsuit,"
Politico, April 18, 2023, https://www.politico.com/news/2023/04/18/fox-news
-reaches-settlement-with-dominion-in-defamation-lawsuit-00092621.

25 John B. Bader, *Taking the Initiative: Leadership Agendas in Congress and the
'Contract with America'* (Washington, DC: Georgetown University Press,
1996); Newt Gingrich and Dick Armey, *Contract with America: the Bold Plan
by Rep. Newt Gingrich, Rep. Dick Armey and the House Republicans to Change
the Nation* (New York: Times Books, 1994).

26 *The Social Network*, directed by David Fincher (2010; Culver City, CA: Sony
Pictures, 2011), DVD; Claire Hoffman, "The Battle for Facebook," *Rolling
Stone*, September 15, 2010, https://www.rollingstone.com/culture/culture
-news/the-battle-for-facebook-242989/.

27 Katherine A. Kaplan, "Facemash Creator Survives Ad Board," *Harvard
Crimson*, November 19, 2003, https://www.thecrimson.com/article/2003/11
/19/facemash-creator-survives-ad-board-the/.

28 Nicolas Carlson, "At Last—the Full Story of How Facebook Was Founded,"
Business Insider, March 5, 2010, https://www.businessinsider.com/how
-facebook-was-founded-2010-3; Hoffman, "The Battle for Facebook."

29 "Permanent Suspension of @realDonaldTrump," Twitter, Inc., January 8,
2021, https://blog.twitter.com/en_us/topics/company/2020/suspension; Nick
Clegg, "In Response to Oversight Board, Trump Suspended for Two Years;

Will Only Be Reinstated if Conditions Permit," Meta, June 4, 2021, https://about.fb.com/news/2021/06/facebook-response-to-oversight-board -recommendations-trump/.

30 Tomás Mier, "All the Celebrities Who've Quit Twitter Because of Elon Musk," *Rolling Stone*, December 1, 2022, https://www.rollingstone.com /culture/culture-lists/elon-musk-twitter-celebrities-quit-1234634670/; Irina Ivanova, "These Formerly Banned Twitter Accounts Have Been Reinstated Since Elon Mush Took Over," *CBS News*, November 21, 2022, https://www .cbsnews.com/news/twitter-accounts-reinstated-elon-musk-donald-trump -kanye-ye-jordan-peterson-kathy-griffin-andrew-tate/.

31 Julia Carrie Wong, "Former Facebook Executive: Social Media Is Ripping Society Apart," *Guardian*, December 12, 2017, https://www.theguardian .com/technology/2017/dec/11/facebook-former-executive-ripping-society -apart (internal quotations omitted).

32 Maxwell L. Stearns, Todd J. Zywicki, and Thomas J. Miceli, *Law and Economics: Private and Public* (St. Paul, MN: West Academic, 2009), 50.

33 "Mark Zuckerberg Stands for Voice and Free Expression," Meta, October 17, 2019, https://about.fb.com/news/2019/10/mark-zuckerberg-stands-for-voice -and-free-expression/.

34 "Read Sacha Baron Cohen's Scathing Attack on Facebook in Full: 'Greatest Propaganda Machine in History,'" *Guardian*, November 22, 2019, https:// www.theguardian.com/technology/2019/nov/22/sacha-baron-cohen-facebook -propaganda ("It's time to finally call these companies what they really are—the largest publishers in history. And here's an idea for them: abide by basic standards and practices just like newspapers, magazines and TV news do every day.").

35 47 U.S.C. § 230.

36 Twitter v. Taamneh, 598 U.S. ___ (2023); Gonzalez v. Google, 598 U.S. ___ (2023) (per curiam).

37 Frank Pasquale, *The Black Box Society: The Secret Algorithms That Control Money and Information* (Cambridge, MA: Harvard University Press, 2016).

38 "All Sides Media Bias Chart," AllSides, accessed August 4, 2022, https:// www.allsides.com/media-bias/media-bias-chart.

39 Angie Drobnic Holan, "The Principles of the Truth-O-Meter: Politifact's Methodology for Independent Fact-Checking," Politifact, last updated April 18, 2022, https://www.politifact.com/article/2018/feb/12/principles -truth-o-meter-politifacts-methodology-i/; "Fact Checks," Snopes, accessed October 12, 2022, https://www.snopes.com/fact-check/.

40 "The Chart, Version 1.0: Original Reasoning and Methodology," Ad Fontes Media, accessed August 4, 2022, https://adfontesmedia.com/the-reasoning

-and-methodology-behind-the-chart/ (explaining Vanessa Otero's methodology when designing the Media Bias Chart); "Media Bias Chart," Ad
Fontes Media, accessed March 7, 2023, https://adfontesmedia.com/gallery/
(updated Media Bias Chart).

41 For a more detailed discussion, see Maxwell Stearns, "The Multiple-
Analyst-Generated Media Bias Chart," *Blindspot: A Blog about Law, Politics
and Culture*, January 3, 2020, https://www.blindspotblog.us/post/the
-multiple-analyst-generated-media-bias-chart.

42 "Maxwell Stearns," Ad Fontes Media, accessed October 12, 2022, https://
adfontesmedia.com/maxwell-stearns/.

43 David Mikkelson, "Dragnet: 'Just the Facts. Ma'am,'" Snopes, March 29,
2002, https://www.snopes.com/fact-check/just-the-facts/.

44 Alice E. Marwick, "Why Do People Share Fake News? A Sociotechnical
Model of Media Effects," *Georgetown Law & Technology Review* 2, no. 2
(2018): 474–512; Matthew A. Baum and Phil Gussin, "In the Eye of the
Beholder: How Information Shortcuts Shape Individual Perceptions of
Bias in the Media," *Quarterly Journal of Political Science* 3, no. 1 (2008):
1–31; Josefine Pallavicini, Bjørn Hallsson, and Klemens Kappel, "Polarization in Groups of Bayesian Agents," *Synthese* 1989 (2021): 1–55.

45 Rebecca Shabad, "Trump Booed after Revealing He Got a Covid Booster
Shot," *NBC News*, December 21, 2021, https://www.nbcnews.com/politics
/donald-trump/trump-reveals-he-got-covid-booster-shot-crowd-boos-him
-n1286361.

Chapter 5. The European Tour

1 Prince Harry, The Duke of Sussex, *Spare* (New York: Random House,
2023).

2 Jean-Claude Lamberti, "Montesquieu in America," *European Journal of
Sociology* 32, no. 1 (1991); Donald L. Lutz, "The Relative Influence of
European Writers on Late Eighteenth-Century American Political
Thought," *American Political Science Review* 78, no. 1 (1984).

3 Maurice Duverger, "A New Political System Model: Semi-presidential
Government," *European Journal of Political Research* 8, no. 2 (June 1980):
165–88; Yüksel Alper Ecevit & Ekrem Karakoç, "The Perils of Semi-
presidentialism: Confidence in Political Institutions in Contemporary
Democracies," *International Political Science Review* 38, no. 1 (January 2017): 4–20.

4 Susan E. Scarrow, "Germany: The Mixed-Member System as a Political
Compromise," in *Mixed-Member Electoral Systems: The Best of Both Worlds?*,

eds. Matthew Soberg Shugart and Martin P. Wattenberg (Oxford: Oxford University Press, 2001), 55–69.

5 Sylvia Nasar, *A Beautiful Mind* (New York: Simon & Schuster, 1998).

6 Maxwell L. Stearns, Todd J. Zywicki, and Thomas J. Miceli, *Law and Economics: Private and Public* (Saint Paul, MN: West Academic, 2018): 579–80.

7 Anthony Downs, *An Economic Theory of Democracy* (New York: Harper and Brothers, 1957).

8 Churchill made this statement, which Churchill scholar Richard Langworth attributes to "an unknown predecessor," on November 11, 1947. Richard M. Langworth, "Churchill's 'Democracy is the Worst Form of Government . . .'" *Richard M. Langworth* (blog), June 20, 2022, https://richardlangworth.com/worst-form-of-government; "The Worst Form of Government," *International Churchill Society*, February 25, 2016, https://winstonchurchill.org/resources/quotes/the-worst-form-of-government/.

9 Kenneth Arrow, *Social Choice and Individual Values*, 2nd ed. (New York: John Wiley & Sons, 1963); Stearns, Zywicki, Miceli, *Law and Economics*, 541–74.

10 Susan Ratcliffe, *Concise Oxford Dictionary of Quotations* (Oxford: Oxford University Press, 2011), 389.

11 "Key Dates of the Glorious Revolution: 1689–1714," *UK Parliament*, last accessed October 18, 2022, https://www.parliament.uk/about/living -heritage/evolutionofparliament/parliamentaryauthority/revolution/keydates /keydates1689-1714/; Yann Allard-Tremblay, "Proceduralism, Judicial Review and the Refusal of Royal Assent," *Oxford Journal of Legal Studies* 33, no. 2 (Summer 2013): 379–400.

12 "Dissolution of Parliament," *UK Parliament*, last accessed October 18, 2022, https://www.parliament.uk/about/how/elections-and-voting/general /dissolution/; "Past Prime Ministers: James Callaghan," *Gov.uk*, last accessed October 18, 2022, https://www.gov.uk/government/history/past-prime -ministers/james-callaghan; "What Is a Vote of No Confidence?," *BBC*, October 20, 2022, https://www.bbc.com/news/uk-politics-46890481.

13 Steven Erlanger, "Britain Votes to Leave E.U.; Cameron Plans to Step Down," *New York Times*, June 23, 2016, https://www.nytimes.com/2016/06 /25/world/europe/britain-brexit-european-union-referendum.html; "Background to the UK's EU Referendum 2016," *UK Parliament*, last accessed October 18, 2022, https://www.parliament.uk/business/publications /research/eu-referendum/background-uk-eu-referendum-2016/.

14 Erlanger, "Britain Votes to Leave E.U."; "EU Referendum: Results," *BBC News*, last accessed October 18, 2022, https://www.bbc.co.uk/news/politics /eu_referendum/results.

15 Kylie MacLellan, "UK Election Result 'Blew Away' Argument for Second Brexit Vote: Labour's Starmer," *Reuters*, January 5, 2020, https://www .reuters.com/article/us-britain-eu-starmer/uk-election-result-blew-away -argument-for-second-brexit-vote-labours-starmer-idUSKBN1Z40F3.

16 Gerald A. Dorfman, "Britain's New Odd Couple Coalition Government," *Forbes*, May 12, 2010, https://www.forbes.com/2010/05/12/david-cameron -prime-minister-coalition-opinions-contributors-gerald-a-dorfman.html?sh =557aa0e032c9.

17 Jen Kirby, "A Short History of the Long Road to Brexit," *Vox*, January 31, 2020, https://www.vox.com/2020/1/31/21083573/brexit-news-boris-johnson -timeline-eu-uk; "Timeline of Events in Britain's Exit from the European Union," *AP*, December 24, 2020, https://apnews.com/article/europe-general -elections-elections-referendums-david-cameron-f673af169925d30e524169e f92c4f386.

18 Karla Adam and William Booth, "Boris Johnson Survives but Is Weakened by No-Confidence Vote," *Washington Post*, June 6, 2022, https://www .washingtonpost.com/world/2022/06/06/boris-johnson-tory-leadership-vote/; Richard Kelly, "Votes of No Confidence," *UK Parliament*, July 12, 2022, https://commonslibrary.parliament.uk/votes-of-no-confidence/.

19 Karla Adam, "The Queen and Her 15 Prime Ministers," *Washington Post*, September 8, 2022, https://www.washingtonpost.com/world/interactive /2022/queen-prime-ministers/; "The Prime Ministers Who Served under Queen Elizabeth II," *AP*, September 8, 2022, https://apnews.com/article /queen-elizabeth-ii-prime-ministers-9b1d631878dfcc594af1fe69cc838dca.

20 William Booth and Karla Adam, "How Liz Truss Became the Shortest- Serving Prime Minister in U.K. History," *Washington Post*, October 20, 2022, https://www.washingtonpost.com/world/2022/10/20/liz-truss -shortest-prime-minister-uk/.

21 Max Colchester and David Luhnow, "Rishi Sunak Becomes U.K. Prime Minister Amid Growing Economic, Political Crisis," *Wall Street Journal*, October 25, 2022, https://www.wsj.com/articles/rishi-sunak-takes-over-as-u -k-prime-minister-amid-growing-economic-and-political-crisis-116666 98079.

22 Sascha O. Becker, Thiemo Fetzer, and Dennis Novy, "Who Voted for Brexit? A Comprehensive District-Level Analysis," *Economic Policy* 32, no. 92 (October 2017): 601–50, https://doi.org/10.1093/epolic/eix012.

23 Maxwell L. Stearns, "Direct (Anti-)Democracy," *George Washington Law Review* 80, no. 2 (2012): 311–84.

24 Debra Ronca, "How the London Eye Works," HowStuffWorks, accessed November 17, 2022, https://adventure.howstuffworks.com/london-eye.htm.

25 Norman Schofield and Itai Sened, *Multiparty Democracy: Elections and Legislative Politics* (Cambridge: Cambridge University Press, 2006).

26 Mauro F. Guillén, "Symbolic Unity, Dynastic Continuity, and Countervailing Power: Monarchies, Republics, and the Economy," *Social Forces* 97, no. 2 (December 2018): 607–48; Rodney Brazier, "Legislating about the Monarchy," *Cambridge Law Journal* 66, no. 1 (March 2007): 86–105.

27 Mancur Olson, "Dictatorship, Democracy, and Development," *American Political Science Review* 87, no. 3 (September 1993).

28 Alex Lacamoire, Jonathan Groff, and original Broadway cast of *Hamilton*, "You'll Be Back," YouTube, February 18, 2020, https://www.youtube.com /watch?v=PyD6jeDBoDo.

29 *Palais Bourbon: A Palace for Democracy*, Assemblée Nationale, last accessed October 19, 2022, https://www.assemblee-nationale.fr/histoire/images /PalaisBourbon-r_UK.pdf.

30 Olivier Duhamel, "France's New Five-Year Presidential Term," Brookings, March 1, 2001, https://www.brookings.edu/articles/frances-new-five-year -presidential-term/.

31 Yüksel Alper Ecevit and Ekrem Karakoç, "The Perils of Semi-presidentialism," *International Political Science Review* 38, no. 1 (January 2017): 4–20; Robert Elgie, "An Intellectual History of the Concepts of Premier-Presidentialism and President-Parliamentarism," *Political Studies Review* 18, no. 1 (February 2020): 12–29.

32 Over twenty parties are represented in the current National Assembly and Senate. "Liste des Sénateurs par Groupes Politiques," Sénat, last accessed October 19, 2022, https://www.senat.fr/senateurs/grp.html; "Les Groupes Politiques Actuels," Assemblée Nationale, last accessed October 19, 2022, https://www.assemblee-nationale.fr/dyn/les-groupes-politiques; "France," Parties and Elections in Europe, last accessed October 19, 2022, http://www .parties-and-elections.eu/france.html.

33 Code Électoral (Electoral Code), Title I (France); "France," International Foundation for Electoral Systems: Election Guide, last accessed October 19, 2022, https://www.electionguide.org/countries/id/75/; Dylan Difford, "How Do Elections Work for France's Parliament, the French National Assembly?," Electoral Reform Society, May 30, 2022, https://www.electoral-reform.org.uk /how-do-elections-work-for-frances-parliament-the-french-national-assembly/.

34 Abby LaBreck, "French Election 2022 Analysis: A Transatlantic Perspective," *Harvard International Review*, September 23, 2022, https://hir.harvard .edu/french-election-2022-analysis/.

35 "Marine Le Pen: EU Has More to Lose on Brexit, but I Don't Want Frexit," *Euronews*, July 2, 2020, https://www.euronews.com/2020/02/06/marine-le

-pen-eu-has-more-to-lose-on-brexit-but-i-don-t-want-frexit; Jon Henley and Jennifer Rankin, "'Frexit in All but Name': What a Marine Le Pen Win Would Mean for EU," *Guardian*, April 15, 2022, https://www.theguardian.com/world/2022/apr/15/frexit-what-marine-le-pen-win-mean-eu.

36 Jules Darmanin, "Le Pen's National Rally Wins Seats, Airtime and Money in French Vote," *Politico*, June 20, 2022, https://www.politico.eu/article/marine-le-pen-national-rally-win-seat-airtime-money-france-legislative-election/.

37 Joseph Ataman, Saskya Vandoorne, and Oliver Briscoe, "May Day Protests Erupt in Paris as France Seethes about a Hike in the Retirement Age," *CNN*, May 1, 2023, https://www.cnn.com/2023/05/01/europe/france-pension-protests-explainer-intl/index.html.

38 Alberto Alesina, Edward Glaeser, and Bruce Sacerdote, "Work and Leisure in the United States and Europe: Why So Different?," *NBER Macroeconomics Annual* 20 (2005): 1–64, https://www.journals.uchicago.edu/doi/epdf/10.1086/ma.20.3585411; Dominique Méda, "Three Scenarios for the Future of Work," *International Labour Review* 158, no. 4 (2019), https://doi.org/10.1111/ilr.12157.

39 "Le Pen Would Beat Macron if French Presidential Vote Repeated: Poll," *France24*, May 4, 2023, https://www.france24.com/en/live-news/20230405-le-pen-would-beat-macron-if-french-presidential-vote-repeated-poll; Oliver Haynes, "There's Only One Winner from Macron's Hardline Response to Pension Protests: The Far Right," *Guardian*, April 12, 2023, https://www.theguardian.com/commentisfree/2023/apr/12/emmanuel-macron-pension-protests-far-right-reform-marine-le-pen.

40 "Holocaust Ad Campaign Backfires," *CNN*, August 6, 2001, http://www.cnn.com/2001/WORLD/europe/08/06/germany.holocaust/index.html; "'Holocaust Never Happened' Ad Prompts Lawsuit and Controversy," *Jewish Telegraphic Agency*, August 2, 2001, https://www.jta.org/archive/holocaust-never-happened-ad-prompts-lawsuit-and-controversy.

41 Ian Kershaw, *Hitler* (New York: Routledge, 2014), 37–61, 117–18; "Third Reich: An Overview," *Holocaust Encyclopedia: United States Holocaust Memorial Museum*, last accessed October 25, 2022, https://encyclopedia.ushmm.org/content/en/article/third-reich-an-overview.

42 Johanna Hornung, Robin Rüsenberg, Florian Eckert, and Nils C. Bandelow, "New Insights into Coalition Negotiations—the Case of German Government Formation," *Negotiation Journal* 36, no. 3 (Summer 2020): 331–52, https://doi.org/10.1111/nejo.12310.

43 For a general discussion of the German electoral scheme, see Eric Lagenbacher, "The Political and Electoral System of Germany," *American*

German Institute, July 12, 2021, https://aicgs.org/2021/07/the-political-and
-electoral-system-of-germany/.

44 "Chancellery," *The Federal Chancellor*, last accessed October 20, 2022,
https://www.bundeskanzler.de/bk-en/chancellery/federal-chancellors-since
-1949.

45 Germany employs the Sainte-Laguë / Schepers method to convert votes to
seats. "Election of Members and the Allocation of Seats," Deutscher
Bundestag: Parliament, last accessed October 20, 2022, https://www
.bundestag.de/en/parliament/elections/arithmetic.

46 Vladimír Dančišin, "Negative Vote Weight and the No-Show Paradox in
Party-List Proportional System" (working paper no. 1/2014, Presov
University Institute of Political Science, Presov Slovakia, 2014), https://www
.researchgate.net/publication/266030551_NEGATIVE_VOTE_WEIGHT
_AND_THE_NO-SHOW_PARADOX_IN_PARTY-LIST_PROPORT
IONAL_SYSTEM; Ian Stewart, "Electoral Dysfunction: Why Democracy
Is Always Unfair," *New Scientist*, April 28, 2010, https://www.newscientist
.com/article/mg20627581-400-electoral-dysfunction-why-democracy-is
-always-unfair/.

47 See chapter 10 at pp. 260–64.

48 Bundesverfassungsgericht (German Federal Constitutional Court), Case
No. 2 BvC 1, 7/07, July 3, 2008, 121 BVERFGE 266, 297 (Germany);
Zweiundzwanzigstes Gesetz zur Änderung des Bundeswahlgesetzes (Law
Amending the Federal Electoral Law), May 3, 2013, BGBI I (Germany);
Erik Kirschbaum, "Germany Passes New Election Law to Help Small
Parties," *Reuters*, February 21, 2013, https://www.reuters.com/article/us
-germany-election/germany-passes-new-election-law-to-help-small-parties
-idUSBRE91K16420130221.

49 "Distribution of Seats in the 20th German Bundestag," Deutscher Bundestag: Parliament, last accessed October 25, 2022, https://www.bundestag.de
/en/parliament/plenary/distributionofseats; Rina Goldenberg, "A Look at
Germany's Political Parties," *Deutsche Welle*, October 5, 2021, https://www
.dw.com/en/spd-green-party-fdp-cdu-left-party-afd/a-38085900.

50 "AK Party to Submit Election Law Proposal to Parliament by March," *Daily
Sabah*, December 7, 2021, https://www.dailysabah.com/politics/elections/ak
-party-to-submit-election-law-proposal-to-parliament-by-march; Willem
Maas, "Dutch Elections Show the Promise and Perils of Proportional
Representation," *Conversation*, June 10, 2021, https://theconversation.com
/dutch-elections-show-the-promise-and-perils-of-proportional-representation
-157290; "Turkish Parliament Passes Law Reducing Required Votes Threshold to 70%," *Reuters*, March 31, 2022, https://www.reuters.com/world/middle

-east/turkish-parliament-passes-law-reducing-required-votes-threshold-7
-2022-03-31/?.

51 "Election of the Federal Chancellor," Deutscher Bundestag: Parliament, last
accessed December 1, 2022, https://www.bundestag.de/en/parliament
/function/chancellor.

52 Volker Witting, "Germany Passes Law to Shrink its XXL Parliament," *Deutsche Welle*, March 17, 2023, https://www.dw.com/en/germany
-passes-law-to-shrink-its-xxl-parliament/a-64471203; Fabian Michl and
Johanna Mittrop, "Farewell to 'Personenwahl,'" *Verfassungsblog: On Matters
Constitutional*, January 19, 2023, https://verfassungsblog.de/farewell-to
-personenwahl/.

53 Witting, "Germany Passes Law to Shrink its XXL Parliament."

54 Witting, "Germany Passes Law to Shrink its XXL Parliament"; Michl and
Mittrop, "Farewell to 'Personenwahl'"; Geir Moulson, "German Lawmakers Approve Plan to Shrink Bloated Parliament," *AP*, March 17, 2023,
https://apnews.com/article/germany-electoral-reform-parliament-bundestag
-0e96c6ef6a4d55d6f8f473c3251e5615.

55 See chapter 6 at pp. 151–52, 162.

56 Stearns, Zywicki, and Miceli, *Law and Economics*, 622–23.

Chapter 6. Democratic Variations

1 Adam Taylor, "Has the Global Jewish Population Finally Rebounded from
the Holocaust? Not Exactly," *Washington Post*, July 2, 2015, https://www
.washingtonpost.com/news/worldviews/wp/2015/07/02/has-the-global
-jewish-population-finally-rebounded-from-the-holocaust-not-exactly/;
"Documenting Numbers of Victims of the Holocaust and Nazi Persecution,"
United States Holocaust Memorial Museum, last accessed October 27, 2022,
https://encyclopedia.ushmm.org/content/en/article/documenting-numbers
-of-victims-of-the-holocaust-and-nazi-persecution. Estimates for the
Armenian Genocide place losses between 664,000 and 1.2 million deaths.
"The Armenian Genocide (1915–16): Overview," United States Holocaust
Memorial Museum, last accessed October 27, 2022, https://encyclopedia
.ushmm.org/content/en/article/the-armenian-genocide-1915-16-overview.

2 Yitzhak Reiter, "Narratives of Jerusalem and Its Sacred Compound," *Israel
Studies* 18, no. 2 (2013): 118; Philologos [pseud.], "A Wail of a Wall Story,"
Forward, January 12, 2001, 11.

3 Benjy Singer, "Temple Mount—What the Rabbis Say," *Jerusalem Post*,
August 12, 2019, https://www.jpost.com/israel-news/temple-mount-what
-our-rabbis-really-say-598372; Ruth Margalit, "The Politics of Prayer at the

Temple Mount," *New Yorker*, November 5, 2014, https://www.newyorker .com/news/news-desk/furor-temple-mount.

4 Catharina Raudvere, *Islam: An Introduction* (London: I.B. Tauris, 2015), 44–46.

5 Raudvere, *Islam*, 44–46.

6 "The Fourteen Stations of the Via Dolorosa," Terra Sancta Museum, accessed October 30, 2022, https://www.terrasanctamuseum.org/en/discover -more/the-fourteen-stations-of-the-sorrowful-way/.

7 See chapter 5 at p. 130.

8 See chapter 5 for a discussion of the core and yolk metaphor. Norman Schofield and Itai Sened, *Multiparty Democracy* (Cambridge: Cambridge University Press, 2006).

9 *Current Knesset Members: Factions*, The Knesset, accessed October 30, 2022, https://knesset.gov.il/mk/eng/mkindex_current_eng.asp?view=1.

10 Michael Freedman, "Vote with Your Rabbi: The Electoral Effects of Religious Institutions in Israel," *Electoral Studies* 68 (2020): 102241, https://doi.org/10 .1016/j.electstud.2020.102241; Christina Pazzanese, "Will a Historically Diverse New Coalition Bring Big Changes to Israel?," *Harvard Gazette*, June 7, 2021, https://news.harvard.edu/gazette/story/2021/06/harvard-analysts-discuss -israels-historically-diverse-new-coalition/; Itamar Rabinovich, "Religion and Politics in Israel," *The Caravan: Hoover Institution*, December 6, 2018, https://www.hoover.org/research/religion-and-politics-israel.

11 "'Greencons' are a New Political Alliance for an Uncertain Age," *Economist*, June 28, 2020, https://www.economist.com/europe/2020/06/28/greencons -are-a-new-political-alliance-for-an-uncertain-age.

12 Patrick Kingsley and Isabel Kershner, "Israel's Government Collapses, Setting Up 5th Election in 3 Years," *New York Times*, June 21, 2022, https://www.nytimes.com/2022/06/20/world/middleeast/israel-election -government-collapse.html.

13 This happened once before with Benjamin Netanyahu and Benny Gantz. The 2020 agreement to form an emergency unity government kept Netanyahu as prime minister for eighteen months, after which Gantz would succeed him. Steve Hendrix and Ruth Eglash, "Israeli Leaders Agree to Form Unity Government with Netanyahu Remaining Prime Minister for Now," *Washington Post*, April 20, 2020, https://www.washingtonpost.com /world/middle_east/israeli-leaders-agree-to-form-unity-government-with -netanyahu-remaining-prime-minister-for-now/2020/04/20/855a82cc-7817 -11ea-a311-adb1344719a9_story.html.

14 Isabel Kershner, "Another Israeli Election Looms, and a Familiar Face Plans a Comeback," *New York Times*, October 29, 2022, https://www.nytimes.com

/2022/10/29/world/middleeast/israeli-election.html; "Final 3 TV Polls Before Election All Show Netanyahu Bloc One Seat Short of Majority," *Times of Israel*, October 28, 2022, https://www.timesofisrael.com/final-tv -network-polls-before-election-show-netanyahu-bloc-one-short-of-majority /; Yolande Knell, "Israel Elections: Netanyahu Election Win Propels Far Right to Power," *BBC*, November 2, 2022, https://www.bbc.com/news /world-middle-east-63490806; Richard Allen Greene, "Netanyahu on Brink of Comeback as Israeli Exit Polls Point to Narrow Majority for Ex-PM," *CNN*, November 2, 2022, https://www.cnn.com/2022/11/01/middleeast /israel-election-intl/index.html.

15 Alan Shatter, "Undermining the Credibility of Israel's Legal System Is No Way to Celebrate Israel's Seventy-Fifth Anniversary," *Israel Journal of Foreign Affairs* (March 2023): 2. https://www.tandfonline.com/doi/full/10 .1080/23739770.2023.2194116; Barak Medina, "The Israeli Supreme Court's Independence Must Be Protected," *Jurist*, February 16, 2023, https://www.jurist.org/commentary/2023/02/barak-medina-israel -constitutional-crisis/.

16 Raffi Berg, "Israel Judicial Reform: Why is there a Crisis?," *BBC*, April 28, 2023 https://www.bbc.com/news/world-middle-east-65086871.

17 Maurice Duverger, "Les Monarchies Républicaines," *Pouvoirs* 78 (1996): 107–20; Steffen Ganghof, "A New Political System Model: Semi-parliamentary Government," *European Journal of Political Research* 57, no. 2 (May 2018): 261–81; Steffen Ganghof, *Beyond Presidentialism and Parliamentarism* (Oxford: Oxford University Press, 2021).

18 Benjamin Netanyahu (1996); Ehud Barak (1999); Ariel Sharon (2001).

19 Yüksel Sezgin, "The Implications of the Direct Elections in Israel," *Turkish Yearbook of International Relations* 30 (2001): 73–74.

20 Alyssa Resar, "The 1992 Consensus: Why It Worked and Why It Fell Apart," *Diplomat*, July 18, 2022, https://thediplomat.com/2022/07/the-1992 -consensus-why-it-worked-and-why-it-fell-apart/; Shannon Tiezzi, "China and Taiwan Leaders Emphasize Kinship, 1992 Consensus in Historic Talks," *Diplomat*, November 7, 2015, https://thediplomat.com/2015/11/china-and -taiwan-leaders-emphasize-kinship-1992-consensus-in-historic-talks/.

21 Hans Stockton, "How Rules Matter: Electoral Reform in Taiwan," *Social Science Quarterly* 91, no. 1 (March 2010): 21–41

22 Yen-tu Su, "The Amendability of Taiwan's Constitution Is Put to the Test," *Constitution Net*, May 30, 2022, https://constitutionnet.org/news/amendability -taiwans-constitution-put-test.

23 Phelim Kine, "Biden Leaves No Doubt: 'Strategic Ambiguity' Toward Taiwan Is Dead," *Politico*, September 19, 2022, https://www.politico.com

/news/2022/09/19/biden-leaves-no-doubt-strategic-ambiguity-toward
-taiwan-is-dead-00057658.

24 The Ethics in Government Act of 1978, Pub. L. No. 95-521, 92 Stat. 1824
(October 26, 1978); Morrison v. Olson, 487 U.S. 654 (1988). For a book
outlining proposals intended to guard against ethical and legal lapses
following the Trump administration, see Bob Bauer and Jack Goldsmith,
After Trump: Reconstructing the Presidency (Washington, DC: Lawfare
Institute, 2020).

25 Jarosław Flis, Wojciech Słomczyński, and Dariusz Stolicki, "Pot and Ladle:
A Formula for Estimating the Distribution of Seats under the Jefferson-
D'Hondt Method," *Public Choice* 182 (2020): 201–27.

26 *Democracy Index 2021: The China Challenge* (New York: Economist Intelligence Unit, 2022), 12 and 40.

27 Steven Levitsky and Daniel Ziblatt, *How Democracies Die* (New York:
Crown Publishing Group, 2018), 3.

28 Jack Nicas, "Chile Says 'No' to Left-Leaning Constitution after 3 Years of
Debate," *New York Times*, September 6, 2022, https://www.nytimes.com
/2022/09/04/world/americas/chile-constitution-no.html.

29 Levitsky and Ziblatt, *How Democracies Die*, 3.

30 *Election FAQs: Brazil General Elections* (Arlington, VA: International
Federation for Electoral Systems, 2022), 2; "Federative Republic of Brazil:
Electoral System," Political Database of the Americas, accessed October 31,
2022, https://pdba.georgetown.edu/ElecSys/Brazil/brazil.html.

31 *Election FAQs*, 1.

32 Scott Mainwaring, "Presidentialism, Multipartism, and Democracy: The
Difficult Combination," *Comparative Political Studies* 26, no. 2 (July 1993):
198–228.

33 Fabio Ramazzini Bechara and Paulo C. Goldschmidt, *Lessons of Operation
Car Wash: A Legal, Institutional, and Economic Analysis* (Washington, DC:
Wilson Center, 2020); Lenin Cavalcanti Guerra, "Brazil's Operation Car
Wash: A Corruption Investigator Is Accused of His Own Misdeeds,"
Conversation, June 27, 2019, https://theconversation.com/brazils-operation
-car-wash-a-corruption-investigator-is-accused-of-his-own-misdeeds-118889.

34 "Brazil President Dilma Rousseff Removed from Office by Senate," *BBC*,
September 1, 2016, https://www.bbc.com/news/world-latin-america
-37237513; Alexandra Rattinger, "The Impeachment Process of Brazil: A
Comparative Look at Impeachment in Brazil and the United States,"
University of Miami Inter-American Law Review, 49 (2018): 129–66.

35 "Brazil," CIA: The World Factbook, last updated October 25, 2022,
https://www.cia.gov/the-world-factbook/countries/brazil/#government.

36 Valerie Wirtschafter and Ted Piccone, "Anti-Democratic Sentiment Boils Over in Brazil," *Brookings*, January 12, 2023, https://www.brookings.edu/blog/order-from-chaos/2023/01/12/anti-democratic-sentiment-boils-over-in-brazil/.

37 Jack Nicas, "What Can U.S. Democracy Learn From Brazil?," *New York Times*, November 5, 2022, https://www.nytimes.com/2022/11/05/world/americas/brazil-election-us-democracy.html; Belén Fernández, "Opinion: Brazil, It Is Time to Wake Up from Your Bolsonaro Nightmare," *Al Jazeera*, October 1, 2022, https://www.aljazeera.com/opinions/2022/10/1/brazil-it-is-time-to-wake-up-from-bolsonaros-nightmare; Tom Phillips, "'It's Over': Jair Bolsonaro Reportedly Accepts Defeat in Brazil Election," *Guardian*, November 2, 2022, https://www.theguardian.com/world/2022/nov/02/jair-bolsonaro-reportedly-accepts-defeat-brazil-election.

38 Jacques Crémer and Djavad Salehi-Isfahani, *Models of the Oil Market* (New York: Routledge, 2001); Amelia Cheatham, Diana Roy, and Rocio Cara Labrador, "Venezuela: The Rise and Fall of a Petrostate," *Council on Foreign Relations*, December 29, 2021, https://www.cfr.org/backgrounder/venezuela-crisis.

39 "Bolivarian Republic of Venezuela: Chronology of Presidents," *Political Database of the Americas*, last updated January 31, 2007, https://pdba.georgetown.edu/Executive/Venezuela/pres.html.

40 Kenneth M. Roberts, "Populism, Political Conflict, and Grass-Roots Organization in Latin America," *Comparative Politics* 38, no. 2 (January 2006): 141–44.

41 Michael R. Kulisheck and Brian F. Crisp, "The Legislative Consequences of MMP Electoral Rules in Venezuela," in *Mixed-Member Electoral Systems: The Best of Both Worlds?*, eds. Matthew Soberg Shugart and Martin P. Wattenberg (Oxford: Oxford University Press, 2001), 404–31; John Polga-Hecimovich, "Guest Contributor: How Did Venezuela's MUD Get Its Supermajority?," *Global Americans*, December 14, 2015, https://theglobalamericans.org/2015/12/venezuelas-mud-get-supermajority/; Ley Orgánica de Procesos Electorales [Electoral Law] art. 8 (Venezuela); Constitución de la República Bolivariana de Venezuela [Constitution] art. 186 (Venezuela).

42 David Daley, *Ratf**ked: Why Your Vote Doesn't Count* (New York: Liveright, 2016).

43 John Polga-Hecimovich, "Guest Contributor: How Did Venezuela's MUD Get Its Supermajority?," *Global Americans*, December 14, 2015, https://theglobalamericans.org/2015/12/venezuelas-mud-get-supermajority/.

44 Raúl Jiménez and Manuel Hidalgo, "Forensic Analysis of Venezuelan Elections during the Chávez Presidency," *PLOS One* 9, No. 6 (2014): e100884, https://doi.org/10.1371/journal.pone.0100884.

45 Margarita López Maya and Luis E. Lander, "Participatory Democracy in Venezuela: Origins, Ideas, and Implementation," in *Venezuela's Bolivarian Democracy: Participation, Politics, and Culture Under Chávez*, eds. David Smilde and Daniel Hellinger (Durham, NC: Duke University Press, 2011), 61–62.

46 Chávez's successor, Nicolás Maduro, has been described as a dictator, and Maduro's second term election in 2018 was regarded as fraudulent, with some countries, including the United States, recognizing Juan Guaidó as Venezuela's rightful leader. The United Socialist Party of Venezuela (PSUV) dominated until the opposition party, Democratic Unity Roundtable (MUD), secured a majority in the National Assembly in 2015. This proved a Pyrrhic victory as Maduro transferred legislative power to the "National Communal Parliament," which the defeated outgoing PSUV majority had created. Daniel Lansberg-Rodríguez, "President Maduro and His Imaginary Parliament," *Foreign Policy*, December 22, 2015, https://foreignpolicy.com/2015/12/22/president-maduro-and-his-imaginary-parliament-venezuela-elections/; William Neuman and Nicholas Casey, "Venezuela Election Won by Maduro amid Widespread Disillusionment," *New York Times*, May 20, 2018, https://www.nytimes.com/2018/05/20/world/americas/venezuela-election.html.

47 Lee Drutman, *Breaking the Two-Party Doom Loop* (New York: Oxford University Press, 2020).

48 Paul Kirby, "Giorgia Meloni: Italy's Far-Right Wins Election and Vows to Govern for All," *BBC*, September 26, 2022, https://www.bbc.com/news/world-europe-63029909.

Chapter 7. Reinventing the House of Representatives

1 States with single-member House districts: Alaska, Delaware, North Dakota, South Dakota, Vermont, and Wyoming. "Directory of Representatives," United States House of Representatives, accessed November 14, 2022, https://www.house.gov/representatives.

2 Arizona, California, Colorado, Hawaii, Idaho, Michigan, and Washington currently employ nonpartisan districting commissions. "Redistricting Commissions," Ballotpedia, accessed November 14, 2022, https://ballotpedia.org/Redistricting_commissions.

3 James M. Buchanan and Gordon Tullock, *The Calculus of Consent: Logical Foundations of Constitutional Democracy* (Ann Arbor, MI: University of Michigan Press, 1965), 43–46, 105–13.

4 The current system, called the Method of Equal Proportions, assigns seats 51–435 to states based on their "priority value." The population of each state

is multiplied by a series of declining "multipliers" to assess each state's successive valuation. Seats are allocated in succession based on which state has the highest "Computing Apportionment," a process repeated until all seats are filled. "Computing Apportionment," United States Census Bureau, last revised November 22, 2021, https://www.census.gov/topics/public-sector /congressional-apportionment/about/computing.html.

5 Reynolds v. Simms, 377 U.S. 533 (1964).

6 For a comprehensive study of thresholds, including the frequency with which they have been changed across several democratic nations, see Judah Troen, "The National Electoral Threshold: A Comparative Review across Countries and Over Time," *The Knesset Research and Information Center*, January 1, 2019. Examples, as of the time the study was published, include the Netherlands below 1 percent, yielding thirteen parties, and Israel at 3.25 percent, yielding thirteen parties. Until 2017 reforms, Moldova had varying thresholds (6, 9, or 11 percent) based on whether parties run alone or as coalitions.

7 R. H. Coase, "The Problem of Social Cost," *Journal of Law & Economics* 3 (October 1960): 3–15, http://www.jstor.com/stable/724810; R. H. Coase, *The Firm, The Market, and the Law* (Chicago: University of Chicago Press, 1988), 174–79.

8 Maxwell L. Stearns, Todd J. Zywicki, and Thomas J. Miceli, *Law and Economics: Private and Public* (Saint Paul, MN: West Academic, 2018), 147–48.

9 Glen O. Robinson, "Public Choice Speculations on the Item Veto," *Virginia Law Review* 74, no. 2 (March 1988): 407–12.

10 See Katherine Schaeffer, "Single-Party Control in Washington Is Common at the Beginning of a New Presidency, but Tends Not to Last Long," *Pew Research Center*, February 3, 2021, https://www.pewresearch.org/fact-tank /2021/02/03/single-party-control-in-washington-is-common-at-the -beginning-of-a-new-presidency-but-tends-not-to-last-long/; Drew DeSilver, "Nothing Lame about This Lame Duck: 116th Congress Had Busiest Post-election Session in Recent History," *Pew Research Center*, January 21, 2021, https://www.pewresearch.org/fact-tank/2021/01/21/nothing-lame -about-this-lame-duck-116th-congress-had-busiest-post-election-session-in -recent-history/; Thomas H. Moore, "Weld Quits Nomination Fight," *CNN: All Politics*, September 15, 1997, https://www.cnn.com/ALLPOLITICS/1997 /09/15/weld.quits/; Lawrence Hurley, "Supreme Court Nominee Out in Cold as Election Heats Up," *Reuters*, July 19, 2016, https://www.reuters.com /article/us-usa-election-garland-idUSKCN0ZZ17L.

11 Notable examples include President Clinton's 1995 debt ceiling confronta-tion with House Republicans and the Senate Republicans' delay of President Obama's judicial appointments. As this book goes to press, it has also

338   NOTES TO PAGES 181–185

included President Biden's debt ceiling negotiations. Robert Schlesinger, "A Debt Ceiling History Lesson," *US News*, October 11, 2013, https://www .usnews.com/opinion/articles/2013/10/11/the-history-of-raising-the-debt -ceiling-from-ronald-reagan-to-bill-clinton-and-newt-gingrich?context =amp; Hurley, "Supreme Court Nominee Out in Cold as Election Heats Up"; Peter Baker, "Initial Takeaway from the Spending and Debt Ceiling Deal," *New York Times*, May 28, 2023, https://www.nytimes.com/2023/05 /28/us/politics/debt-ceiling-deal-takeaways.html.

12 For a general discussion of interest group theory, see Stearns, Zywicki, and Miceli, *Law and Economics* at 417–64.

13 For the classic work, see McNollgast, "Legislative Intent: The Use of Positive Political Theory in Statutory Interpretation," *Law & Contemporary Problems* 57, no. 1 (spring 1994): 3–37.

14 See chapter 6 at pp. 146, 157, 167.

15 Buchanan and Tullock, *The Calculus of Consent*.

16 Buchanan and Tullock, *The Calculus of Consent*, 233–49.

17 Lee Drutman advocates enlarging the House to 700. Lee Drutman, *Breaking the Two-Party Doom Loop: The Case for Multiparty Democracy in America* (New York: Oxford University Press, 2020), 193.

18 Caroline Kane, Gianni Mascioli, Michael McGarry, and Meira Nagel, *Why the House of Representatives Must Be Expanded and How Today's Congress Can Make It Happen* (New York: Fordham Democracy and the Constitution Clinic, 2020), 11–14, https://ir.lawnet.fordham.edu/faculty_scholarship /1100; Rein Taagapera, "The Size of National Assemblies," *Social Science Research* 1 (1972): 386–87; "Population Represented by State Legislators," Ballotpedia, accessed March 10, 2023, https://ballotpedia.org/Population _represented_by_state_legislators.

19 Shawn Bowler, David M. Farrel, and Richard Katz, *Party Discipline and Parliamentary Government* (Columbus, Ohio: Ohio State University Press, 1999), 1–18; John M. Carey, "Competing Principals, Political Institutions, and Party Unity in Legislative Voting," *American Journal of Political Science* 51, no.1 (January 2007): 92–107.

20 Notable Republicans who resisted Trump include Senator Mitt Romney (Utah), former-Congresswoman Liz Cheney (Wyoming), and, for a time, Senator Mike Lee (Utah). Maeve Reston, "With Cheney's Impending Ouster, the GOP Chooses Trump over Principle," *CNN*, May 9, 2021, https://www.cnn.com/2021/05/09/politics/trump-cheney-stefanik -republican-party/index.html.

21 Peter Beinart, "Glenn Beck's Regrets," *Atlantic*, January 2017, https://www .theatlantic.com/magazine/archive/2017/01/glenn-becks-regrets/508763/.

22 Upton Sinclair, *I, Candidate for Governor and How I Got Licked* (Berkeley, CA: University of California Press, 1994), 109.

23 *Mr. Smith Goes to Washington*, directed by Frank Capra (1939; Culver City, CA: Columbia Pictures), film.

24 The following are now exempt from the filibuster: Supreme Court nominations; certain other judicial appointments; executive appointments; and programs related to spending, revenue, or the debt limit when submitted as part of a combined Omnibus bill. Drew DeSilver, "Finding 60 Votes in an Evenly Divided Senate? A High Bar, but Not an Impossible One," *Pew Research Center*, August 26, 2022, https://www.pewresearch.org/fact-tank /2022/08/26/finding-60-votes-in-an-evenly-divided-senate-a-high-bar-but -not-an-impossible-one/.

25 Aaron Blake, "How the GOP is Trying to Justify Its Supreme Court Reversal," *Washington Post*, September 21, 2020, https://www.washingtonpost .com/politics/2020/09/21/how-gop-is-trying-justify-its-supreme-court -reversal/.

26 Susan Page, "Inside Nancy Pelosi's War with AOC and the Squad: How the House Speaker Put Rep. Alexandria Ocasio-Cortez in Her Place," *Politico*, April 15, 2021, https://www.politico.com/news/magazine/2021/04/15/nancy -pelosi-alexandria-ocasio-cortez-481704.

27 Chuck Todd, Mark Murray, Carrie Dann, and Melissa Holzber, "The Senate Was Designed to Cool Our Politics Down. No More," *NBC News*, September 22, 2020, https://www.nbcnews.com/politics/meet-the-press /senate-was-designed-cool-our-politics-down-no-more-n1240693.

28 Jennifer Epstein and Carrie Budoff Brown, "Obama Praises 'Gang of 6' Plan," *Politico*, July 19, 2011, https://www.politico.com/story/2011/07/obama -praises-gang-of-six-plan-059377; Rachel Weiner, "Immigration's Gang of 8: Who Are They?," *Washington Post*, January 28, 2013, https://www .washingtonpost.com/news/the-fix/wp/2013/01/28/immigrations-gang-of-8 -who-are-they/; Karen Pierog, "S&P Says U.S. Risks Severe Downgrade But It Expects Debt Ceiling Fix," *Reuters*, September 30, 2021, https://www .reuters.com/business/finance/sp-says-it-expects-us-congress-address-debt -ceiling-time-2021-09-30/.

29 See chapter 3 at p. 65.

30 Rucho v. Common Cause, 139 S. Ct. 2484 (2019).

Chapter 8. Reinventing Presidential Elections

1 Arend Lijphart has assessed three dozen democracies, distinguishing majoritarian systems, including the United Kingdom and the United States,

and consensus systems, which combine proportional representation with parliamentary selection of the head of government. Overall, voters report far greater satisfaction with consensus systems. Although noting exceptions, Lijphart observes that the Westminster model and US presidentialism land toward the bottom in voter satisfaction scores. Arend Lijphart, *Patterns of Democracy: Government Forms and Performance in Thirty-Six Countries* 2nd ed. (New Haven, CT: Yale University Press, 2012), 285; Hans-Dieter Klingemann, "Mapping Political Support in the 1990s: A Global Analysis," in *Critical Citizens: Global Support for Democratic Government*, ed. Pippa Norris (Oxford: Oxford University Press, 1999), 31–56; *World Values Survey, 2005–2007* (Stockholm: World Values Survey Association, 2010).

2 These leadership positions are not defined in the Constitution; rather they evolved during the nineteenth and twentieth centuries. "About Parties and Leadership: Majority and Minority Leaders," United States Senate, accessed November 17, 2022, https://www.senate.gov/about/origins-foundations/parties-leadership/majority-minority-leaders.htm.

3 Under the existing calendar, the terms of the president and vice president end at noon on January 20, and the terms of members of Congress end at noon on January 3. U.S. Const. amend. XX, § 1. The date of the presidential election is set as the Tuesday following the first Monday in November, meaning November 2 through November 8. 2 U.S.C. § 7. Allowing two weeks of negotiations for up to five parties under the existing calendar is compressed, and this amendment lets Congress and the House make appropriate adjustments. A full ten weeks of negotiations could operate from November 8 through January 17, requiring near immediate swearing in and leaving only two days prior to Inauguration Day if on January 20, or three days if January 21. Rather than fixing the calendar by constitutional rule, the amendment allows flexibility.

4 In addition to the existing timeline for elections, this amendment implicates the Supreme Court ruling, *INS v. Chadha*, 462 U.S. 919 (1983). That ruling struck down a federal statutory provision creating a one-house veto, which let a single house of Congress invalidate a decision by an administrative agency. The *Chadha* Court identified only four circumstances allowing one House of Congress to act beyond internal administrative processes: initiating impeachments (the House), trying impeachments (the Senate), ratifying treaties (the Senate), and confirming presidential appointments (the Senate). The First Electoral Reform Amendment adds a fifth, letting the Senate set party qualification thresholds in the House. This Amendment adds a sixth, letting the House change the calendar for swearing in its members following a quadrennial election to facilitate coalition negotiations.

5 See chapter 5 at p. 130.
6 "Elections for the Knesset," Knesset, accessed November 17, 2022, https://main.knesset.gov.il/EN/mk/Pages/Elections.aspx; "Early Elections," Bundestag: Federal Returning Officer, last updated January 3, 2022, https://www.bundeswahlleiter.de/en/service/glossar/n/neuwahl.html.
7 Richard Kelly, *Fixed-Term Parliaments Act* (London: House of Commons Library, November 26, 2021), https://researchbriefings.files.parliament.uk/documents/SN06111/SN06111.pdf; David Torrance, "How Is a Prime Minister Appointed?," UK Parliament, October 20, 2022, https://commonslibrary.parliament.uk/how-is-a-prime-minister-appointed/.
8 Beyoncé, performer, "Irreplaceable," by Shaffer "Ne-Yo" Smith, recorded April 2006, track 9 on *B'Day* (*Sony Music*), 2006.
9 Steven Levitsky and Daniel Ziblatt, *How Democracies Die* (New York: Crown, 2018), 149–54.
10 3 U.S.C. § 19.
11 U.S. Const. art. II, § 2, cl. 2.
12 In the language of social choice, restricting range ensures institutional outcomes, helping to explain specific rules employed in judicial decision-making and elections, which must achieve outcomes, on one side, versus legislatures, which can avoid even voting upon proposed bills, on the other. Maxwell L. Stearns, Todd J. Zywicki, and Thomas J. Miceli, *Law and Economics: Private and Public* (Saint Paul, MN: West Academic, 2018), 541–64; Maxwell L. Stearns, "Direct (Anti-)Democracy," *George Washington Law Review* 80 (2012): 311–58.
13 Lijphart, *Patterns of Democracy*, 285; Klingemann, "Mapping Political Support in the 1990s" in *Critical Citizens: Global Support for Democratic Government* at 31–56; Drew DeSilver, "Turnout in U.S. Has Soared in Recent Elections but by Some Measures Still Trails That of Many Other Countries," *Pew Research Center* (November 1, 2022), https://www.pewresearch.org/fact-tank/2022/11/01/turnout-in-u-s-has-soared-in-recent-elections-but-by-some-measures-still-trails-that-of-many-other-countries/; Eileen Fumagalli and Gaia Narciso, "Political Institutions, Voter Turnout, and Policy Outcomes," *European Journal of Political Economy* 28, no. 2 (2012): 162–73, https://doi.org/10.1016/j.ejpoleco.2011.10.002.
14 Danielle Allen, "The Results of Our National Election May Tell a Story of Division. Ballot Measures Tell a Different Tale," *Washington Post*, November 5, 2020, https://www.washingtonpost.com/opinions/state-ballot-measures-show-unity/2020/11/05/dc85eee4-1f8b-11eb-90dd-abd0f7086a91_story.html; David Daley, *Unrigged: How Americans Are Battling Back to Save Democracy* (New York: Liveright Publishing, 2021), 187–200; Matthew

Oberstaedt, "Andrew Yang And Ranked Choice Voting," FairVote Action, https://fairvoteaction.org/andrew-yang-and-ranked-choice-voting/.

15 Shaun Bowler, David M. Farrell, and Robin T. Pettitt, "Expert Opinion on Electoral Systems: So Which Electoral System Is 'Best'?," *Journal of Elections, Public Opinion and Parties* 15, no. 1 (2005): 3–19; Lee Drutman, *Breaking the Two-Party Doom Loop: The Case for Multiparty Democracy in America* (New York: Oxford University Press, 2020), 189, 323n36. Drutman, like Daley, favors RCV, sometimes referred to as single transferrable vote (STV). Based on the Bowler, Farrell, and Pettitt study, with 169 respondents rating systems from one (the best) to seven (the worst), Drutman observes that "The top-ranked system is mixed-member proportional, with an average rating of 2.37 [as compared with single-transferrable voting at 2.6], with fifty-two respondents calling it the best system."

16 Erik J. Engstrom and Samuel Kernell, *Party Ballots, Reform, and the Transformation of America's Electoral System* (New York: Cambridge University Press, 2014), 19–26, 190.

17 Alice Calaprice, *The Ultimate Quotable Einstein* (Princeton, NJ: Princeton University Press, 2011), 475.

18 John R. Hibbing, Kevin B. Smith, and John R. Alford. *Predisposed: Liberals, Conservatives, and the Biology of Political Differences* (New York: Routledge, 2013), 6–7; Jay J. Van Bavel and Andrea Pereira, "The Partisan Brain: An Identity-based Model of Political Belief," *Trends in Cognitive Sciences* 22, no. 3 (2018): 213–24; Caroline Kelly, "Political Identity and Perceived Intragroup Homogeneity," *British Journal of Social Psychology* 28, no. 3 (1989): 239–50; Donald P. Green, Bradley Palmquist, and Eric Schickler, *Partisan Hearts and Minds: Political Parties and the Social Identities of Voters* (New Haven, CT: Yale University Press, 2004).

19 Political Scientist William Riker posited that under specified conditions, legislative coalitions in a parliamentary system become more stable as they approach minimum winning size. Riker demonstrated that subgroups of overweighted coalitions gain greater governance benefits by splintering off and joining parties outside the coalition, bringing the new coalition closer to a simple majority. A similar dynamic helps explain why greatly overweighted coalitions in a two-party system are unstable, at least in periods of greater ideological overlap among the parties. William H. Riker, *The Theory of Political Coalitions* (New Haven, CT: Yale University Press, 1962).

20 See chapter 3 at p. 59.

21 Some helpful sources: Frank Cunningham, *Theories of Democracy: A Critical Introduction* (London: Routledge, 2002); Renske Doorenspleet, *Rethinking*

the Value of Democracy: A Comparative Perspective (Cham, Switzerland: Palgrave Macmillan, 2019).

22 Pacific States Tel. & Tel. Co. v. Oregon, 223 U.S. 118 (1912).

23 Phillip B. Kurland and Gerhard Casper, eds., *Landmark Briefs and Arguments of the Supreme Court of the United States: Constitutional Law* (Arlington, VA: University Publications of America, 1975), 64: 667–69.

24 Stearns, "Direct (Anti-)Democracy" at 313.

25 George Orwell, *Animal Farm* (New York: Harcourt Brace and Company, Inc, 1946), 112.

Chapter 9. Reinventing Presidential Removal

1 U.S. Const. art. II, § 4; U.S. Const. art. I, § 3., cl. 7; U.S. Const. art. I, § 2, cl. 5.

2 *Hearing on Bill before the House Select Committee to Investigate the January 6th Attack on the U.S. Capitol*, 117th Cong. (June 2022); Josh Chafetz, "Trump's Second Impeachment Defends the Constitution. Senate Conviction Should Be Next," *NBC News*, January 14, 2021, https://www.nbcnews.com/think/opinion/trump-s-second-impeachment-makes-constitutional-sense-senate-conviction-must-ncna1254207.

3 *United States v. Nixon*, 418 U.S. 683 (1974); "This Day in History: Nixon Resigns," *History*, November 24, 2009, https://www.history.com/this-day-in-history/nixon-resigns.

4 Michael J. Gerhardt, *The Federal Impeachment Process: A Constitutional and Historical Analysis*, 3rd ed. (Chicago: University of Chicago Press, 2019), 105–19; Michael J. Gerhardt, "Putting the Law of Impeachment in Perspective," *St. Louis University Law Journal* 43 (1999): 905–30; Frank O. Bowman, III and Stephen L. Sepinuck, "High Crimes & Misdemeanors: Defining the Constitutional Limits on Presidential Impeachment," *South Carolina Law Review* 72 (September 1999): 1517–600.

5 *Lessons from the Mueller Report, Part III: "Constitutional Processes for Addressing Presidential Misconduct": Hearing before the H. Comm. on the Judiciary*, 116th Cong., 15-23 (2019) (statement of Dr. John C. Eastman, Founding Director, The Claremont Institute's Center for Constitutional Jurisprudence); *The Impeachment Inquiry into President Donald J. Trump: The Constitutional Grounds for Presidential Impeachment: Hearing before the H. Comm. on the Judiciary*, 116th Cong., 50-105 (2019) (statement of Jonathan Turley, Shapiro Professor of Public Interest Law The George Washington University Law School); Josh Blackmun, "Opinion: Trump Acts Like a Politician. That's Not an Impeachable Offense," *New York Times*, January 23,

344 NOTES TO PAGES 222–228

2020, https://www.nytimes.com/2020/01/23/opinion/trump-impeachment
-defense.html?searchResultPosition=1; 166 *Congressional Record*, S579,
S609–S616 (daily ed. January 27, 2020) (statement of Alan Dershowitz,
Felix Frankfurter, professor emeritus of Harvard Law School).

6 Gary L. McDowell, "High Crimes and Misdemeanors: Recovering the
Intentions of the Founders," *George Washington Law Review* 67 (March 1999):
626–49; Laurence H. Tribe, "Defining 'High Crimes and Misdemeanors':
Basic Principles," *George Washington Law Review* 67 (March 1999): 712–34.

7 18 U.S.C. § 2381; U.S. Const. art. III, § 3, cl. 1.

8 U.S. Const. art. I, § 3, cl. 7.

9 See chapter 3 at p. 64.

10 "President Dan Quayle? Yes, It Almost Happened, for a Few Hours Back in
1991," *Reuters*, December 6, 2011, https://www.reuters.com/article
/idUK193101583620111206.

11 Alana Wise, "House Approves 25th Amendment Resolution Against
Trump, Pence Says He Won't Invoke," *NPR*, January 12, 2021, https://www
.npr.org/sections/trump-impeachment-effort-live-updates/2021/01/12
/955750169/house-to-vote-on-25th-amendment-resolution-against-trump.

12 Angie Drobnic Holan, "Lie of the Year: If You Like Your Healthcare Plan,
You Can Keep It," *PolitiFact*, December 12, 2013, https://www.politifact.com
/article/2013/dec/12/lie-year-if-you-like-your-health-care-plan-keep-it/.

13 "George Bush Declares Mission Accomplished," *History* video, 1:29, May 1,
2003, https://www.history.com/speeches/george-w-bush-declares-mission
-accomplished.

14 Richard K. Betts, "Two Faces of Intelligence Failure: September 11 and
Iraq's Missing WMD," *Political Science Quarterly* 122, no. 4 (2007): 603.

15 Betts, "Two Faces of Intelligence Failure;" Bruce Reidel, "9/11 and Iraq; The
Making of a Tragedy," *Brookings*, September 17, 2021, https://www
.brookings.edu/blog/order-from-chaos/2021/09/17/9-11-and-iraq-the
-making-of-a-tragedy/; David E. Sanger and Scott Shane, "Panel's Report
Assails C.I.A. for Failure on Iraq Weapons," *New York Times*, March 29,
2005, https://www.nytimes.com/2005/03/29/politics/panels-report-assails
-cia-for-failure-on-iraq-weapons.html; Amy Gershkoff and Shana Kushner,
"Shaping Public Opinion: The 9/11 Iraq Connection in the Bush Administration's Rhetoric," *Perspectives on Politics* 3, no. 3 (September 2005): 525–37.

16 Articles of Impeachment Against William Jefferson Clinton, H.R. Res. 611,
105th Cong. (December 19, 1998).

17 Office of the Independent Council, Volume III: Document Supplement Part
A: William J. Clinton Statements, Referral to the U.S. House of Representatives 58 (August 17, 1998).

18 Dylan Matthews, "George W. Bush Really Did Lie about WMDs, and His Aides Are Still Lying for Him," *Vox*, March 20, 2019, https://www.vox.com /policy-and-politics/2019/3/20/18274228/ari-fleischer-iraq-lies-george-w -bush-wmds.

19 Glenn Kessler, Salvador Rizzo, and Meg Kelly, "Trump's False or Mislead- ing Claims Total 30,573 over 4 Years," *Washington Post*, January 24, 2021, https://www.washingtonpost.com/politics/2021/01/24/trumps-false-or -misleading-claims-total-30573-over-four-years/.

20 See chapter 8 at p. 198.

21 Clinton v. Jones, 520 U.S. 681, 702–6, 708–10 (1997).

22 3 U.S.C. § 19.

23 See chapter 5 at p. 135.

24 "Motion of No-Confidence in the Government," The Knesset: Lexicon, accessed December 1, 2022, https://m.knesset.gov.il/en/about/lexicon/pages /noconfidence.aspx.

25 See chapter 6 at p. 147.

Chapter 10. Achieving Coalition Governance

1 Susan Svrluga, "George Mason Law School to Be Renamed the Antonin Scalia School of Law," *Washington Post*, April 1, 2016, https://www .washingtonpost.com/news/grade-point/wp/2016/03/31/george-mason-law -school-to-be-renamed-the-antonin-scalia-school-of-law/; Larry S. Gibson, *Young Thurgood: The Making of a Supreme Court Justice* (Amherst, NY: Prometheus Books, 2012), 107; "Thurgood Marshall Law Library," University of Maryland Francis King Carey School of Law, accessed March 15, 2023, https://www.law.umaryland.edu/library/.

2 Jill Lepore, "The United States' Unamendable Constitution," *New Yorker*, October 26, 2022, https://www.newyorker.com/culture/annals-of-inquiry /the-united-states-unamendable-constitution (counting nineteen states); Carl Hulse, "A Second Constitutional Convention? Some Republicans Want to Force One," *New York Times*, September 4, 2022, https://www.nytimes .com/2022/09/04/us/politics/constitutional-convention-republican-states .html (pointing out counting challenges); "Graham: We Need a Balanced Budget Amendment to the Constitution More than Ever," Lindsey Graham, January 25, 2022, https://www.lgraham.senate.gov/public/index.cfm/2022/1 /graham-we-need-a-balanced-budget-amendment-to-the-constitution-more -than-ever (counting twenty-seven states); "Progress Map," Convention of States Action, accessed December 5, 2022, https://conventionofstates.com/ (providing tracking data); Jay Riestenberg, "U.S. Constitution Threatened as

Article V Convention Movement Nears Success," Common Cause, last modified 2023, https://www.commoncause.org/resource/u-s-constitution -threatened-as-article-v-convention-movement-nears-success/ (counting twenty-eight states).

3 Thomas H. Neale, Congressional Research Service, *The Article V Convention to Propose Constitutional Amendments: Contemporary Issues for Congress* (March 29, 2016), 7, https://crsreports.congress.gov/product/pdf/R/R42589 /15/; Reid Wilson, "Conservatives Prepare New Push for Constitutional Convention," *Hill*, December 8, 2021, https://thehill.com/homenews/state -watch/584835-conservatives-prepare-new-push-for-constitutional -convention/.

4 Thomas Zimmer, "The US Senate Presents a Long-Term Threat to US Democracy," *Guardian*, January 24, 2022, https://www.theguardian.com /commentisfree/2022/jan/24/us-senate-v-liberal-democracy-the-battle-in -the-heart-of-washington-dc.

5 Sanford Levinson, *Our Undemocratic Constitution: Where the Constitution Goes Wrong (And How We the People Can Correct It)* (New York: Oxford University Press, 2006), 11–24.

6 Reynolds v. Sims, 377 U.S. 533 (1964); Karcher v. Daggett, 462 U.S. 725 (1983); Evenwel v. Abbott, 578 U.S. 54 (2016).

7 See chapter 7 at p. 187.

8 Missouri v. Holland, 252 U.S. 216 (1920).

9 Gibbons v. Ogden, 22 U.S. 1 (1824); U.S. Term Limits, Inc. v. Thornton, 514 U.S. 779 (1995).

10 U.S. Const. art. V.

11 For a proposal to amend the amending clause, see Jedediah Britton-Purdy, "The Constitutional Flaw That's Killing American Democracy," *Atlantic*, August 28, 2022, https://www.theatlantic.com/ideas/archive/2022/08 /framers-constitution-democracy/671155/.

12 Rein Taagepera, "The Size of National Assemblies," *Social Science Research* 1, no. 4 (December 1972): 385–401.

13 Taagepera, "The Size of National Assemblies," 385–401.

14 Caroline Kane et al., Democracy and the Constitution Clinic, *Why the House of Representatives Must Be Expanded and How Today's Congress Can Make It Happen* (New York: Fordham University, 2020), 1–25.

15 Kane et al., *Why the House of Representatives Must Be Expanded*; see chapter 10 at pp. 250–52.

16 Trilochan Sastry, "Civil Society, Indian Elections and Democracy Today," (Working Paper No. 465, Indian Institute of Management Bangalore,

July 2014), https://ruralindiaonline.org/bn/library/resource/civil-society
-indian-elections-and-democracy-today/.

17 Kane et al., *Why the House of Representatives Must Be Expanded*, 12.

18 See chapter 7 at pp. 182–86.

19 Lee Drutman, *Breaking the Two-Party Doom Loop: The Case for Multiparty Democracy in America* (New York: Oxford University Press, 2020), 175–205; Lee Drutman and Stephan Kyburz, "Episode #39: Fixing the House with Proportional Representation," March 30, 2023, produced by *Rules of the Game*, podcast, 22:01, https://rulesofthegame.blog/fixing-the-house-with -proportional-representation/.

20 See chapter 3 at pp. 64–66, 72.

21 Commission on the Practice of Democratic Citizenship, *Our Common Purpose: Reinventing American Democracy for the 21st Century* (Cambridge, MA: American Academy of Arts & Sciences, 2020), 24–26.

22 The Supreme Court has greenlighted partisan gerrymandering. Rucho v. Common Cause, 139 S.Ct. 2484 (2019).

23 Katharine Q. Seelye, "Gingrich Explores New Way to Limit Terms in Congress," *New York Times*, February 16, 1995, https://www.nytimes.com /1995/02/16/us/gingrich-explores-new-way-to-limit-terms-in-congress .html.

24 U.S. Term Limits, Inc. v. Thornton, 514 U.S. 779 (1995).

25 Clifton Williams, "Expressio Unius Est Exclusio Alterius," *Marquette Law Review* 15, no. 4, 191 (June 1931): 191–96; John Mark Keyes, "Expressio Unius: The Expression That Proves the Rule," *Statute Law Review* 10, no. 1 (Summer 1989): 1–25.

26 Linda Greenhouse, "'Because We Are Final' Judicial Review Two Hundred Years after Marbury," *Proceedings of the American Philosophical Society* 148, no. 1 (Mar. 2004): 38–52.

27 See chapter 7 at p. 181.

28 Maxwell L. Stearns, Todd J. Zywicki, and Thomas J. Miceli, *Law and Economics: Private and Public* (St. Paul, MN: West Academic Publishing, 2018), 585–96.

29 For some relevant studies, see Michael P. Olson and Jon C. Rogowski, "Legislative Term Limits and Polarization," *Journal of Politics* 82, no. 2 (April 2020), https://www.journals.uchicago.edu/doi/10.1086/706764; Andrew C. W. Myers, "State Legislatures, Term Limits, and Polarization," *Stanford Institute for Economic Policy Research* (November 2021), https://www .andrewcwmyers.com/documents/Myers_term_limits.pdf; Gerald C. Wright, "Do Term Limits Affect Legislative Roll Call Voting?," *State Politics*

and Policy Quarterly 7, no. 3 (fall 2007): 256–80, https://www.jstor.org/stable /40405603.

30 Maxwell L. Stearns, "Direct (Anti-)Democracy," *George Washington Law Review* 80 (2012): 311–84.

31 Bush v. Palm Beach County Canvassing Board, 531 U.S. 70 (2000); Bush v. Gore, 531 U.S. 98 (2000); Michael Abramowicz and Maxwell L. Stearns, "Beyond Counting Votes: The Political Economy of Bush v. Gore, *Vanderbilt Law Review* 54, no 5. (October 2001): 1849–952.

32 Jim Heath Channel, "Election 2000 Florida, Florida, Florida," YouTube video, 17:52, November 13, 2011, https://www.youtube.com/watch?v =OOaaUackKFQ.

33 Thomas E. Mann, "Reflections on the 2000 U.S. Presidential Election," *Brookings*, January 1, 2001, https://www.brookings.edu/articles/reflections -on-the-2000-u-s-presidential-election/.

34 Brandon Draper, "Popular Fallacy: A Public Choice Analysis of Electoral College Reform," *International Journal of Public Law and Policy* 1, no. 1 (January 2011): 49–82.

35 "Agreement among the States to Elect the President by National Popular Vote," National Popular Vote, accessed December 6, 20222, https://www .nationalpopularvote.com/written-explanation; "About Us," FairVote, accessed December 6, 2022, https://fairvote.org/who-we-are/about-us/.

36 "Status of National Popular Vote Bill in Each State," National Popular Vote, accessed June 7, 2023, https://www.nationalpopularvote.com/state-status; Christopher Ingraham, "Minnesota Lawmakers Bring National Popular Vote One Step Closer to Reality," *Minnesota Reformer*, May 24, 2023, https://minnesotareformer.com/2023/05/24/minnesota-lawmakers-bring -national-popular-vote-one-step-closer-to-reality/.

37 U.S. Const., amend. XXIII.

38 Drew Desilver, "Turnout Soared in 2020 as Nearly Two-Thirds of Eligible U.S. Voters Cast Ballots for President," *Pew Research Center*, January 28, 2021, https://www.pewresearch.org/fact-tank/2021/01/28/turnout -soared-in-2020-as-nearly-two-thirds-of-eligible-u-s-voters-cast-ballots-for -president/; Monica Potts, "Turnout Was High Again. Is This the New Normal?," *FiveThirtyEight*, November 15, 2022, https://fivethirtyeight.com /features/turnout-was-high-again-is-this-the-new-normal/.

39 "Ranked Choice Voting," FairVote, accessed December 8, 2022, https:// fairvote.org/our-reforms/ranked-choice-voting/; "Ranked-Choice Voting & Nonpartisan Primaries," Forward Party, accessed December 8, 2022, https://www.forwardparty.com/principle_ranked_choice_voting; "Overview of Strategies and Recommendations," Our Common Purpose, accessed

December 8, 2022, https://www.amacad.org/ourcommonpurpose/report
/section/3.

40 Sarah John and Caroline Tolbert, Fairvote, *Socioeconomic and Demographic
Perspectives on Ranked Choice Voting in the Bay Area* (April 2015), 7,
https://fairvote.app.box.com/v/perspectives-on-rcv-bay-area; Martha
Kropf, "Using Campaign Communications to Analyze Civility in Ranked
Choice Voting Elections," *Politics & Governance* 9, no. 2 (2021): 289–90,
https://www.cogitatiopress.com/politicsandgovernance/article/view/4293
/4293.

41 *State of Alaska 2022 Primary Election: Election Summary Report Official Results*
(August 16, 2022), https://www.elections.alaska.gov/results/22PRIM
/ElectionSummaryReportRPT.pdf; *RCV Detailed Report: General Election
State of Alaska* (November 8, 2022), https://www.elections.alaska.gov/results
/22GENR/US%20REP.pdf.

42 "United States House of Representatives Special Election in Alaska, 2022,"
Ballotpedia, accessed December 6, 2022, https://ballotpedia.org/United
_States_House_of_Representatives_special_election_in_Alaska,_2022;
"United States House Election in Alaska, 2022 (June 11 Top-Four Pri-
mary)," Ballotpedia, accessed December 6, 2022, https://ballotpedia.org
/United_States_House_of_Representatives_special_election_in_Alaska,
_2022_(June_11_top-four_primary); *State of Alaska 2022 Primary Election:
Election Summary Report Official Results* (August 16, 2022), https://www
.elections.alaska.gov/results/22PRIM/ElectionSummaryReportRPT.pdf;
RCV Detailed Report: General Election State of Alaska (November 8, 2022),
https://www.elections.alaska.gov/results/22GENR/US%20REP.pdf;
Barbara Barrett, "Ranked Choice Voting Lifts Unexpected Hopeful in
Alaska Election," *Pew Charitable Trusts: Stateline* (September 2, 2022),
https://www.pewtrusts.org/en/research-and-analysis/blogs/stateline/2022
/09/02/ranked-choice-voting-lifts-unexpected-hopeful-in-alaska-election.

43 Liz Ruskin, "Gross, a Top Four Candidate for US House, Calls It Quits,"
Alaska Public Media, June 20, 2022, https://alaskapublic.org/2022/06/20
/gross-a-top-four-candidate-for-us-house-calls-it-quits/.

44 Aaron Hamlin, "RCV Fools Palin Voters into Electing a Progressive
Democrat," Center for Election Science, September 16, 2022, available from
Wayback Machine, https://web.archive.org/web/20230606002141/https:
/electionscience.org/commentary-analysis/rcv-fools-palin-voters-into
-electing-a-progressive-democrat/.

45 David McCune and Adam Graham-Squire, "Mathematical Flaws in
Ranked Choice Voting Are Rare But Real," *ProMarket,* May 3, 2023,

https://www.promarket.org/2023/05/03/mathematical-flaws-in-ranked
-choice-voting-are-rare-but-real/.

46 Jim Geraghty, "Who Really Wins under Ranked-Choice Voting?," *National Review*, September 1, 2022, https://www.nationalreview.com/the-morning
-jolt/who-really-wins-under-ranked-choice-voting/?utm_source
=Sailthru&utm_medium=email&utm_campaign=MJ_20220901&utm
_term=Jolt-Smart.

47 Aaron Hamlin, "RCV Fools Palin Voters into Electing a Progressive Democrat."

48 "Ranked Choice Voting Information," FairVote, accesses December 6, 2022, https://fairvote.org/our-reforms/ranked-choice-voting-information/#where
-is-ranked-choice-voting-used (listing, as international examples, Australia (Federal House and state and local), Ireland (President and Parliament), Malta (Parliament), New Zealand (Mayor and City Council), Northern Ireland (Regional Parliament and local), Scotland (all government elections), India (President and National Senate), Nepal and Pakistan (National Senate), Sri Lanka (President), and London (Mayor).

49 See chapter 8 at pp. 206–9.

50 "Research and Data on RCV in Practice," FairVote, accessed December 6, 2022, https://fairvote.org/resources/data-on-rcv/; Joseph Anthony and David C. Kimball, "Public Perceptions of Alternative Voting Systems: Results from a National Survey Experiment" (Working Paper, Midwest Political Science Association, 2021), https://papers.ssrn.com/sol3/papers.cfm
?abstract_id=3854047; André Blais, Carolina Plescia and Semra Sevi, "Choosing to Vote as Usual" (working paper, 2021), https://papers.ssrn.com
/sol3/papers.cfm?abstract_id=3784822.

51 "Final-Five Voting," Institute for Political Innovation, accessed June 7, 2023, https://political-innovation.org/final-five-voting/.

52 Åsa von Schoultz, "Electoral Systems in Context: Finland," in *Oxford Handbook of Electoral Systems* (Oxford: Oxford University Press, 2017), 601–26; "Experience of PR Open List System?," ACE Project, January 24, 2012, https://aceproject.org/electoral-advice/archive/questions/replies
/58678269#118098376.

53 Alex Tausanovitch, "It's Time to Talk about Electoral Reform," Center For American Progress, January 31, 2023, https://www.americanprogress.org
/article/its-time-to-talk-about-electoral-reform/

54 "Approval Voting," Center for Election Science, accessed June 7, 2023, https://electionscience.org/library/approval-voting/.

55 Jack Santucci, *More Parties or No Parties: The Politics of Electoral Reform in America* (New York: Oxford University Press, 2022), 6.

Chapter 11. Parliamentary America

1 Ezra Klein, *Why We're Polarized* (New York: Avid Reader Press, 2020).
2 See chapter 3 at pp. 76–81; see chapter 4 at p. 85.
3 Ian G. Anson, "Partisanship, Political Knowledge, and the Dunning-Kruger Effect," *Political Psychology* 39, no. 5 (October 2018): 1173–92; Elizabeth Kolbert, "Why Facts Don't Change Our Minds," *New Yorker*, February 27, 2017, https://www.newyorker.com/magazine/2017/02/27/why-facts-dont-change-our-minds.
4 David Daley, *Ratf**ked: Why Your Vote Doesn't Count* (New York: Liveright Publishing, 2016), 97.
5 Michael Abramowicz and Maxwell L. Stearns, "Beyond Counting Votes: The Political Economy of Bush v. Gore," *Vanderbilt Law Review* 54, no. 5 (2001): 1850–952.
6 Chris Wilson, "These 3 Counties Could Have Flipped the 2016 Election for Hillary Clinton," *Time*, February 23, 2017, https://time.com/4678962/2016-election-donald-trump-hillary-clinton/.
7 Rucho v. Common Cause, 139 S. Ct. 2484 (2019); Dobbs v. Jackson Women's Health Organization, 142 S. Ct. 2228 (2022); New York State Rifle & Pistol Association Inc. v. Bruen, 142 S. Ct. 2111 (2022); Carson v. Makin, 142 S. Ct. 1987 (2022); Students for Fair Admissions v. Harvard, 980 F.3d 157 (1st Cir. 2020); Students for Fair Admissions v. University of North Carolina, 567 F. Supp. 3d 580 (M.D.N.C. 2021); Students for Fair Admissions v. University of North Carolina, 142 S. Ct. 896 (2022) (granting cert.).
8 Alexandra Jaffe, "Kellyanne Conway: WH Spokesman Gave 'Alternative Facts' on Inauguration Crowd," *NBC News*, January 22, 2017, https://www.nbcnews.com/storyline/meet-the-press-70-years/wh-spokesman-gave-alternative-facts-inauguration-crowd-n710466.
9 Students for Fair Admissions, Inc. v. President & Fellows of Harvard College, 143 S. Ct. 2141, 2176 (2023).
10 Regents of the University of California v. Bakke 438 U.S. 265 (1978).
11 Grutter v. Bollinger, 539 U.S. 306 (2003); Gratz v. Bollinger, 539 U.S. 244 (2003).
12 Heather McGee, *The Sum of Us: What Racism Costs Everyone and How We Can Prosper Together* (New York: One World, 2021), 2; Richard Rothstein, *The Color of Law: A Forgotten History of How Our Government Segregated America* (New York: Liveright, 2017); Brooks v. School Dist. of City of Moberly, 267 F.2d 733 (8th Cir. 1959).
13 Parents Involved in Community Schools v. Seattle School Dist. No. 1, 551 U.S. 701, 748 (2007).

14 Dobbs v. Jackson Women's Health Organization, 142 S. Ct. 2228 (2022).

15 Burgess Everett, Marianne Levine, and Sarah Ferris, "Graham's Abortion Ban Stuns Senate GOP," *Politico*, September 13, 2022, https://www.politico .com/news/2022/09/13/grahams-abortion-ban-senate-gop-00056423; Lisa Lerer and Elizabeth Dias, "How Democrats Used the Abortion Debate to Hold off a Red Wave," *New York Times*, November 10, 2022, https://www .nytimes.com/2022/11/10/us/politics/abortion-midterm-elections-democrats -republicans.html.

16 Planned Parenthood of Southeastern Pennsylvania v. Casey, 505 U.S. 833 (1992).

17 Planned Parenthood of Southeastern Pennsylvania v. Casey, 505 U.S. 833, 843, 866 (1992).

18 *Majority of Public Disapproves of Supreme Court's Decision to Overturn Roe v. Wade*, Pew Research Center (July 6, 2022), https://www.pewresearch.org /politics/2022/07/06/majority-of-public-disapproves-of-supreme-courts -decision-to-overturn-roe-v-wade/.

19 *National: Most Say Leave Roe v. Wade as Is*, Monmouth University (September 20, 2021), https://www.monmouth.edu/polling-institute/reports /monmouthpoll_us_092021/; *Majority of Public Disapproves of Supreme Court's Decision to Overturn Roe v. Wade*, Pew Research Center.

20 Transcript of Oral Argument at 108–11, Dobbs v. Jackson Women's Health Organization, 142 S. Ct. 414 (2022) (No. 19-1392).

21 Dobbs v. Jackson Women's Health Organization, 142 S. Ct. 2228, 2304 (2022) (Kavanaugh, J., concurring); Executive Order 14076, 87 Fed. Reg. 42,053 (July 8, 2022).

22 Katherine Schaeffer, "Key Facts about Americans and Guns," Pew Research Center, September 13, 2021, https://www.pewresearch.org/fact-tank/2021 /09/13/key-facts-about-americans-and-guns/.

23 Brady Handgun Violence Prevention Act, 18 U.S.C. §§ 921–22; Andrew Goddard, "A View through the Gun Show Loophole," *Richmond Journal of Law and Public Interest* 12, no. 4 (2009): 357–61.

24 "Grades and Endorsements," NRA-PVF, accessed December 8, 2022, https://www.nrapvf.org/grades/ https://www.nrapvf.org/grades/; David Siders and Olivia Beavers, "Republicans Pledge Allegiance to a Hobbled NRA," *Politico*, May 25, 2022, https://www.politico.com/news/2022/05/25 /nra-republicans-texas-shooting-trump-00035260.

25 Bipartisan Safer Communities Act, Public Law 117-159, 136 Stat. 1313 (June 25, 2022).

26 "Mass Shootings in 2022," Gun Violence Archive, accessed December 9, 2022, https://www.gunviolencearchive.org/reports/mass-shooting; Ash-

ley R. Williams, "More Mass Shooters Are Using Semi-automatic Rifles—Often Bought Legally," *USA Today*, July 12, 2022, https://www .usatoday.com/story/news/nation/2022/07/12/mass-shootings-weapons-legal -what-to-know/7814081001/.

27 "Global Firearms Holdings," Small Arms Survey, March 29, 2020, https:// www.smallarmssurvey.org/database/global-firearms-holdings; Christopher Ingraham, "There Are More Guns than People in the United States, According to a New Study of Global Firearm Ownership," *Washington Post*, June 19, 2018, https://www.washingtonpost.com/news/wonk/wp/2018/06 /19/there-are-more-guns-than-people-in-the-united-states-according-to-a -new-study-of-global-firearm-ownership/.

28 John R. Lott, *More Guns, Less Crime: Understanding Crime and Gun Control Laws*, 3rd ed. (Chicago: University of Chicago Press, 2010).

29 District of Columbia v. Heller, 554 U.S. 570, 576–79, 595–605, 626–29 (2008).

30 U.S. Const., amend. II.

31 District of Columbia v. Heller, 554 U.S. 570, 627–28 (2008); New York State Rifle & Pistol Ass'n v. Bruen, 142 S. Ct. 2111, 2132–33 (2022).

32 Wang-Sheng Lee and Sandy Suardi, "Australian Firearms Buyback and Its Effect on Gun Deaths" (Working Paper No. 17/08, Melbourne Institute of Applied Economic and Social Research, August 2008); Dan Karpenchuk, "Canada Announces Proposed Pricing for Mandatory Gun Buyback Program," *WBFO NPR*, August 1, 2022, https://www.wbfo.org/national -international/2022-08-01/canada-announces-proposed-pricing-for -mandatory-gun-buyback-program.

33 A variation on "Misery acquaints a man with strange bedfellows." Shakespeare, *The Tempest*, 2.2.

34 Elizabeth Warren, "Expand the Supreme Court," *Boston Globe*, December 15, 2021, http://ct.symplicity.com/t/wrn/642e107461a3b7019544be0d95 27d3cb/2665571418/realurl=https:/www.bostonglobe.com/2021/12/15 /opinion/expand-supreme-court/; Jeffrey L. Fisher, "The Supreme Court Reform That Could Actually Win Bipartisan Support," *Politico*, July 21, 2022, https://www.politico.com/news/magazine/2022/07/21/supreme-court -reform-term-limits-00046883; Roger C. Cramton, "Reforming the Supreme Court," *California Law Review* 95 (2007): 1313–34, 1323.

35 See chapter 7 at p. 175.

36 Lee Drutman, *Breaking the Two-Party Doom Loop: The Case for Multiparty Democracy in America*, (New York: Oxford University Press, 2020), 191–95.

37 See chapter 7 at p. 187.

38 See chapter 6 at pp. 156–57.

39 U.S. Const., amend. I ("Congress shall make no law . . . abridging the freedom of speech, or of the press").

40 "It's Difficult To Make Predictions, Especially about the Future," Quote Investigator, accessed December 9, 2022, https://quoteinvestigator.com/2013/10/20/no-predict/.

41 William Faulkner, *Requiem for a Nun* (New York: Vintage Books, 2011), 73.

Conclusion

Epigraphs. Francis Scott Key, "The Star-Spangled Banner," in *Yale Book of American Verse* (New Haven, CT: Yale University Press, 1912), 4–5. Sara Bareilles, vocalist, "Brave," by Sara Bareilles and Jack Antonoff, recorded 2013, track 1 on *The Blessed Unrest*, Epic, compact disc.

1 White House, "Remarks by President Biden at Signing of the Juneteenth National Independence Day Act," June 17, 2021, https://www.whitehouse.gov/briefing-room/speeches-remarks/2021/06/17/remarks-by-president-biden-at-signing-of-the-juneteenth-national-independence-day-act.

2 See chapter 11 at p. 291.

INDEX

abortion, 272, 275–78
Adams, John, 57, 59–61, 87
Adams, John Quincy, 59, 61–63, 64, 87, 88, 225
Ad Fontes Media Bias Chart, 85, 100–106
adjustment mandate seats, 131–33
advertising: and newspapers, 89, 103, 289; and social media, 21, 84, 94, 98, 100
Affordable Care Act, 227
Alaska, ranked-choice voting in, 261–63, 320n41
Albany Regency, 88
Aldrich, John, 66, 138
Alien Enemies Act, 87
Alito, Samuel, 272
Allen, Danielle, 206
Allende, Salvador, 154
American exceptionalism, 2–3, 5
American Rescue Plan, 314n26
Anderson, John, 17, 38, 39
Anti-Federalist Papers, 86
apportionment: and Hamilton and Jefferson, 153–54; process of, 77–79, 175–76; replacement of at-large voting with, 64–65. *See also* gerrymandering; proportional representation
Apportionment Act of 1842, 64–65

approval voting, 264, 265
Armenian genocide, 144
Arrow, Kenneth, 114–15, 179
Articles of Confederation, 2, 23, 86, 246, 296
assault rifles, 279, 280
association, right of, 198
at-large voting: and bloc voting, 71–72, 163; as reform option, 4, 164, 193, 253, 254–55; replacement with single-member districts, 64–66; in Venezuela, 163
Australian ballots, 62

Barak, Ehud, 148
Barrett, Amy Coney, 272, 277, 283
Begin, Menachem, 143
Bell, John, 68
Ben-Gvir, Itamar, 147
Bennett, Naftali, 147
bias, media, 82–83, 85, 86–87, 100–106
Biden, Joe: and debt ceiling, 337n11; and electoral swings, 116; executive orders by, 314n26; and foreign relations, 152; and hypothetical centrist faction, 22; and Juneteenth, 69; legislative challenges, 180; legislative successes, 314n26; and 2020 election, 39, 42–43, 49, 70, 193

250–52; multimember districts, 4, 26, 245, 252–55; prestige and power of, 243–44; redistricting of, 245; and term limits, 4, 26, 245, 255–56. *See also* Electoral Reform Amendments and House of Representatives
How Democracies Die (Levitsky and Ziblatt), 154–55

ideology: and cognition, 210; and high-valence candidates, 73–76; in Media Bias Chart, 101–5; and misinformation, 228; and personality, 210; voters' commitment to, 40–41
impeachment: of Clinton, 218, 228, 230, 318n10; and criminality, 222; effect of no-confidence votes on, 221, 223–24; and Framers, 61, 203, 217–19, 222–23, 229; as ineffective, 61, 203–4, 217–19, 222–23, 233; of Johnson, 218, 318n10; of Trump, 218, 318n10
ineffectiveness and maladministration, 220, 224–25, 226
Inflation Reduction Act, 314n26
instant-runoff voting, 206, 256–57, 260–61. *See also* ranked-choice voting
INS v. Chadha, 340n4
Ireland: coalitions in, 147; party thresholds in, 337n6
Israel: coalitions in, 145–47, 199, 201; country comparison, 140, 142–50, 165, 166, 167–68; party thresholds in, 337n6; protests in, 147–48; ratio of legislators to voters in, 252; semi-parliamentary system in, 140, 148–49, 182

Italy: country comparison, 167; number of parties in, 182
iterative game, 256

Jackson, Andrew, 59, 61–63, 87, 88
Jackson, Rachel, 63
January 6 insurrection, 40, 41, 81, 82, 218
Japan: ratio of legislators to voters in, 251; and Taiwan, 150–51
Jay, John, 86
Jefferson, Thomas, 27–28, 57, 59–61, 87, 88, 153–54, 156
Johnson, Andrew, 59, 68, 218, 318n10
Johnson, Boris, 116, 118
Jolly, David, 42
Jones, Paula Corbin, 230
judicial branch: and separation of powers, 12–15; in Taiwan, 151; in Venezuela, 162
Juneteenth, 69

Kansas-Nebraska Act of 1854, 67
Kasich, John, 45–47
Kavanaugh, Brett, 79, 272, 283
Kennedy, Anthony, 15, 79–80
Kennedy, John F., 49, 73, 91
Klein, Ezra, 28
Knesset, 143, 145–49, 167–68
Ku Klux Klan, 69

Lapi, Eduardo, 163
Lapid, Yair, 147
legislative branch: in country comparison matrix, 113, 165, 166–68; and separation of powers, 12–15. *See also* House of Representatives; Senate
Legislative Yuan (Taiwan), 151–54
Le Pen, Marine, 126